Guerrilla Analytics

A Practical Approach to Working with Data

Guerrilla Analytics

A Practical Approach to Working with Data

Enda Ridge

AMSTERDAM • BOSTON • HEIDELBERG
LONDON • NEW YORK • OXFORD • PARIS
SAN DIEGO • SAN FRANCISCO • SINGAPORE
SYDNEY • TOKYO
Morgan Kaufmann is an Imprint of Elsevier

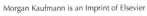

Acquiring Editor: Steve Elliot
Editorial Project Manager: Kaitlin Herbert
Project Manager: Priya Kumaraguruparan
Designer: Mark Rogers

Morgan Kaufmann is an imprint of Elsevier
225 Wyman Street, Waltham, MA 02451, USA

British Library Cataloguing-in-Publication Data
A catalogue record for this book is available from the British Library

Library of Congress Cataloging-in-Publication Data
Application submitted

ISBN: 978-0-12-800218-6

For information on all MK publications
visit our website at http://www.mkp.com

Contents

Part 4
Building Guerrilla Analytics Capability   203

List of Figures

Table of War Stories

Preface

WHY THIS BOOK?

Data analytics involves taking some data and exploring and testing it to produce insights. You can put a variety of names on this process from Business Intelligence to Data Science but fundamentally the approach does not change. Understand a problem, identify the right data, prepare the data appropriately, and run the appropriate analysis on it to find insights and report on them. This is difficult. You are probably seeing this data for the first time. Worse still, the data usually has issues you will only uncover during your journey. Meanwhile, the problem domain must be understood so the data that represents it can be understood. But what is discovered in the data often helps define the problem domain itself.

Faced with this open-ended challenge, many analysts become lost in the data. They explore multiple lines of enquiry. One line of enquiry can invalidate or confirm a previous line. The structure and exceptions in the data are discovered during the process and must be accounted for. Many of the analyses themselves can be executed in a multitude of ways, none of which are categorically correct but instead must be interpreted and justified. Just when you thought you had a handle on the problem, new data arrives and everything you have already done is potentially invalidated. This makes planning, executing, and reproducing data analytics challenging.

If you have ever been in this situation then this book is for you.

WHAT THIS BOOK IS AND WHAT IT IS NOT

First of all, let me cover what this book is not.

- This book is not a prescriptive guide to either specific technologies or analytics techniques. For that you will have to read widely in fields such as machine learning, statistics, database programming, scripting, web development, and data visualization. It is my belief that while technology continues to improve at pace, the fundamental principles of how to do data analytics change little.
- This is not a project management book. I certainly believe project management of analytics needs more attention. Analytics projects are complex and fast-paced and it seems that established project management techniques can struggle to cope with them. This book will help you in areas such as tracking of work but it does not take a project management focus in the presentation of any of its material.
- This book is not about "Big Data." It is also not about little data or medium data. Debates about whether Big Data is something new or indeed something

at all are left to others. As you will see, this book's principles and its practice tips are applicable to all types of data analysis regardless of the scale.

- This book is not about how to build large data warehouses and web-based Business Intelligence platforms. These techniques are also well covered in the literature having been tackled in academia and the software development industry for several decades.

My goal in writing this book is to help people who have been in the same situation as me. I want them to benefit from my experiences and the lessons I have learned, very often the hard way. This book aims to help you in the following three ways.

- **How to do:** This book is a guiding reference for data analysts who must work in dynamic analytics projects. It will help them do high-quality work that is reproducible and testable despite the many disruptions in their project environment and the typically open-ended nature of analytics. It will guide them through each stage of a data analytics job with overarching principles and specific practice tips.
- **How to manage:** This book is a how-to for data analytics managers. It will help them put in place light weight workflows and team conventions that are easy to understand and implement. Teams managed with this book's principles in mind will avoid many of the pain points of analytics. They will be well coordinated, their work will be easily reviewed and their knowledge will be easily shared. The team will become safely independent, freeing up the manager to communicate and sell the team's work instead of being mired in trying to cover every detail of the team's activities.
- **How to build:** Finally, this book is a guide for those with the strategic remit of building and growing an analytics team. Chapters describe the people, processes, and technology that need to be put in place to grow an agile and versatile analytics team.

WHO SHOULD READ THIS BOOK?

Data analytics is a hugely diverse area. Nonetheless, the fundamentals of how to do data analytics, manage analytics teams, and build analytics capability do not change significantly. You will benefit from reading this book if you work in any of the following roles.

- **Data Analyst or Data Scientist:** You are somebody who works directly with data and needs guidance on best practice for doing that work in an agile, controlled, reproducible way. If you have ever experienced been "lost in the data" or losing track of your own analyses and data modifications then this book will help you. If you have ever been frustrated with repeated conversations with your colleagues about where data is stored, what it means, or how your colleague analyzed it then this book will help you both.
- **Analytics Manager:** You are somebody who has several direct reports and you are responsible for guiding and reviewing their analytics work. You have

to jump into many different work products from different team members to review their correctness. You do not have time to waste on facing a different approach, coding convention, data location, or test structure every time you sit down to review a piece of work. Your project resources come and go and you want to facilitate fast transitions and handovers with minimal overhead. You need to be able to explain your team's work with confidence to customers but do not have time to be down in all the details of that work.

- **Senior Manager:** You are somebody who is busy interfacing with a customer and perhaps architecting a high-level approach to a customer's problems. You need to know that your team's work products are reproducible, tested, and traceable. You need to sell the quality, versatility, and speed of mobilization of your team to your customers.
- **Team Director/Chief Information Officer/Chief Data Officer:** You are somebody who wants to build the best analytics team possible to solve customer problems and respond to a wide variety of analytics challenges. To support this ambition, you need a uniformity of skills and methods in your analytics teams for flexibility of resourcing and sharing of knowledge. You want your teams to produce to high standards without suffocating them with rules or requiring they use expensive niche tools. You want your teams to have the right training and toolsets at their fingertips so they can get on with the work they do best.
- **Researcher:** You gather and analyze experimental data for research and publication purposes. This could be algorithm design in computer science, instrumentation data in physics, or any field requiring gathering data to test hypotheses. With such an open-ended exploratory approach to your work, you may struggle to coordinate multiple parallel lines of inquiry, multiple versions of analyses, and experiment result data. This book helps you do all of that so you can focus on reproducible and repeatable publication of results.
- **Research Director:** You are somebody who runs a team of researchers working on multiple concurrent research projects. Your concern is that research is reproducible and sharable among your teams so that the body of knowledge of your team and lab grows over time. You do not have time to be down in the details but you want to know that your team's work is of publication quality in an academic context or can be easily transferred into production in an industry context.

HOW THIS BOOK IS ORGANIZED

I have designed the book so that each chapter is as self-contained as possible and chapters can be read in any order. The book is organized into four parts.

Part 1 Principles introduces Guerrilla Analytics and the Guerrilla Analytics Principles. Begin here if you need an introduction to why analytics is difficult, what can go wrong, and how to mitigate the risks of things going wrong.

- Introducing Guerrilla Analytics
- Guerrilla Analytics: Challenges and Risks
- Guerrilla Analytics Principles

Part 2 Practice covers how to apply the Guerrilla Analytics Principles across the entire analytics workflow. Read any of these chapters if you are working in a particular stage of the Data Analytics Workflow. For example, jump into "Data Load" if you have just received some data from a customer. Look through "Creating Work Products" if you are beginning a piece of work that you will deliver to your customer.

- Data Extraction
- Data Receipt
- Data Load
- Analytics Coding for Ease of Review
- Analytics Coding to Maintain Data Provenance
- Creating Work Products
- Reporting
- Consolidating Knowledge in Builds

Part 3 Testing discusses how to test analytics work to discover defects. Begin with the introduction, if testing is new to you.

- Introduction to Testing
- Testing Data
- Testing Builds
- Testing Work Products

Part 4 Building Guerrilla Analytics Capability is all about the people skills, technology, and processes you need to put in place to establish and grow a Guerrilla Analytics team. Pick up one of these chapters if you are setting up a Guerrilla Analytics environment or are looking to hire and train a team in this book's techniques.

- People
- Process
- Technology

Throughout the book, many of the points will be illustrated with simple examples. "War stories" will describe instances of how things can go badly wrong without the Guerrilla Analytics Principles. The war stories cover a variety of domains to appeal to as many readers as possible.

DISCLAIMER

It is important to state that the examples and war stories from this book are fictional and based on a decade of experiences, conversations, projects, and study. While drawn from real-world experiences, they are not particular to any of my employers or clients, past or present, and should not be interpreted as such.

Part 1

Principles

Chapter 1

Introducing Guerrilla Analytics

Having read this chapter, you will understand

- what data analytics is in a very general sense
- the projects in which data analytics is applied
- the type of analytics that is "Guerrilla Analytics"
- examples of Guerrilla Analytics projects

1.1 WHAT IS DATA ANALYTICS?

The last decade has seen phenomenal growth in the creation of data and in the analysis of data to provide insight. Social media and search giants such as Facebook and Google probably spring to mind. These analytics innovators gather immense amounts of data to understand Internet search and social habits so that they can better target online advertising for their customers. Online digital media is generating hours of content and streaming it around the globe for major sporting events such as the FIFA World Cup and the Olympics. In the Financial Services industry, firms process and store billions of financial transactions every day and analyze those transactions to gain an edge in the market over their competitors. Ubiquitous Telco operators store data on our call patterns to analyze it for indicators of customer churn and up-selling opportunities. Every time you book a hotel, flight, or go to the supermarket, loyalty card data is analyzed to better understand customer-purchasing habits and to better target marketing opportunities.

And this growth in data and analytics is not restricted to businesses. Scientific research centers are also creating immense amounts of experimental data in fields such as particle physics, genetics, and pharmacology. Government departments too are not exempt from this trend.

The complexity and pace of change have created a market for data analytics teams in consulting services firms to help their clients both cope with and profit from new data-driven opportunities.

Unsurprisingly, given the growth in data generation, the last decade has also seen a proliferation of the skills and tools needed for extracting value from data. Names for this field include Data Analytics, Data Mining, Quantitative Analysis, Big Data, Machine Learning, Business Intelligence, Artificial Intelligence, and Data Science. Vendors are frantically racing to provide enterprise grade tools to support work in these fields and to distinguish their offerings from those of their competitors. Universities are trumpeting degree programs that will train a generation of graduates to be conversant in these new technologies and skills.

All of this marketing noise, vendor hype, and pace of change can be confusing and overwhelming for somebody who just wants to get started in data and answer questions to solve problems. Big Data, data velocity, unstructured data, NoSQL, key-value stores, predictive modeling, social network analysis – it is very hard to know where to begin.

Before we get into the details, it will be helpful to step back and think a little about what "data analytics" can mean and agree on what it means to us in this book. Wikipedia, for example, defines "data analytics" as:

> ... a process of inspecting, cleaning, transforming, and modelling data with the goal of discovering useful information, suggesting conclusions, and supporting decision making. Data analysis has multiple facets and approaches, encompassing diverse techniques under a variety of names, in different business, science, and social science domains. (Anon n.d.)

This definition acknowledges the wide range of activities encompassed by the term data analytics. Tom Davenport's book "Competing on Analytics" offers the following definition.

> By analytics we mean the extensive use of data, statistical and quantitative analysis, explanatory and predictive models, and fact-based management to drive decisions and actions. The analytics may be input for human decisions or may drive fully automated decisions. (Davenport, 2006)

Again this is a broad definition. Clearly there are many different opinions on what data analytics is and what it should be called. Let's step back and define data analytics for the purposes of this book.

1.1.1 Data Analytics Definition

First and foremost, this book is a practitioner's book. We, therefore, need a practical definition of data analytics, so we can agree on what is in scope for discussion and what should be left to academic debate.

> Data analytics is any activity that involves applying an analytical process to data to derive insight from the data.

Figure 1 illustrates this definition. A customer and/or a third party provides raw data to an analytics team. Analysis is done on the data, producing some modified data output. This output is returned to the customer to provide the customer with insight.

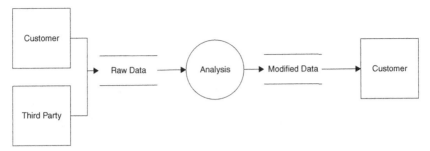

FIGURE 1   Definition of data analytics

1.1.2   Examples of Data Analytics

Such a general definition of data analytics means we can recognize analytics in many scenarios. Here are just a small number of data analytics activities.

- A phone company's customer complaints team keys in 500 poorly scanned customer complaint letters for their data team. The data team reports back on what the common complaint theme is in those letters. They have converted data that was difficult to access into usable data, which was then enriched with complaint keywords. They now have an insight into the common complaint themes from their customers.
- My dad gives me a spreadsheet of household purchases and I tell him how much he spends on groceries per month. I have taken data in the form of dates and purchases and summarized them by month to provide insight into spending patterns.
- Emma, the IT administrator, is concerned about user access controls. She gives Aaron, the data analyst, a year of system log activity. Aaron reports back how users can be grouped based on their activity and what the likely activity is at a particular time on a particular day of the week. Emma now has an insight into who is doing what on the systems she manages.
- Feargus is always looking for new indie bands. An online streaming music website trawls through its user data, mining song plays to make recommendations to Feargus on new artists that he might like.
- A utilities contractor receives its subcontractors' expense claims in hundreds of spreadsheets every month. These spreadsheets are brought together in a database, cleaned, and used to report on subcontractor expenses and search for potentially fraudulent expense claims.
- A financial services firm called OlcBank, having mis-sold financial products to their customers, is tasked with reconstructing the history of its product sales for inspection by a third party and a government regulator.
- A manufacturing plant Widget Inc., suspicious of fraud in its material purchase approvals wants to search its financial and manufacturing data for evidence of fraud.

There are several points to note from these examples of data analytics activities.

- **Technology agnostic:** First, there is no mention of any specific technology involved in the data analytics process. The analyst may be dragging formulas in a spreadsheet. They may be pushing data through the latest parallel streaming data processor. They may be training a troop of analytical monkeys to manipulate the data as required. Our definition is independent of the technology used and should not be confounded with the latest technology trend.
- **Activity agnostic:** Second, there is no differentiation between different types of data analytics activities. Some work is descriptive analytics that creates a summary and profile of data. Other work is data mining that trawls through data looking for patterns. Some work is predictive analytics that builds a model of the data and uses it to make predictions about new data. Some work is combinations of these things. The details of what is done with the data do not matter as long as the data is used to produce insight at some level of sophistication.
- **Scale agnostic:** Third, there is no attempt to comment on the scale or type of the data being analyzed. The work can deal with 100 rows in a spreadsheet table, 10,000 text documents describing insurance claims or some social media data feed approaching scales currently called "Big Data" (Franks, 2012).

This book is aimed at people involved in taking a variety of types of data from a variety of sources, analyzing it with a variety of methods of varying sophistication and returning it to their customers with insight. This insight can be used to make recommendations and take actions.

I cannot emphasize enough the importance of our general data analytics definition. It may surprise you how many activities can be considered as data analytics and how often people fail to recognize that they are working with data and doing analytics!

1.2 TYPES OF DATA ANALYTICS PROJECTS

Data analytics projects exist on a spectrum. At one end of this spectrum we have projects that are close to traditional software engineering projects. By traditional software engineering I mean the production of websites and web applications, desktop software applications, and data warehouses. To develop these analytics applications, a data model is carefully specified, coded, tested, and rolled out through development, user acceptance, and production environments. A presentation layer or application layer is programmed to sit on top of this data and present it to users so they can interact with it. Users may be customers on a website who see recommendations that match their purchasing habits. Users might be online banking customers who see analytics summarizing the performance of their investments or internal business employees who need insights related to their business's operations. Typical projects are those that manage data feeds, populate data warehouses or implement analytics and management reporting layers on top of warehouses. The development team involved in these projects typically has a variety of roles including database developers, application layer developers, testers as well as data analysts determining how best to extract value from the data. These projects produce software applications in the general sense that we all encounter and use every day on our computers and mobile devices.

At the other end of the spectrum, there are more ad-hoc data analytics projects. These involve taking some sample of data, exploring and analyzing it, and turning around some insight and recommendations based on the analysis. This type of work occurs in many fields. In research, you gather data and analyze it to test hypotheses and ultimately support the publication of research papers. In finance, quantitative analysts gather multiple data sources and mesh them together to present new financial models that give their trading teams an advantage. An organization's internal analytics team is often required to produce one-off ad-hoc support for internal business customers and these analyses often drive key business decisions. In consulting, short-term projects help a client understand the value in their data and inform the client's decision to invest in an analytics platform or an extension to their data warehouse. Inspired by a Harvard Business Review blog (Redman and Sweeney, 2013), I refer to the former projects as **Data Factory** projects and the latter as **Data Lab** projects.

In **Data Factory** projects, the team typically has their own development environment that is well-stocked with the necessary software engineering tools. These projects may be project managed with any number of well-established techniques for software development. The requirements of the project are generally well understood and agreed at a high level. Ultimately, the output is some software application that users will interact with to consume the data analytics insights provided. The team consists of process-oriented engineers who strive for engineering goals such as consistency, testing, and scalability.

In **Data Lab** project types, the data is often completely unknown and the project objective is simply to determine where the data is and what can or should be done with the data. Specification of an analysis or a data model is therefore pointless except on the shortest timescales and needs to be frequently revised as the project progresses. As the data is better understood, requirements change and business rules are revised. As a variety of analyses come into project scope, a wide variety of analytical tools must be applied to the data. The team is composed of "data scientists" whose goals are to find value and insight and to create and test hypotheses in one-off projects.

As Redman and Sweeney (2013) mention, the Data Lab and the Data Factory are complementary entities as illustrated in Figure 2. Innovation and data exploration happen in the lab. Productionized data analytics is rolled out in the factory. This is similar to a typical pharmaceutical company, for example. New drugs are developed and trialed in industrial labs. Then these drugs are

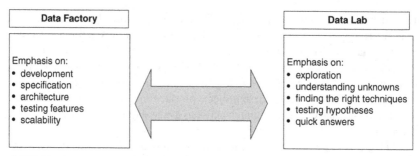

FIGURE 2   Spectrum of data analytics projects

mass-produced in factories and distributed to pharmacies and hospitals. Google advocates a similar complimentary approach to the interplay between their research and engineering (Spector et al., 2012).

1.3 INTRODUCING GUERRILLA ANALYTICS PROJECTS

Data Factory type analytics projects can leverage well-established software engineering approaches because they have so much in common. Collier (2011), for example, gives data warehouse development an analytics perspective. Tools and techniques from software engineering, such as version control, testing, and refactoring, are applicable to data factory projects.

The techniques and tools to use in Data Lab type projects are also well covered by texts on data analytics and machine learning (Witten et al., 2011). Analysts in a data lab have suites of algorithms to choose from and research fields devoted to improving those algorithms and tuning them to work on new data problems.

However, there is a large class of projects where some of the expectations of both the factory and the lab are present. These projects have many of the characteristics of the lab in that the data is not understood and must be explored. They also have many of the requirements of a factory in terms of repeatable and tested analyses that can be easily rolled out to end users. The project environment is extremely dynamic in terms of available resources (both people and technology), changing requirements, and changing data. In these scenarios, the Data Lab approach begins to fail.

- Teams with a range of skill sets and experiences are sharing code and data. There is no longer an individual data scientist coding analytics in isolation.
- The advanced analytics toolkits may not be available if the team is located on the customer's site.
- Clean data is not immediately identifiable or available for experimentation and the data keeps changing.
- Every experiment performed may be subject to external scrutiny and test.
- Every experiment performed may need to be explained to a customer in the context of previous experiment results.

In these scenarios the Data Factory approach also begins to struggle.

- There is no time for detailed data modeling, specifications, and requirements.
- Any requirements that do exist will probably change frequently.
- Helpful engineering tools such as test frameworks and refactoring methods may not be available or may never be made available in a project with short timescales.
- There is little role division – every team member has to be able to contribute to a bit of everything.

These projects are best described with phrases such as "extremely agile," "highly dynamic," "having many disruptions". These projects are where you need **Guerrilla Analytics**.

Think about guerrilla warfare. It is fought with small independent teams having limited weapons at their disposal. Guerrilla fighters are agile and move through a landscape making attacks on their larger enemy. They do not conduct battle in accordance with the conventional rules of engagement.

Our data analysts in these types of projects are similar to guerrillas. They often have limited tools. They do not have the time to produce detailed analytics plans and specifications. Instead they must be agile and go for quick wins under their tight timelines. They must deploy a wide variety of available analytical weapons against their foe – complex data that refuses to yield insights.

1.4   GUERRILLA ANALYTICS DEFINITION

Guerrilla Analytics is data analytics performed in a very dynamic project environment that presents the team with varied and frequent disruptions and constrains the team in terms of the resources they can bring to bear on their analytics problem.

The project environment can be dynamic for the following reasons.

- **Data changes** because of updates, corrections, and discovery of a requirement for new data sources.
- **Requirements change** because as the project progresses, the team and customer's understanding of the problem evolves.
- **Resources change** because these are real-world projects where staff go on leave or change roles and teams are composed of individuals with a wide range of experience and skills.

The project can be constrained in several ways too.

- Time is usually limited and so a "good enough" answer has to be reached quickly and justified.
- Toolsets will often be limited either because of circumstances at a customer's site or because it is simply impossible to anticipate the required tools for an almost infinite number of analytical scenarios.

The next sections elaborate on the typical characteristics of a project requiring Guerrilla Analytics.

1.4.1 Changing Data

Data in real-world projects is always subject to change. The data provided to the team can be replaced, appended to, or updated at a fairly high frequency. For example, in a dynamic data environment you may receive a delivery of several datasets that are critical to the project. After working on those datasets for several days, you could receive another delivery of those same datasets containing the very latest data. Alternatively, perhaps the earlier datasets were incomplete in some way or contained errors. Perhaps new data fields were discovered and added to the project scope.

1.4.2 Changing Requirements

Requirements in real-world analytics projects change at a high frequency. This is common in projects where the data is poorly understood. It is only as the first analyses and data explorations are completed that the analytics team and their customers better understand what can be done with the data. This presents a challenge for the guerrilla analyst who has to develop their analytics in a flexible and agile manner that can accommodate changing requirements while respecting the need for backwards compatibility with previous analyses.

1.4.3 Changing Resource

Highly dynamic resourcing means that you cannot guarantee who your team members will be and the team composition may change during the course of the project. This is very common in professional services and pre-sales functions where the work pipeline is usually quite "lumpy" and hard to predict. Your team is often dictated by who is available at the office. Similarly, in research, collaborative teams are very often composed of researchers from a variety of institutions and departments. The researchers available may be on relatively short-term contracts as they build their cases for academic tenure. You therefore have teams with a moving composition during the lifetime of the project and your projects need to be able to cope with the challenges they present.

1.4.4 Limited Time

Projects requiring Guerrilla Analytics are typically subject to tight timelines, particularly at the start of the project. Analyses can be due within a day or even an afternoon. Progress needs to be demonstrated within days of the project commencing. The guerrilla analyst therefore faces the challenge of developing and releasing work products in a staged manner so they can be interrupted and delivered at multiple time points.

1.4.5 Limited Toolsets

The toolsets available to a Guerrilla Analytics team are often restricted. This can be due to the team being located on a customer's site and subject to their customer's IT policies and available software licenses. It can also be due to tight project timelines where it can often take IT days or weeks to provision software. Since analytics projects are so varied, the right tool for the job is often not known in advance. A Guerrilla Analytics team must be prepared to do the best with what they have available.

1.4.6 Analytics Results Must be Reproducible

It is imperative that despite the obstacles presented above, the work products of the analytics team are reproducible. That is, when the team releases any given dataset, analysis, report, or other work product then the team must be capable of recreating that work product. While reproducibility is desirable in most work, in Guerrilla Analytics projects it is usually a critical requirement.

1.4.7 Work Products must be easily explained

It is one thing to be able to reproduce work products. It is another to be able to easily explain how that work product was derived. Explaining the derivation of a result entails three things.

- Understanding what data was used in creating the work product and where that data came from.
- Knowing how the data was filtered, cleaned, augmented, or any other modifications.
- Quantifying the impact of data modifications on analyses and populations.

1.5 EXAMPLE GUERRILLA ANALYTICS PROJECTS

You are probably wondering where such demanding and difficult sounding projects could occur. Not all projects will have all of the characteristics and requirements laid out in the Guerrilla Analytics definition of the previous section. Nonetheless, projects that have some combination of these characteristics and requirements are actually very common. Here are some examples, which you may recognize in your own work.

- **Forensic Data Analytics:** A financial event needs to be investigated. This could be an accounting fraud involving manipulation of accounts. It could be the circumstances leading up to a bankruptcy. It could be instances of bribery or price fixing. In all cases, legal pressures and scrutiny from one or more parties will require that all data analytics results are clearly derived, tested for correctness, and verifiably complete. However, the sensitivity of the data may mean that much of the analytics work has to be done in the unfamiliar territory of a client site. Timescales for the data analytics will often be very tight with teams usually arriving to analyze data within days of the alleged events. Because the need for such investigations is unpredictable, the analytics team is usually assembled from available resources. The team may not have worked together before. There will not be established team processes and procuring tools may take too much time under these timescales.

- **Data Analytics for Research:** Research is the ultimate unknown. Its very aim is to better understand some phenomenon. This is usually done by preparing hypotheses, designing an experiment to test the hypotheses, and gathering data from the experiment execution. The reality of modern research both in industry and academia is that it is a business. Like any business, its research outputs are measured and their quality and reputation leads to further funding from sponsors. In this competitive environment, successful research directors build labs that follow a particular line of research. There will be research contributions from summer undergraduate interns, graduate students, postgraduate researchers on short-term contracts, and collaborators from other research labs. In such an environment, a research director's team must produce reproducible analytics under tight publication timelines in such a way that knowledge and analyses can be handed off to other team members and the lab's capability can be grown.

- **Data Journalism:** Data journalism is a relatively new field (Rogers, 2012) pioneered by news publications such as the *Guardian* and the *New York Times*. Simply put, data journalism is about using available data sources to drive or support a compelling news article. The analytics to support data journalism faces many of the Guerrilla Analytics challenges. As news articles are released to a huge public audience, data journalists must ensure that their data, analyses, and conclusions are traceable, reproducible and that the data sources contributing to an article have good provenance. As publication deadlines are tight and breaking news is difficult to predict, data journalists often find themselves facing dynamic requirements, resourcing, and data.

- **Business Analytics and Management Information (MI):** Many organizations have their own internal business analytics team. One of the roles of this team is to provide ad-hoc analyses. These help answer business questions, drive strategy decisions, and provide insights and MI that are not yet available in productionized reports from the organization's data warehouse. We see this in many areas. A loyalty card provider may want to better understand its customer segmentation in light of new products launched by its rival. In banking, a retail bank is embarking on rationalizing its branches nationwide and wants to better understand customer profiles and activities at various branches. In all cases, the requirements are dynamic as they are driven by business exploration. In manufacture, an industrial engineer considering a change in a production process may first want to understand where there are bottlenecks and the current inefficiencies of the manufacturing process.

Data provenance and analytics traceability and reproducibility are critical because the analytics are usually reported to key business stakeholders and are the basis for important business decisions. These internal analytics teams are often extremely busy and have many internal customers to service. They need to be agile in their resourcing and produce analytics that are easily shared and swapped between team members. Since any of their work products may be further developed or may become critical in the boardroom, they also need to maintain their provenance, traceability, and reproducibility despite the very dynamic environment.

- **Quantitative Analytics:** The majority of modern financial trading functions are supported by quantitative analytics teams. These teams gather market data and other relevant third-party data, and use advanced analytics techniques to produce statistical models and recommendations that are relied on by traders. As markets move quickly, so must the quantitative analytics and underlying data. Analyses in these environments may have to stand up to regulatory scrutiny and internal audit despite the very dynamic nature of the work and the challenging demands of traders.
- **Analytics Pre-Sales and Proof of Concept:** In many scenarios, the value of analytics must be established before a customer commits to a sale or an internal stakeholder can secure a budget. This process is called pre-sales and a typical approach is to produce a proof of concept on a sample of the customer's data so they can justify investment in analytics to their business and stakeholders. Since funding is usually limited for a pre-sale, the analytics pre-sales team will face challenges of quickly and cheaply producing analytics. Having won a pre-sale however, there is often an expectation of a quick transition from the pre-sale "lab" to the production "data factory". Pre-sales teams therefore need to be able to mobilize quickly, explore several analyses in parallel, and consolidate the knowledge they acquire so it can be passed on to an implementation team if the sale is successful.

This is a small sample of scenarios from which you can see how prevalent Guerrilla Analytics projects are in research, industry, and consulting and professional services.

1.6   SOME TERMINOLOGY

This book is deliberately not prescriptive in its recommendations. The field of data analytics is too varied and too fast moving to make this a book about a specific programming language or technology. The book is also deliberately general so that data analysts and analytics and senior managers can benefit from its recommendations regardless of their particular industry sector. Before we progress, I want to lay out some common terminology used in the book.

- **Data Manipulation Environment (DME):** This is any environment in which data is modified and analyzed. The term is deliberately general as it covers relational databases, NoSQL databases, statistical environments such as R and SAS, and quite possibly scripts being run on a file system with a language such as AWK (Dougherty and Robbins, 1997) or Perl (Christiansen et al., 2000). This book's definition of data analytics focuses on the manipulation of data to provide insight. The DME is where this happens.

- **Data Analytics Environment:** The data analytics environment is everywhere that the data analytics team works. This is primarily two places. It is their project folder on a file system and it is their DME(s) as described above.

- **Dataset:** This is a general data structure that is manipulated in a DME. In a relational database, it would be a "table." In R it could be a "data frame." In a NoSQL document database it would be a JSON or XML document. Again, we wish to keep this term as general as possible as the book's principles apply to all data structures.

- **Data Field:** A dataset in the form of a table contains columns of data. A dataset in the form of a NoSQL document contains arbitrary attributes. For example, a "person" document could have first name, last name, and age attributes. In the general sense, this book refers to table columns and document attributes as data fields. This allows us to explore Guerrilla Analytics without being distracted by the underlying data modeling paradigm.

- **The Team:** When we refer to the team, we mean the data analytics team as opposed to any broader project team that they might be embedded in or collaborating with.

- **The Customer:** The customer is anybody who uses the insights created by the data analytics team. Examples include a business analyst or forensic accountant who is working with our analytics team, a client for whom we are engaged to do work or even the reader of a publication. Again, we keep things general and simple to avoid the distraction of internal and external stakeholders, team members, and clients.

- **Work Product:** A work product is a self-contained piece of analytics work. It does not necessarily get delivered to a customer. Typical analytics work products can encompass one or more program code files, spreadsheets, dashboards, data samples, presentations, and reports. When we speak of a work product we are referring to all the components that combine to define an atomic analytics output.

- **Business Rule:** This is a rule about the data that has been agreed between the team and the customer. Business rules are where the data and business understanding interface. Example business rules include "the field called EXP_DATE is the expiry date of an item" or "All financial product description records must have at least one corresponding financial product detail record."

- **Data Flow:** A data flow is one or more data manipulations executed in the production of a work product. A typical data flow takes some raw data, modifies it in one or more ways into derived data, and finally turns it into a presentation format for delivery to the customer.

- **Code:** Code or program code refers to the program commands written to manipulate and visualize data. Again, in the interest of generality, this does not refer to any specific programming language.

1.7   WRAP UP

This chapter introduced Guerrilla Analytics. You should have an understanding of the following.

- There is a wide variety of fields involved in what can be considered data analytics.
- To ensure that the scope of this book is clear, we defined data analytics very generally as "any activity that involves applying an analytical process to data to derive insight from the data."
- We discussed the spectrum of projects that involve data analytics. This spectrum ranges from the "data lab" where data is explored and analyses are trialed through to the "data factory" where the outputs of the lab are scaled up and rolled out through software applications.
- We introduced a type of analytics project that has many of the characteristics and challenges of the lab but is expected to produce outputs with the traceability, reproducibility, and provenance of the factory. These are the projects that require Guerrilla Analytics.
- We gave examples of common Guerrilla Analytics projects and explained the guerrilla warfare metaphor.
- We introduced some common general terminology that will be used throughout the book.

Chapter 2

Guerrilla Analytics: Challenges and Risks

2.1 THE GUERRILLA ANALYTICS WORKFLOW

We introduced Guerrilla Analytics in the previous chapter. Recall that Guerrilla Analytics projects are characterized as having some or all of the following.

- Highly dynamic data
- Highly dynamic requirements
- Highly dynamic resourcing

The project requirements and constraints are such that:

- There is limited time
- There are limited toolsets
- Results must be reproducible
- Results must be transparent and traceable

What does the analytics workflow look like in these types of projects? At a high level, data is received and work is done to understand it, prepare it, and produce analyses. This is no different from the workflow followed in many methodologies such as CRISP-DM (Chapman et al., 2000; Shearer, 2000) that is reproduced in Figure 3.

Not surprisingly, given what we now know about Guerrilla Analytics, its reference model is more iterative. It is as if somebody keeps moving the goalposts on us. We have to accommodate these disruptions while producing testable, reproducible analytics. Figure 4 summarizes the reality of data analytics in a Guerrilla Analytics project. Overall, data goes through the same lifecycle. Data is extracted from some source system and loaded into the team's Data Manipulation Environment (DME). It is then analyzed and perhaps consolidated before being issued in a formal report or smaller work product.

Some characteristics of this process immediately stand out.

- **Highly iterative:** Because the project data is poorly understood initially, it is necessary to commence analysis with the available data and the current understanding of that data. Because the customer is typically working very closely with the analytics team there is frequent feedback and requests

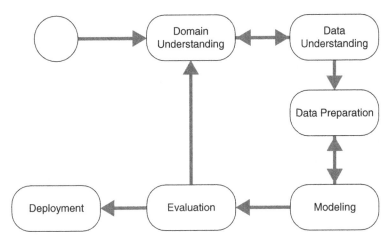

FIGURE 3   The CRISP-DM reference model (Jensen, 2012)

for changes to the analyses. This changes the reporting and work product requirements, which then drives new analytics or even requests for new data. Such change requests typically happen at any point in the Guerrilla Analytics workflow.

- **People are involved:** People are closely involved in the review of outputs and in data generation. Spreadsheets are often an unavoidable element of these projects as team members or customers mark up and modify outputs, which must then be fed back into the data environment.

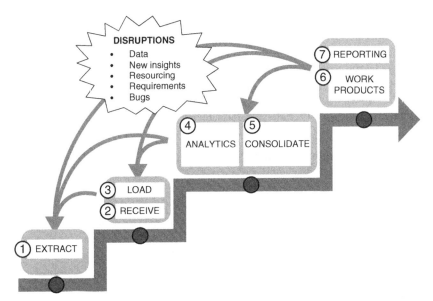

FIGURE 4   The Guerrilla Analytics workflow

- **Dynamic data:** These projects often have to begin and demonstrate progress before a definitive and verifiably correct dataset is available to the team. This means that the data is always changing. It is delivered piecemeal, replaced, and updated throughout the project. New data must feed into the analyses, but old data must also be preserved so that the impact on existing work products and understanding can be assessed. Guerrilla Analysts have to cope with this.

Despite these dynamics, Guerrilla Analytics projects often demand the following.

- **Testing of analyses:** Evidence of checking and testing of analyses is usually required. At the very least, the analytics work should be amenable to review and audit.
- **Reproduction of analyses:** Despite disruptions such as moving data and requirements, the team need to be able to preserve and reproduce any analysis.

At this point you are probably thinking this seems impossible. How can you possibly maintain visibility of your workings and reproducibility of your analyses with these constraints and disruptions and still get any work done?

This book aims to answer these questions. Before doing so, we will examine what specifically makes Guerrilla Analytics particularly difficult.

2.2 CHALLENGES OF MANAGING ANALYTICS PROJECTS

We have seen how complex Guerrilla Analytics projects can become. This complexity can lead to the project team becoming overwhelmed. If the result is not a failure of the project it is at least a very stressful and chaotic experience for the team. To manage this, you need to first understand what makes Guerrilla Analytics projects so challenging. This section identifies and describes the following challenges. The way to address these challenges will be the subject of Part 2 of this book.

In terms of data, the challenges include:

- Tracking multiple data inputs
- Versioning multiple data inputs
- Tracking multiple data work products
- Working with data generated by people
- External data sources

Analysis done on this kind of data presents its own challenges.

- Version control of analytics
- Creating analytics that is reproducible
- Testing and reviewing analytics
- Foreign data environment

Managing a team in this environment involves:

- Upskilling a team quickly
- Reskilling a team quickly

The subsequent sections now examine these topics.

2.2.1 Tracking Multiple Data Inputs

Your team is receiving data from a variety of sources. These sources could be some or all of the following.

- **Relational database extracts of database tables.** These may arrive as refreshes of existing data every couple of weeks. There may be both additions to and corrections of existing data tables.
- **Front-end reports from a variety of systems.** Even a simple report can be produced with a variety of report generation options. Consider the simple act of printing an office document. You can adjust page sizes, optionally include comments, and optionally hide certain parts of the document.
- **Web-scraped data.** This must be tracked to a particular date and time of extraction because web pages are dynamic and can often change by the hour.
- **Spreadsheets.** Being spreadsheets, they have no clear version control apart from their file names, may contain embedded text boxes and images, and probably contain several sheets within a given workbook file. If spreadsheets are reviewed and marked up by an end user for inclusion in your team's data, then you have additional problems of data quality and version tracking.
- **Large numbers of unstructured data sources.** Example includes email archives or document archives where documents are in a variety of file formats such as Microsoft Office and Adobe PDF.

The challenge is how to store and log receipt of these data sources and where to load them in the data environment so that their origins are easily identifiable. How can all of this be easily communicated to the team so that everybody can quickly find the right data with a minimum of documentation overhead?

2.2.2 Versioning Multiple Data Inputs

It is unavoidable that multiple versions of data will be issued to the team. Systems are live and so data needs to be updated during the course of the project. When mistakes are made in data deliveries, the data needs to be reissued with corrections. This is complicated when data can only be provided piecemeal because of resource constraints or the need to secure data release approvals. Meanwhile, spreadsheets of analyses are ongoing and need to be incorporated back into your DME at each revision.

How should these data versions be distinguished from one another? How should the team maintain older work products based on previous versions of the data but incorporate the new data into subsequent work products? Version control of data can get very complex. Which system is lightweight enough to deal with this complexity, but easy for a team to pick up and understand?

2.2.3 Tracking Multiple Data Work Products

Very early in the project, the analytics team will begin producing work products and issuing them to customers. Because Guerrilla Analytics projects are very dynamic, many work products will go through several iterations with the customer. During the course of these iterations, the underlying data itself can change for the reasons already discussed.

How should the team track these work products their iterations, the changes introduced in each iteration, and the impact of those changes? When a work product is returned to the team for discussion, modification, or correction, can the team easily and quickly determine how that work product was created, and where it is stored in their DME?

2.2.4 Data Generated by People

In a typical Guerrilla Analytics project, there will be data inputs from business users, accountants, analysts, and others. These people are not data analysts by trade, they do not benefit from the use of data analytics tools, and do not understand the complex nature of data.

Should this type of data be treated differently to data from warehouses and databases that have better controls? What additional checks should be put in place? How can you improve the interface between these team members and the DME?

2.2.5 External Data

The team will sometimes need to source external data. This could be data scraped from websites or it could be data from a third-party provider such as customer credit scores. These data sources present their own challenges because you are not working directly with the data provider in the same way as you are working with your customer. Websites change. External data providers have their own data formats and conventions that you must work with when you purchase their data.

How do you track and control such data sources? What do you do to maintain an efficient interface between these sources and your team's own data work?

2.2.6 Version Control of Analytics

A key challenge for an analytics project is how to produce reproducible work products against moving data sources and changing business rules and requirements. Some type of version control is required so you can say that a particular work product was produced against a particular version of the data with a particular version of business rules and team understanding.

How do you implement sufficient version control against both program code and data without swamping the analytics team in cumbersome process and administrative overhead? What is a basic process you can implement in the event that version control software is not available to you? Do you archive away data or keep everything available for the lifetime of the project?

2.2.7 Creating Analytics that is Reproducible

All the team's work products should be reproducible. That means you must know which versions of data, analytics code, analytics libraries, common custom code, and programming languages were combined to produce a version of a given work product. How do you do this in a lightweight manner that a team can understand and remember? Do you need to produce documentation with every work product? What about outputs such as spreadsheets, presentations, and reports? How do you maintain a link between a chart in a presentation and all the underlying code and data that created that particular chart? More difficult still, how do you do this for a single number that is quoted in a paragraph of text?

2.2.8 Testing and Reviewing Analytics

Even if a piece of analytics work can be reproduced, the work can typically involve many steps and the use of several tools. A team that has not worked together before will have different coding styles. There is much variety in the modularity with which data can be manipulated. You could have one analyst who uses one large piece of code, while another may break down the analysis into several smaller steps.

Is it clear what steps were taken in the analytics code? Can a reviewer of the work see the impact of analysis steps like filtering, deriving data fields, and removing records such as duplicates? How do you have confidence that the data has been correctly interpreted? How much modularity of the work is enough and how much is a burden on the team?

2.2.9 Foreign Data Environment

Very often, a Guerrilla Analytics team will find itself in a foreign data environment. By this I mean that their work will have to be done away from their home data lab on systems that belong to the customer. This is particularly true in forensic work, pre-sales work, and work with certain types of sensitive data such as employee and customer data. The customer will not want the data to leave their systems and so the analytics team must go to the data. Now the challenge is to produce analytics outside the team's comfort zone of their familiar data environment. Perhaps version control software is not available. Perhaps workflow tracking software is not available. Perhaps the DME itself is from a vendor that the team are unfamiliar with.

In these circumstances, how does a team do the best it can to deliver? What are the minimum lightweight tools and processes it needs so that the team can get up and running quickly, and start demonstrating value add for the customer?

2.2.10 Upskilling a Team Quickly

Because resourcing is dynamic, it is quite likely that many of the team have not worked together before. Furthermore, even when you establish a team, you may find that some team members leave or are replaced during the course of the project. Teams are often of mixed skills including data scientists and statisticians, database developers, and web developers to name a few.

Assuming you can create a process and team rules to cover all of the aforementioned challenges, are these processes and rules easy for the team's new joiners to pick up? How do you get to a minimal set of team guidelines so that the team can quickly upskill itself and remain agile and independent in the face of the challenges of the project environment?

2.2.11 Reskilling a Team Quickly

It is one thing to get a new team member up to speed quickly or have a handover of work run smoothly. However, on a busy and very dynamic project, even established team members' knowledge of the project can go out of date. New data is arriving frequently. New interpretations of that data are being agreed and implemented in the DME. Other team members may be working on similar analyses.

How do you set up sufficient communication channels so that team members are kept abreast of these changes and updates? Where do you store this evolving knowledge?

2.3 RISKS

Project risk is an uncertain event or condition that, if it occurs, has a positive or negative effect on one or more project objectives such as scope, schedule, cost, and quality.

(PMI, 2013)

Given the challenges of analytics projects just described, it is not surprising that so many are chaotic and stressful. These challenges introduce risks to delivery, the mitigation of which will be discussed in the rest of the book. These risks include the following.

- Losing the link between data received and its storage location
- Losing the link between raw data and data derived from raw during the analyst's work

- Inability to reproduce work products because the original source datasets cannot be found or have been modified
- Inability to easily navigate the analytics environment because it is cluttered with stray files and datasets or is overly complex
- Conflicting changes to datasets
- Changes to raw data
- Out of date documentation misleads the team
- Failure to communicate updates to team knowledge
- Multiple copies of files and work products
- Fragmented code that cannot easily be executed without the author's oversight
- Inability to identify the source of a dataset
- Lack of clarity around derivation of an analysis
- Multiple versions of tools and libraries in use but no way to know when a particular version was used

The next sections will elaborate on these risks and their effects, which you will hopefully recognize from your own project experiences and lessons learned.

2.3.1 Losing the Link Between Data Received and its Storage Location

This risk arises when data is stored in a variety of locations on the file system and imported into a variety of locations in the DME. This may happen because of time pressures, a lack of agreed guidelines, overwhelmingly complex guidelines, or simply laziness.

Figure 5 illustrates a folder structure that arises when a team is not managing this risk. There is no way to easily identify the sources of the datasets. Furthermore, data from various data sources has been mixed together. There are orphaned files and potentially duplicate files. Mapping this received data into the DME would be challenging.

Effect: Source data cannot be identified and so any derived analyses are not fully traceable.

War Story 1: The missing link

Paul was leading an analytics team working in pre-sales for an insurance fraud management solution. His team was working on a large tranche of data from the customer, searching it for fraud to demonstrate the value of the solution to the customer and hopefully secure a sale. Timelines were quite tight but the volume and complexity of data meant it took 2 days to process everything. Things had been going smoothly albeit with some long hours. The solution was performing well and all that was needed was to demonstrate a successful run on one last tranche of data. Data arrived with the team on Friday afternoon. The team eagerly extracted it, imported it, and set it up for the 2-day analytics run. Everybody went home for the weekend looking forward to the shiny new analyses that would greet them on Monday morning. What actually greeted Paul's team on Monday morning were some surprisingly familiar results. The same analyses produced the week previously had appeared again from the weekend run.

Paul hadn't been keeping an eye on his data receipts. The team was carelessly decrypting and unzipping raw data deliveries in various folders with names such as temp, temp1, copy_of_temp, etc. In all the confusion and looking forward to the weekend, they ended up running a long and expensive analysis on an old copy of the data. Needless to say, Paul's customer was not impressed that several days of project time were lost and a demo to key stakeholders had to be postponed. A missing link between data received and data processed can cause a team to go extinct.

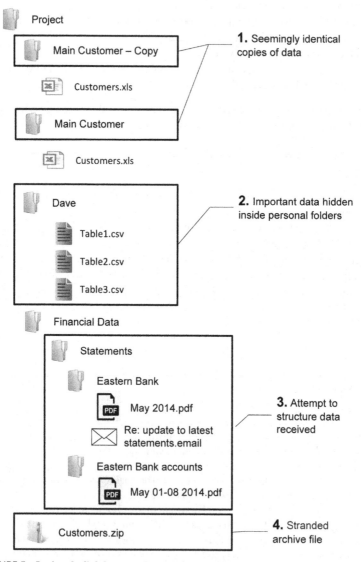

FIGURE 5   Losing the link between data received and its storage location

2.3.2   Losing the Link Between Raw Data and Derived Data

Your team will clean and manipulate raw data to produce "derived" data for every work product they create. This risk arises when the team cannot identify how derived data was created from raw data. In the typical project, lots of code is quickly written to get to a clean dataset with the required characteristics for analysis. The team then eagerly moves on to working out and delivering the analysis. However, during this process, the code files to clean and prepare the data are scattered and even lost.

Effect: Results cannot be easily reproduced and the team cannot confidently say whether a required business rule was applied.

War Story 2: This work product will self destruct

Natasha was an analyst in a small team working on a particularly intense project for a financial regulator. She was facing a mission impossible. Her job was to produce some initial baseline customer population numbers by the next day. This wasn't as easy as it sounds. There were many variations on business rules, each leading to a slightly different population of customers. The pressure was really on because the regulator needed a response from Natasha's customer the next day. She had a late finish around 6 am but the population was published and all was well. She had explored many alternative analyses in parallel, at speed and come up with a forensically sound result for the regulator. Success! That is, until she came back to the office the next day.

Which of the 20 code snippets was the one that produced the answer delivered to the customer? Had Natasha even saved the final code? The delivered work product was lost and only existed as the data sample she had exported from the DME and given to the customer.

It was probably another 2 days before Natasha was able to reproduce her own work product using a combination of sleep-deprived memory and searches through code files on the analytics server.

2.3.3   Inability to Reproduce Work Products Because Source Datasets have Disappeared or been Modified

Time and again, teams move datasets after they have been imported into the DME. The reasons given are usually something to do with archiving away a result, making space for a data refresh, or replacement of an incorrect dataset.

Effect: Any modification or movement of a dataset has the potential to break an unknown number of data processes and work products that may already depend on that data source. These breakages may not be discovered until somebody tries to re-run code to reproduce a work product.

2.3.4   Inability to Easily Navigate the Analytics Environment

This risk arises because of a lack of discipline in where data and analyses are stored on the file system and in the DME.

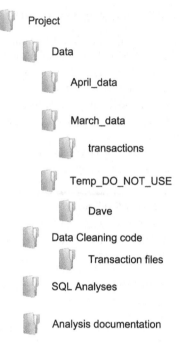

Project
　　Data
　　　　April_data
　　　　March_data
　　　　　　transactions
　　　　Temp_DO_NOT_USE
　　　　　　Dave
　　Data Cleaning code
　　　　Transaction files
　　SQL Analyses
　　Analysis documentation

FIGURE 6 **A complex project folder structure**

Figure 6 shows a project structure you often encounter. The creators of this project folder structure meant well. They thought about everything that was happening in the project, they classified the activities, and then they implemented this classification in the project folder structure. However, the dynamic nature of a Guerrilla Analytics project means that there will never be one stable classification of project activities. Work streams that once looked separate will later merge. New tools will be introduced as a project need arises so a separation of "SQL analysis" does not make sense. Separation of data cleaning and data analytics means you cannot easily execute the end-to-end data flow. Finally, because data folders are not sensibly time-stamped it is difficult to determine the order in which data arrived with the team. The problems go on.

Effect: An overly complex environment overwhelms analysts and defeats the purpose for which the complexity was introduced – being able to easily locate the data and analyses associated with a work product.

2.3.5 Conflicting Changes to Datasets

This risk arises when several analysts are working on the same datasets. One team member is producing a dataset that is to be used by other team members. This could be an analysis that the rest of the team are depending on or a convenience dataset that the analyst is providing to the rest of the team.

Effect: Without a clear process to separate datasets that are in development from datasets that have been released to the team, it is inevitable that users of these datasets are repeatedly interrupted. Users find that the dataset they need is either not available because it is being rebuilt, or its contents are in flux because its creator is in the middle of developing the dataset.

2.3.6   Changing of Raw Data

There is often a temptation to modify raw data when working under tight time-lines. Typically this happens when a flaw is spotted in the data and it is considered quicker to edit a minor fix in the raw data rather than applying a data flow to repair the flaw. It is important to realize that all analyses derive from the raw data received by the team.

Effect: Changes to the raw data can break any number of work products based on that raw data in ways that may not be discovered for quite a while.

War Story 3: A gremlin in the data

Christine was a junior data analyst working to support a team of marketing researchers at O' Garbanny Associates. The analytics team was along for the duration of a marketing campaign, taking survey data and web logs to provide insight on the success of the campaign targeting. Once a week, Christine would receive a large extract of survey responses and import them into the DME for cleaning, profiling, and analysis. There would always be data quality problems, but the team would handle those in program code, where business rules agreed with the customer were explicit and version controlled. This process ran smoothly. That is, until one day when the established numbers on customer preferences began to decrease dramatically.

How could this have happened? The team always just appended to their store of survey data and cleaned it up. No data was ever deleted. Was it a poorly implemented business rule? Perhaps it was a change to the data-cleaning libraries?

A senior team member spent several hours reviewing Christine's work. Meanwhile, the team manager had to explain a late delivery of the marketing report that was usually quickly turned around within half a day. That's when Christine mentioned the "fix" to the raw data. A single tiny flaw in the data had been throwing off one of Christine's data joins so she went into the raw data and edited it directly. The seemingly minor "fix" had resolved Christine's issue but had dramatically broken other analyses derived from the same raw data.

From that incident onwards, the team had a rule that they would never modify raw data. If you have a gremlin changing your raw data, then it's impossible to keep your work products reproducible and stable.

2.3.7   Out of Date Documentation Misleads the Team

One way that teams attempt to minimize the types of risks discussed so far is to better document their code and analytics. This is a good thing to aim for but is rarely practical. In a very dynamic environment it is quite likely that documentation will go out of date. Keeping pace with the fast-moving project introduces a significant administrative overhead on the team. The result is that documentation takes second priority to delivery.

Effect: Documentation rapidly goes out of data and actually misleads the team rather than helping them.

2.3.8   Failure to Communicate Updates to Team Knowledge

As the project progresses, there will be breakthroughs in understanding the data. New business rules will be discussed with the customer and implemented by the team. Fixes or modifications will be requested to existing analyses.

Effect: If these changes and requests are not communicated within the analytics team, work products may not be up to date with the latest knowledge and so are incorrect or contradictory. It reflects very poorly on a team that delivers two different interpretations of the same data.

2.3.9   Multiple Copies of Files and Work Products

It is natural for a work product to go through several iterations and versions. It is also common for a work product to have several components such as a report, analytics code, and perhaps a presentation to communicate the report's findings. As each of these components is iterated, a workspace can quickly become cluttered with older and redundant files.

Figure 7 may look familiar. There are multiple copies of the same file or at least files with similar names. There seems to have been several occasions

FIGURE 7   A confusing work product folder structure

when a "final" version of a file was produced. An attempt was made at an overly complex version number of some of the analysis files. The work product folder sits in the root of the project alongside other similarly named folders.

Effect: Reviewers and anybody who inherits the work product will struggle to know which versions of which files are relevant to the delivered analysis.

2.3.10   Fragmented Code that Cannot be Executed Without the Author's Input

Program code should execute from start to finish without interruption. This happens every time program code executes behind the scenes in the applications you use on your mobile device, desktop, etc. You do not need to be involved in what the program is doing. Analytics code often ends up different. Code files are written that must be executed under the supervision of a user, step by step, avoiding some steps and adjusting others. It is perhaps due to the nature of analytics coding, which involves summarizing and profiling data to understand how best to analyze it. It may also be due to a lack of analytics coding tools to allow easy refactoring and testing of code.

Whatever the reason, the result is a file of program code snippets, some of which are relevant to a work product and some of which are the analyst's experimentations and learning about the data during the course of the work product's development.

Effect: Fragmented analyses are time consuming to review and reproduce. The code cannot be executed without the guidance of the original author. If the author leaves the project, the specific knowledge of how to execute and reproduce the work product is lost.

War Story 4: Schrödinger's code

Andrew had done some excellent analysis that resulted in a few rules for dividing up a customer population into segments. His client was in the loyalty card business and needed to create some new offers targeted at particular customer groups. The derivation of the populations was not very complex: just combinations of some filters provided by the client in addition to the rules that Andrew had derived.

Using a single data query, Andrew modified his code several times to deliver the various populations to the customer. The customer loved it. Unfortunately for the rest of the team, Andrew's populations were not reproducible and Andrew was on holidays. His code was a collection of cuts and pastes, as well as code commented out to switch filters on and off. The more you tried to produce one population with his quantum code, the less you knew about one of the other populations. When the client asked for variations of the populations and Andrew wasn't around, the team were unable to answer simple questions about the data their own team had delivered. Nobody wanted to lift the lid on that piece of work.

2.3.11   Inability to Identify the Source of a Dataset

In traditional software engineering, it is relatively easy to jump between units of program code using a modern development environment. You can easily tell which piece of code calls another piece of code and navigate this "call hierarchy" through the code base. Analytics code is different. Analytics code is tightly coupled to the data because it changes the data it operates on. But code is usually held completely separately from the data. This makes it time consuming to investigate how a piece of data was created by one or more pieces of code. Keeping the link between data and the code that generated the data is critical.

Effect: The DME becomes cluttered with datasets of unknown origin that the team is afraid to delete. These make it difficult to navigate to the datasets that actually matter in the project.

2.3.12   Lack of Clarity Around Derivation of an Analysis

This risk arises when a data flow does not have a clear breakdown of the critical data manipulations into modular steps. It occurs for two main reasons.

The first is that much analytics involves the use of multiple tools. You may have to manipulate some data with a language like SQL, for example. You may then have to visualize this data in a spreadsheet. Finally you may produce a number that appears in the text of a written report. Without a clear connection between these components of the analysis, it is difficult to find where a particular data manipulation occurred or a filter was applied.

The second source of this risk is that analysts often try to do too much too quickly. That is, several data steps are combined into a single big data step. The reason given is to save storage space in the data environment or to improve the efficiency of analytics code and save time. The challenge here is to balance the need for space and speed with the clarity of the steps taken to produce an analysis.

Effect: If more time is spent trying to unravel and understand an analysis, then it would have made more sense to break down that analysis into manageable data steps in the first instance.

2.3.13   Multiple Versions of Tools and Libraries

There are various factors that influence an analytics output including the version of raw data, version of program code, and the application of business rules. A factor that is often overlooked is the tools and libraries that are used by the analytics code. Perhaps the analytics code uses version 2.7 of a language in combination with version 8.1 of a third-party library. If a team is working in a dynamic environment and is under pressure to solve problems, they will likely need various versions of languages and libraries.

Effect: Not being clear on which versions of a language and a helper program library are being used in an analytics work product can result in a work product that cannot be reproduced.

2.4   IMPACT OF FAILURE TO ADDRESS ANALYTICS RISKS

The failure to address some or all of these analytics risks has many adverse effects on the analytics project.

With any of these risks you increase the likelihood that the team's analytics outputs are incorrect, contradictory, or inconsistent. There is also a detrimental effect on team efficiency. The team spends a disproportionate amount of time trying to communicate their work to one another, find their own data, and reproduce their own analyses. In terms of reviewing, managers and reviewers require a detailed description of a work product from its author before they can begin. Team members struggle to handover work and so rolling off and onto the project is unnecessarily difficult. Team members can get left behind in terms of the latest changes in the DME because new versions of data knowledge are not communicated effectively.

Failure to address these risks leads to environment inefficiency. If there is no confidence in the source of datasets and no identification of raw data, then datasets are generally kept lying around in case they are needed in the future. This eventually leads to a cluttered environment that everybody is afraid to modify and struggles to navigate.

Overall, stress and frustration ensue. The team is working hard and doing their best for the customer, but appear to be forever chasing their own tail trying to understand and trace their own data and their own work products.

If you are to deliver a Guerrilla Analytics project successfully and minimize unnecessary stress and chaos, you need a way to mitigate these risks. This is where you need the Guerrilla Analytics Principles.

2.5   WRAP UP

In this chapter you learnt about the challenges of a Guerrilla Analytics project and the risks introduced by these challenges. This chapter has covered the following.

- We described the Guerrilla Analytics workflow and distinguished it from the analytics workflow described by CRISP-DM.
- We saw how at every stage of the Guerrilla Analytics workflow, data provenance is threatened by the dynamic nature of the Guerrilla Analytics project and the constraints placed on the team.
- We described the typical challenges involved in managing Guerrilla Analytics projects.
- We looked at the risks to the project that arise because of those challenges.
- We finished by describing the detrimental impact of failing to manage a Guerrilla Analytics project's risks.

Chapter 3

Guerrilla Analytics Principles

3.1 MAINTAIN DATA PROVENANCE DESPITE DISRUPTIONS

The previous chapter's challenges and risks may have been familiar to you. You may have finished that chapter feeling a little depressed by all of these challenges and risks posed by analytics projects. Nonetheless, we cannot escape the fact that analytics work is complex and Guerrilla Analytics projects even more so. There are so many moving parts across the data, the requirements, the understanding of the data, and in the team itself. This is made worse by the constraints on available tools, resourcing, and the requirement for reproducible and traceable work products.

Looking back through the multitude of challenges and risks described in the previous chapter, you may have noticed a common theme.

- There are many disruptions presented to the team. Examples include data refreshes, changing resources, unforeseen data issues, and changing requirements as data understanding grows.
- These disruptions present risks and the effects of these risks are confusion, incorrect analyses, wasted time in repeated communication, inefficiencies, and ultimately project chaos. The team loses track of the latest data and business rules. Code bases are poorly maintained and versioned.

The key insight that drives the Guerrilla Analytics Principles is that the primary cause of these risks is a lack of data provenance. Data provenance is the ability to trace where data came from, how it was changed, and where it ended up. If data provenance could be maintained then a team would be robust against the inevitable disruptions to their work because they would know the following.

- All data and versions ever received by the team and any associated issues affecting that data.
- All versions of business rules derived by the team or dictated by the customer and when those rules came into effect.
- All data manipulations and changes performed on the raw data received by the team to produce work products issued by the team.
- Every work product created by the team as well as when it was created, who worked on it, and who it was delivered to.

- All work products would be reproducible, given the raw data and the particular business rules that were known at the time the work product was created.

The good news is that maintaining data provenance is possible despite the disruptions of a Guerrilla Analytics project. It requires keeping in mind only a small number of guiding rules when doing analytics work. These are the Guerrilla Analytics Principles.

3.2   THE PRINCIPLES

3.2.1   Overview

The Guerrilla Analytics Principles are as follows.

- **Principle 1:** Space is cheap, confusion is expensive.
- **Principle 2:** Prefer simple, visual project structures over heavily documented and project-specific rules.
- **Principle 3:** Prefer automation with program code over manual graphical methods.
- **Principle 4:** Maintain a link between data on the file system, data in the analytics environment, and data in work products.
- **Principle 5:** Version control changes to data and program code.
- **Principle 6:** Consolidate team knowledge in version-controlled builds.
- **Principle 7:** Prefer analytics code that runs from start to finish.

The Guerrilla Analytics Principles are not prescriptive. As discussed earlier, data analytics is a wide-ranging field that encompasses many activities and technologies. Instead, the principles aim to help you make the right decisions in coordinating your analytics work so that data provenance is preserved. The resulting benefit is that the challenges and risks of the Guerrilla Analytics project can be addressed.

As we elaborate on these principles throughout the book, you will see that they borrow from fields such as Agile, Extreme Programming (Kent Beck, 1999), Test-Driven Development (Beck, 2002), Continuous Integration (Duvall et al., 2007), and Continuous Delivery (Humble and Farley, 2011). A familiarity with these topics would certainly help but is not necessary in understanding and implementing the Guerrilla Analytics Principles. The subsequent sections now explain the principles in more detail.

3.2.2   Principle 1: Space is Cheap, Confusion is Expensive

Data takes up storage space and storage space costs money. While this consideration is important, especially with large data volumes, it is surprising how teams will scrimp on trivial amounts of storage space.

Teams can lose hours of project time because they failed to retain a back-up copy of data on the file system, when data had been lost from the Data Manipulation Environment. Similarly, I have seen hours lost in tracing the source of a work product because an analyst jumped straight into modifying a spreadsheet from a customer without taking a copy of the original file. Often, as work product versions evolve, the older versions are overwritten and replaced instead of archived. This causes confusion if multiple versions are "in the wild" with the customer and cannot now be reproduced.

This principle emphasizes that when faced with space considerations, always think about the impact on loss of data provenance. Ultimately, this is more expensive for the team than trivial amounts of storage space.

3.2.3 Principle 2: Prefer Simple, Visual Project Structures Over Heavily Documented and Project-specific Rules

If project folder structures are complex, then busy data analysts will not have time to understand and follow them. If database structures are complex, then new team members struggle to roll onto the project and agility is compromised. Not only do team members struggle to "find things," they become overwhelmed when deciding where to "put things." This problem is exacerbated when your teams move between several projects and find that each project has its own specific rules and conventions.

The more visual and simple a project structure is, the easier it is to understand and follow. This principle applies to all project folders, data environment structures, and team conventions.

For example, consider the project structures shown in Figure 8. In the first folder structure on the left, it is impossible to know where to store data. The data folder seems to be categorized by type of data and then by receipt date. Analytics work is scattered in a variety of folders, again with a nonsense categorization by analytics programming language. The project has been broken up into many components and some of them seem to overlap. The result is that rather than incorrectly storing an analysis, data or documentation, the teams instead create their own structures that each of them understands individually. Over time, the project's structures deteriorate to the point that nothing can be easily found.

In the second scenario on the right, the core functions of the project have been identified and assigned a single folder. All data goes in one place. All analyses go in one place. You do not have to think about where to locate things because it is obvious. Each team member has his/her own workspace for everything temporary he/she may need to do.

You could think of this principle as "convention over configuration." The approach is straightforward and the simple naming convention is understood by looking at the project folder rather than remembering some complex project

FIGURE 8   **A complex project structure and a simple, visual project structure**

configuration guideline. Similar conventions should be applied in the Data Manipulation Environment.

3.2.4   Principle 3: Prefer Automation with Program Code Over Manual Graphical Methods

Program code is arguably the most expressive tool we have for clearly and definitively describing our analytics work. Program code explicitly describes how data is being changed, the rules that are being applied, and the correctness checks that are done.

However, there are also analytics tools that allow you to work through a graphical user interface rather than use program code to manipulate data. Use of these tools has implications for data provenance.

Think about data manipulated in a spreadsheet. A typical workflow could involve copying data to a new worksheet, dragging a formula down a column to apply it to some cells, and then pivoting the final worksheet. These manual operations of copying and dragging are not captured anywhere in the spreadsheet and so are difficult to reproduce.

This principle states that as far as possible, analytics work should be done using program code.

3.2.5 Principle 4: Maintain a Link Between Data on the File System, in the Analytics Environment, and in Work Products

When aiming to preserve data provenance, it is helpful to think of data flowing through your team and your analytics environment. Imagine a data point arrives with your team (perhaps accompanied by several million other data points). The data is stored on a file system before being imported into the Data Manipulation Environment. The data is then manipulated in several ways such as cleaning, transformation, and combination with other data points. The data then leaves the team as one of the team's work products. At each of these touch points, the data is potentially being changed by one or more team members and one or more processes. Problems arise when a work product's data is incorrect or is questioned by the customer. Errors could have been introduced at any stage of the data's journey from raw to work product.

This principle emphasizes that you should strive to maintain the traceability of the data on this journey. You should be able to look at a data point in an output work product and quickly trace its origins back to its raw source, if necessary.

3.2.6 Principle 5: Version Control Changes to Data and Program Code

If Guerrilla Analytics is essentially about preserving data provenance in spite of disruptions, then we must consider the factors that affect data provenance. The provenance of analytics work is broken if any of the following change.

- **Raw data:** If raw data changes then all analyses built on top of that raw data may also change. A raw data change could consist of renaming a dataset, changing a dataset location, or changing the contents of the dataset in terms of either its fields or field values.
- **Code that manipulates the data:** If you modify your analytics code then your analyses will change. These modifications could arise because of a change in business logic, addition of cleaning rules or any seemingly innocent modification of analytics program code.
- **Common routines applied to the data:** Your analysis code may call out to common routines built by the team such as cleaning routines. If those routines change then your analysis will also potentially change.
- **External software and libraries used by the code:** Your analysis may use a third-party library or a particular version of a programming language. If those libraries and languages are updated or changed by the team then potentially your analysis outputs will also change.
- **Tuning parameters:** Many analyses, particularly statistical analyses and machine-learning algorithms, have a variety of tuning parameters that change their behavior. In a clustering problem, for example, you may specify the number of clusters or threshold distances between clusters as an input to the algorithm. In a statistical model, you may specify a significance or

power level for statistical tests. Changing these types of input parameters will change the outputs of the process.

This principle emphasizes that you should control changes in any of these factors. You can do this by putting in places a few simple checks and rules.

- Never modify raw data after it has been imported into the Data Manipulation Environment.
- Once analytics code has been used for a work product, never modify that code. When the code needs to be revisited, make a new version of the code.
- Be clear on the versions of common routines used by your code and make sure that those common routines are themselves version controlled.
- Be clear on the versions of program languages and libraries used by your code and never replace those languages and libraries. If languages and libraries need to be upgraded then do so while also keeping the older versions available for reproducing existing analytics work products.
- Record input parameters to algorithms and statistical tests so that they can be rerun and produce the same outputs.

Subsequent chapters will elaborate on this principle throughout the analytics workflow.

3.2.7   Consolidate Team Knowledge in Version-controlled Builds

As the project progresses, understanding of the data will grow and evolve. For example, team members may learn that a particular data source needs to be deduplicated before it can be used. The customer may specify a certain business rule that they would like to see in all work products. A coded field value such as "MPR100" might have an agreed business translation. These pieces of team knowledge must be centralized somewhere in the team for consistency and efficiency.

An analytics build is a centralized and version controlled data structure or analytics functionality that captures team knowledge and version controls it.

Consistency is achieved because data knowledge now resides in one location. Efficiency is achieved because much of the hard work of preparing data and solving technical problems has already been done and is published to the entire team in the build.

Builds are version controlled because team knowledge grows and changes during the project. Older work products were built on older knowledge represented in older versions of the build.

3.2.8   Principle 7: Prefer Analytics Code that Runs from Start to Finish

Analytics code by its nature is exploratory. A data analyst will summarize and profile data and apply many transformations to it as they seek to understand the data. Creating an analytics model is an iterative process of creating new variables, scaling them, and testing whether they are good predictors for a variety of model types, such as regression or decision trees. If not managed carefully, this exploratory nature of the work can lead to poor coding practices. Code snippets to profile data and test hypotheses linger in final work product code. These snippets clutter program code files with code that is not needed to reproduce the work product. They very often break code execution with the result that reproducing the work product necessitates a time-consuming stepping over the older code snippets. Code reviews are more time consuming than necessary because a reviewer must work out which snippets to avoid. Since code is cumbersome to execute, execution is delayed or avoided and this increases the risk of bugs and broken data provenance going undetected.

A simple principle of delivering code that executes from start to finish eliminates these problems while still accommodating the need for data exploration and iterative model development.

3.3 APPLYING THE PRINCIPLES

Guerrilla Analytics projects can be successfully managed and the risks of the project environment can be mitigated by following the Guerrilla Analytics Principles. The question then becomes, how to implement these principles and how to manage a Guerrilla Analytics team.

First of all, let us acknowledge that a top-down management approach to Guerrilla Analytics projects will not work. Analytics projects are complicated and Guerrilla Analytics projects are arguably more so. The natural human reaction is to "manage" this complexity through rules and conventions. This is a top-down approach. Some typical symptoms of a top-down management approach and their impact include the following.

- **Controlling complexity with project folders:** A complex project folder structure that is for the convenience of management instead of the reality of data analytics work. Management attempts to "standardize" an analytics project structure with categorizations that often look like the following.
  - Requiring that emails be stored in a "communications" location separate from the work they are related to. The intention is to be able to easily identify all communications with the customer. The effect is that links have to be created between communications and their associated data and work products in another project location.
  - Requiring that stages in the analytics workflow such as data cleaning have a distinct tree of folders separate from other stages in the data analytics workflow. The effect is that it becomes very difficult to group together all code files associated with a particular work product.
  - Deciding that folders should be categorized by programming language so you have folders such as "SQL code." Presumably Python code, Java code, spreadsheet analyses, Tableau dashboards, and all other data manipulation languages get their own project folders too?

- **Controlling delivery with process:** Imagine a cumbersome process that analysts must follow to create and deliver their work. In one instance, to improve traceability of work products, the team was instructed to copy all delivered work products into a deliverables folder. Needless to say that under pressure, quick fixes were made to work product copies in this deliverables folder rather than the original project location. Deliverables went out of sync with their original code and data. The impact here was confusion and inconsistency in delivered work products.
- **Pushing administration down to analysts:** Analysts are busy summarizing their work for project managers because only the analysts can keep pace with the details of the high volume of outputs being released to the customer. Detailed data dictionaries, data logs, and requirements documents are requested in an attempt to maintain oversight of what the team is doing. These documents cannot be produced and maintained at the pace of the project's delivery and evolving understanding and so the documentation goes out of date and is not useful.

You may have many examples of your own. Perhaps as a manager you are guilty of inflicting top-down control on your team so that you and your stakeholders have more comfort in your team's outputs. This approach simply doesn't work. It takes analysts away from the activities where they can add most value. The manager and project manager are often little wiser in their understanding of their team's outputs. The processes themselves are complicated and amount to little more than a box-ticking exercise. This approach does not scale and the team simply will not follow the top-down process in a highly dynamic Guerrilla Analytics project.

I have thought a lot about these challenges over the years and tried several approaches to managing Guerrilla Analytics projects with the input of the teams I have managed. A successful Guerrilla Analytics management approach should have the following characteristics.

- **Bottom up:** There should be a structure and order to the project that emerges from the work of the analysts and complements the work of the analysts rather than being imposed to suit a project management agenda. If done correctly, this bottom-up approach can also satisfy project management requirements.
- **Not disruptive:** As far as possible, the analysts should be able to satisfy the requirements of coordinating the project and reducing the analytics risks without having to interrupt their workflow for documentation, box checking, or some other burdensome administration.
- **Simple and lightweight:** There should be minimal overhead of documentation, rules, and conventions that the team needs to absorb and remember.
- **Consistent:** As far as possible, all data should be treated in a similar fashion, all code should follow some basic conventions, and all work products should have a similar structure. This minimizes what the team needs to learn and so keeps the team flexible and agile.

The subsequent chapters will describe how to implement Guerrilla Analytics Principles throughout the analytics workflow. As you go through the workflow stages, note how these four management characteristics are always present.

3.4 WRAP UP

This chapter has introduced and described the Guerrilla Analytics Principles. You should now be familiar with the following topics.

- **Maintaining data provenance despite disruptions:** What makes Guerrilla Analytics projects particularly challenging is the variety and frequency of disruptions. Data is changing, business rules are evolving, resource is changing, and requirements are changing. This causes data provenance to break. The team loses track of where data is located, how that data was changed, and where analyses based on that data were delivered. If data provenance can be maintained, many of the risks and challenges of an analytics project with frequent disruptions are mitigated and overcome.
- **The Guerrilla Analytics Principles:** These are a small set of lightweight rules of thumb that promote data provenance and so help in the management of the risks and challenges of a Guerrilla Analytics project.
- **Managing Guerrilla Analytics projects:** To apply the Guerrilla Analytics Principles successfully, a management approach must be adopted, that is:
  - Bottom up
  - Simple and lightweight
  - Not disruptive
  - Consistent

Part 2

Practice

Chapter 4

Stage 1: Data Extraction

4.1   GUERRILLA ANALYTICS WORKFLOW

Data Extraction is the first stage in the Guerrilla Analytics workflow (Section 2.1), as illustrated in Figure 9. It involves taking data out of some system or location so it can be brought into the analytics team's Data Manipulation Environment (DME). The place the data is extracted from is called the "source" and the environment it is brought into is called the "target." Data extraction also involves validating that the extracted data is correct and complete.

Data extraction is quite a broad set of activities. These are the main types of data extraction to consider:

- **System data extractions:** These involve connecting to the back-end database that underlies some application and taking a copy of the data in the application at a point in time. Some systems will provide a mechanism to dump data out of the system consistently. Other systems will require custom program code to query data out of the system. Back-end data extractions are desirable in a project because they provide data in its most raw form, and therefore in a form that is most flexible for the analytics team. The data has not yet been presented in the application layer, where it is often modified for user convenience. However, in this type of data extraction you will typically encounter a variety of database systems, each of which will have their own flavors of programming languages and their own custom data structures.
- **Front-end data extractions:** These involve connecting to the application front-end as a user and capturing some data that the application presents. This data is typically in the form of business intelligence reports. Some applications conveniently provide a method to export and save reports in a variety of file formats such as PDF and spreadsheets. Some applications allow you to construct custom reports by graphically arranging reporting elements. Other web applications may have to be "scraped" to grab the data that is presented in the application. Scraping is the process of using an automated method to simulate human interaction with a web page, capturing the web page information that is presented by the application. A web scraper could, for example, automatically click through all train timetables presented on a company's website and scrape those timetables into a series of datasets.

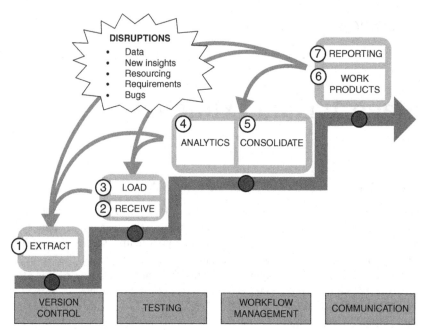

FIGURE 9 The Guerrilla Analytics workflow

- **Optical character recognition (OCR):** Despite the fact that we now live in a "data" age, there are still many occasions on which data is trapped in scanned documents. That is, printed, typed, or even hand-written documents have been scanned into an electronic file format. This is still common with legal documentation and in legacy storage in financial institutions. OCR is an automated process for turning these scanned documents into "real" digital content such as text and numbers.

The Extraction stage of the Guerrilla Analytics workflow is sometimes done by the customer's IT team as they prepare data for your team. Nonetheless, the Guerrilla Analytics team does on occasion perform data extractions themselves because of the customers' lack of capability. Either way, it is important to understand the processes involved so that data provenance can be preserved at this critical first stage in the analytics workflow.

4.2 PITFALLS AND RISKS

There are several pitfalls and risks to be aware of when extracting data. These depend on the type of data extraction that is taking place.

- **Extracting from a moving target:** The source system is not frozen before an extraction takes place. This means that data continues to be generated as the data extraction is taking place. Checks performed on the extracted data cannot be easily compared to data in the originating source system because the data has "moved on" in the intervening time since the extraction.

- **Inability to assess completeness:** The data is not quantified before extraction. When the data extraction is finished there is nothing to compare the extracted data to, and so there can be no confidence that the extraction is complete and correct.
- **No reproducibility of extraction process:** The scripts to execute the extraction (either custom scripts or commands to the system's data export utility) are not saved properly. If questions arise regarding the extracted data or the extraction needs to be repeated for a data refresh, there is no record of how the data was previously extracted.
- **Nothing to compare to:** Front-end reports are not captured from the system at the time of data extraction. Front-end reports are a useful check for the correctness of the extracted data. They are also helpful when reverse engineering a system and its data relationships, as they effectively present business rules to the user. Both of these advantages can be lost if the captured front-end reports are not in sync with the extracted data.
- **Front-end reports cannot be reproduced:** Many applications are complex. It may be possible to generate a "single" report using a large combination of options and filters. The available options and filters can also depend on the type of user logged into the system. For example, administrators will have more visibility of the system than general users. If front-end reports cannot be reproduced then they are less useful in reverse engineering the system.
- **No record of web pages:** Web pages are dynamic content. Today's *BBC* news page is different from yesterday's. If no raw copy of an extracted web page is saved then it is impossible to check if a web scrape was done correctly.
- **No checks of OCR data:** OCR is prone to errors. A number 3 often gets confused with a number 8, for example. These errors can have serious implications in financial data where numbers are very important! Thought needs to be given as to how OCR documents can be checked for consistency and correctness, especially when OCR data is not in a neat tabular form.

These pitfalls and risks are of concern to the Guerrilla Analytics team because they can invalidate all subsequent work. Under tight timelines, the team cannot afford to make these basic mistakes in acquiring data. The following tips will now guide you in ways to mitigate the effects of these data extraction risks and pitfalls.

4.3 PRACTICE TIP 1: FREEZE THE SOURCE SYSTEM DURING DATA EXTRACTION

4.3.1 Guerrilla Analytics Environment

If you wish to validate that your extracted data are correct and complete, then you need to first determine what correct and complete is. When a system is running and live, then you have a moving target. By the time you have run a data extraction, the data in the system will be newer and different to what were extracted. This leaves you with no source record for meaningful comparison.

4.3.2 Guerrilla Analytics Approach

When a data extraction is being executed, freeze the source system or clone it for the duration of the extraction.

4.3.3 Advantages

With a data extraction from a frozen or cloned system:

- **No moving target:** There is a static copy of the data from which key data characteristics and profiles can be recorded. This addresses Guerrilla Analytics concerns around data provenance.
- **Reports and data in sync:** Because the data is static, so too are the system's reports. It is therefore possible to capture useful front-end reports that are guaranteed to tie out to the underlying system data. This helps begin the process of understanding the data without the need for detailed documentation that can be difficult to acquire.

4.4 PRACTICE TIP 2: EXTRACT DATA INTO AN AGREED FILE FORMAT

4.4.1 Guerrilla Analytics Environment

Extracted data will be loaded into the analytics team's target DME. If the customer's source system and the analytics team's target system are the same, then data transfer is usually feasible using a data export format that the source system provides. Most relational databases, for example, can export their data into binary or text file format. However, it is far more common for the source and target systems to differ. This raises the question of how two different systems can exchange data safely.

Here are some examples of the thorny issues that arise. Consider the date "Tuesday 17th March 2002." Do we extract that as "Tue 17/03/2002" or "2002-03-17"? What about "03-17-02"? In terms of the extracted file format, do we assume that the first row of the file describes data field names, or are those names provided separately? Which characters separate data fields from one another? How are separator characters handled when they appear within a data field? How do we terminate an extracted file so that we know it was not truncated during extraction? There is much to consider and agree on at the outset of data extraction.

4.4.2   Guerrilla Analytics Approach

It is imperative to specify and agree the data format when extracting and exchanging data. The data format covers both the overall format of the file and the format of data fields within the file. There is no right or wrong answer here (although some answers are far better than others). What is important is that the file format is agreed on and is consistent. Some important data field format considerations are:

* What is the agreed date and date time format?
* What is the agreed floating point number format?
* What decimal separators are used, if at all? Some countries use 20,000 while others write 20.000.

Once the data field formats are agreed, then a data file format must be agreed. Perhaps the most common flat text file format in use is the Comma Separated Value (CSV) file format. Surprisingly, there is no agreed standard for a CSV file, so make sure you are clear on exactly how the CSV file is constructed. In terms of the CSV file format, consider:

* **Field separators:** The character or characters that separate fields.
* **Enclosing characters:** The character or characters that enclose fields.
* **Escaping:** How to handle the situation when a separator or enclosing character appears within a field as valid field content.

There are several attempts to agree to a CSV standard and these are useful for further reading (Shafranovich, 2005). Increasingly other self-describing formats are also in use such as XML and JSON. Again there is no right or wrong answer in the choice of formats. What is important is agreement, consistency, and awareness of the risks that can arise.

4.4.3   Advantages

Agreeing and specifying the data extraction format is critical to successful data extraction and transfer to target. Any mistake at this point affects all subsequent work with the data.

* **Reduced risk of corruption:** If field formats are not clearly agreed, data can easily be corrupted at import into the DME. A classic and all too common example is that of dates. The date 4 September (04-09-2010 in one format) becomes 9 April when interpreted as Month-Day format.
* **Ease of interpretation:** Interpretation of the file format is straightforward and unambiguous.
* **Source and target compatibility:** A file format that best suits both the source and target DME system can be agreed on to make data exchange less painful for both parties.

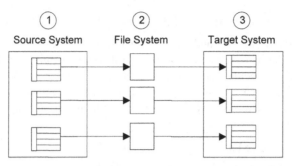

FIGURE 10 The journey of extracted data

4.5 PRACTICE TIP 3: CALCULATE CHECKSUMS BEFORE DATA EXTRACTION

4.5.1 Guerrilla Analytics Environment

If you think about the data's journey, there are three stages it goes through. These are illustrated in Figure 10.

- **Source:** Dataset on the original system, which may have its own proprietary data types.
- **File System:** Extracted datasets in a neutral format for exchange between systems.
- **Target:** Datasets imported into the DME, which again may have their own data types.

It is often a surprise to people to learn that data can easily be corrupted as it moves between these three stages. Databases, warehouses, and other applications are generally not designed for dumping out their data – they are designed for storing and archiving their data. Administrators rarely encounter a requirement to reverse this process and start moving data out of their systems. The process of writing custom code to turn a dataset into a file with an agreed specification can have bugs. The same applies when the data is moved from a file into the DME. At any of these transitions, data can be corrupted or truncated, thus breaking data provenance.

4.5.2 Guerrilla Analytics Approach

Think of when you get change from a purchase in the shops. The cash register reports what your change should be. The sales assistant takes that cash out of the register and usually counts it in front of you to verify it for them and you. They then hand the cash over to you. You might do another quick count of the notes and coins before you put the cash in your pocket. This is a good analogy for data extraction. The source system (cash register) reports that it has a certain amount of data (cash) for extraction. The system administrator (sales assistant) takes that data out of the system and counts it to verify for them and for you that the expected amount of data was taken out of the system. When you receive the cash, you do another count to make sure you did not drop a coin or perhaps that two notes were not stuck together.

The best way to detect errors in data transfer is to calculate checksums on the data before it leaves its original source system, and again calculate checksums on the data after it is loaded into their target destination in the DME. A checksum is a type of calculation on the data such that if the data changes then the result of the checksum calculation changes. Typical checksums for analytics include sums of values and sums of string lengths. Since checksums are so important to the integrity of data at the very beginning of the Guerrilla Analytics workflow, they are given a more detailed treatment in a later chapter on data testing.

War Story 5: The Moving Goal Post

Mary is a junior data analyst on a project. She was asked to go to a client site and extract data from their accounting system. This was to help the client with their expense audit process. Mary successfully got access to the source system, connected up to the database, and began extracting data out into text files to take back to the analytics lab. She was thinking ahead, so asked to work after office hours when the system was not in use and her work would not be a disruption to the client.

Mary did everything by the book. She meticulously calculated checksums, exported the data, and brought it back to the lab. When Mary began her analyses, she noticed something very strange. The data was not consistent at all. Accounts in one dataset did not exist in another dataset. Transactions appeared in one account and not another.

Mary did not know that while the office workers were not on the expenses system, it was still being used by overnight reconciliation processes. The data was changing as she calculated her checksums and exported the data. Working against such a moving goalpost, there was never any chance that she would have a consistent collection of datasets and so could not produce reliable reports. Somewhat sheepishly, Mary had to go back to the client and ask them to freeze their systems while she reran her data extraction. It was a bit of an own goal for Mary.

4.6 PRACTICE TIP 4: CAPTURE FRONT-END REPORTS

4.6.1 Guerrilla Analytics Environment

Data documentation is often of poor quality or out of date. Even when documentation is available, it is difficult to correctly reverse-engineer an extracted system. How do you know which tables to join together when there are often hundreds? How can you know the business rules that are encoded in the data? Does a coded value like "P" mean purchased or procured?

4.6.2   Guerrilla Analytics Approach

When data is extracted from a system, captured front-end reports are a great help in starting the reverse engineering of a system and validating correct interpretation of the underlying data. There are often many methods and options for generating a report. Think of a report where you generate your bank account transactions in your online banking. You may be able to select a particular month of transactions or a date range. You may also be able to set a transaction size range and a number of accounts. When reports are captured, the application options and login used to generate the front-end report should also be recorded so that the same type of report can be regenerated in the future.

4.6.3   Advantages

A set of front-end reports to accompany a data extraction is useful for two reasons.

- **Data validation:** Front-end reports are a good check that data has been extracted correctly. Consider a typical ERP system. If the total monthly sales values in the front-end report are the same as the total monthly sales values calculated from the underlying data, then you have high confidence that the data has been extracted correctly and are being interpreted correctly. This is a huge advantage in Guerrilla Analytics projects where documentation is often scarce and unreliable.
- **Reverse engineering:** Front-end reports are for end users and so they present the underlying data in a human friendly format after it has been joined together. Using keywords and values from a report, you have a starting point from which you can begin to explore the underlying data and test its relationships. This is particularly useful when documentation is lacking or is out of date.

Figure 11 shows an illustrative front-end report and some typically useful areas of the report. The example is a pay slip since that is a front-end report we all hopefully see a few times a year. In area 1, there are several unique identifiers for an individual. These are the employee number, National Insurance (NI) number, and the bank account number. These patterns of letters and digits should be unique in the underlying database. This provides you with a starting point in the underlying data from which you can begin to map out relationships to other datasets.

Area 2 is a report date. This could allow you to filter out any data after this date and simplify the scope of the reverse engineering exercise.

Finally, area 3 is an example of self-consistent data. If we can identify all the deductions for an individual in a given time period, then we know what they should add to the total deductions number on the bottom right of the report. Similarly, other totals allow us to find the right subset of "Payments."

Presented with a report like this and underlying data that is consistent with the report at the time of extraction, the analyst can find an entry point into the data. They can then start to build out relationships to payments and deductions using the available lists, totals, and dates on the report.

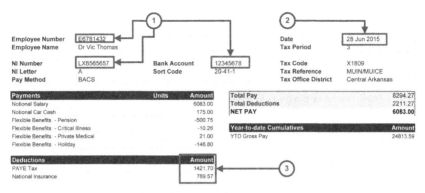

FIGURE 11   Example front-end report

4.7   PRACTICE TIP 5: SAVE RAW COPIES OF WEB PAGES

4.7.1   Guerrilla Analytics Environment

Not all data is extracted from applications. Increasingly, data is provided on "open data" web platforms such as the United States government's www.data. gov website, social media platforms such as *Twitter*, and on news sites such as *BBC* news. Web scraping is the technique of automatically scanning a web page and extracting its content. This content may be free-form text such as news articles. It may also be structured information as presented in tables. It may be a series of blogs, tweets, comments, and other social data streams. This data can change over time since the providers are not obliged to adhere to your data provenance requirements.

Web scraping is difficult because web pages are usually a fairly unstructured data source. Although tools for scraping are improving, it may still take significant ad hoc program code to extract useful structure from a web page.

What should be done when these data sources feed into the data environment?

4.7.2   Guerrilla Analytics Approach

When scraping web data, make sure to save the original raw web page. Think of these as the raw data files from the "source" system.

4.7.3   Advantages

Following this tip, you have two advantages.

- **Permanent record of volatile data:** You have a permanent record of your raw data (the web page).
- **Revisit and improve:** You can revisit your raw data and reapply scraping processes to it in the event that mistakes are discovered in the scraped data. You can still do this when the original web page no longer exists in the same format or with the same content.

4.8 PRACTICE TIP 6: CONSISTENCY CHECK OCR DATA

4.8.1 Guerrilla Analytics Environment

OCR data is error prone. Letters and numbers can be mixed up by the automated OCR software. This is not a huge problem for text as it is rarely critical that every single word is correct. When numbers are incorrectly OCRed, this can create more serious problems. Misplacing a decimal point can make a difference of millions of dollars to a report.

4.8.2 Guerrilla Analytics Approach

When dealing with OCRed data, look for opportunities to check the data for internal consistency. Internal consistency means that rather than comparing the data to some external source, the data is instead compared to itself to make sure that it is consistent with itself.

For example, if a document has a table of numbers with a total, check that the OCR numbers sum up to the total listed in the report. For text data, run a check against a dictionary to find misspelled and unrecognized words.

4.8.3 Advantage

Running these types of checks gives you more confidence in a low-quality data conversion process and will quickly identify errors in the data OCR process.

4.9 WRAP UP

This chapter discussed the first stage of the Guerrilla Analytics workflow – Data Extraction. You learned about the following topics.

The pitfalls of data extraction are as follows:

- It is impossible to reproduce and checksum extracted data because data was extracted from a moving target.
- Inability to assess completeness of extracted data because checksums were not performed at the right time.
- No reproducibility of data extraction because the program code and front-end report generation options were not recorded.
- There is no reference to compare to because no front-end reports were captured.
- Front-end reports cannot be reproduced because the particular user login and reporting options were not recorded.
- There is no record of raw web pages used in scraping.
- There are no checks of OCR data so that the inevitable errors in the OCR process go undetected.

There are several tips that help avoid these pitfalls and mitigate data extraction risks.

- Put the source system in a frozen state.
- Extract data into an agreed file format.
- Calculate checksums before data extraction.
- Capture front-end reports.
- Save raw copies of scraped web pages.
- Do consistency checks on OCR data.

The next chapter will look at how this extracted data is tracked as it makes its way to the analytics team's environment.

Chapter 5

Stage 2: Data Receipt

5.1 GUERRILLA ANALYTICS WORKFLOW

Figure 12 shows the Guerrilla Analytics workflow. At this stage in the workflow, data has been extracted from some source system either by the team or the customer. Data Receipt, as the name suggests, involves receiving this data into the analytics environment. This is typically done in a number of ways. Data may be transferred to the team on storage media such as hard drives or DVDs. Data may be emailed to the team. Occasionally, data may be made available for download from a secure shared location such as an SFTP server. Data may even be made available by providing access to a database. Whatever the means of transfer, this received data must be stored and prepared for use by the team.

5.2 PITFALLS AND RISKS

Surprisingly, there are many pitfalls in what seems a straightforward process. The following pitfalls are common in pressurized and dynamic Guerrilla Analytics environments.

- **Data is lost on the file system:** The location for received data is either a free-for-all left to the creativity of the team or is an overly complex tree of categories that made sense only to its creator. The effect is that it becomes cumbersome if not impossible to track down the original data.
- **Multiple copies of the data exist:** Even when you can locate the data received, you may find that there are multiple similar looking files at that location. This usually arises for two reasons. For example, another team member has the same file open and so the file is locked. As a quick fix, the file is copied so it can be opened and both the decompressed file(s) and the original archive remain on the file system. Multiple copies of data cause confusion.
- **Local copies of data:** Without a clear team convention on where to store data, the data gets scattered across local drives and personal workspace folders.
- **Supporting information is not maintained:** There is no information on traceability of the data such as a history of where the data came from, what the data means, and who received it.

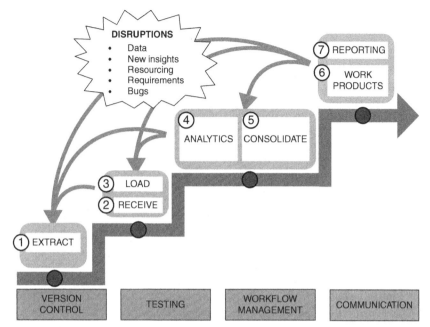

FIGURE 12   The Guerrilla Analytics workflow

- **Original data is renamed:** This happens because data files often have awkward names that only make sense to a machine or the original data provider. Sometimes, particularly in the case of spreadsheets, the name is a long combination of author names versions and dates that are unsightly and awkward to use in program code. System extracts might have coded names that are not immediately self-explanatory, such as TN567 or C1u8. The temptation is to rename these data files to something more user-friendly for the analytics team. However, this breaks the data provenance between the provider of the data as they reference it and the data as the analytics team references it.

War Story 6: A Database for the Database

Simon was a senior manager in charge of a particularly complex project. He decided he needed to control data receipt and avoid the pitfalls discussed above. Simon instructed the team to do data tracking with a data tracking form that had to accompany every piece of data. The whole project team was instructed to use this data tracking form. The form included useful information such as date, receiver, and meaning of data. However, it also included space for other information that was probably unnecessary and difficult to obtain in the given timelines. This included the meaning of data fields, lists of data fields, location in a source system, etc.

While these might make sense in an ideal world, they just weren't possible in a Guerrilla Analytics project. Needless to say, the cumbersome process failed. The project environment was fast moving. Data had to be emailed between team members at a high frequency. Very often the meaning of the data and its fields was not known in advance and the aim of the work was to help understand the fields. The analytics team was held up waiting for data tracking forms that the rest of the team couldn't locate or would partially complete.

Common sense eventually prevailed. Simon's team reduced the forms to the minimum information needed to preserve data provenance – the whole motivation for introducing data tracking in the first place. The analytics team took charge of holding that information (in a database of course) since data provenance affected them the most. The project team found that with a minimum of tracking effort, the vast majority of concerns about data tracking could be allayed.

Figure 13 illustrates a typical folder structure that results when some or all of these pitfalls are encountered. There are several patterns that crop up when a team's received data is not under control.

1. **Multiple copies:** There seems to be two copies of some data called "Main Customer." Both folders contain a spreadsheet with the same file name. There is no easy way to tell if these spreadsheets are identical or if they have been modified in some way. There is no associated documentation we can identify to help understand the data.
2. **Personal folders:** There seems to be data files within a personal folder called "Dave." Although we can probably track down Dave, we would not expect data to reside in this folder. Again there is no documentation available and we have no idea where this data came from. If Dave left the project, his personal folder and this data may be deleted.
3. **Complex folder structures:** Here we have the opposite problem to carelessly leaving data around the project folder. In this case, a team member has recognized that they are accumulating bank statement data and so have begun to structure data folders so that they correspond to the banks providing the statements. At some point, it was decided that statements needed to be identified by their date and so statement files are named by their receipt date. However, these file names are inconsistently formatted. There also seems to be an associated email in one of the data folders.
4. **Orphaned archives:** In the root of the project folder, there is an archive file called "Customer.zip." Is this the archive that was extracted into the folder "Main Customer – Copy" or indeed the folder "Main Customer"? Does the archive even contain data or is it something else?

Although this example seems almost farcical, I have seen many projects that are not very different from this example. Fortunately, following a few simple tips can mitigate a lot of this chaos. The rest of this chapter will now take you through these tips.

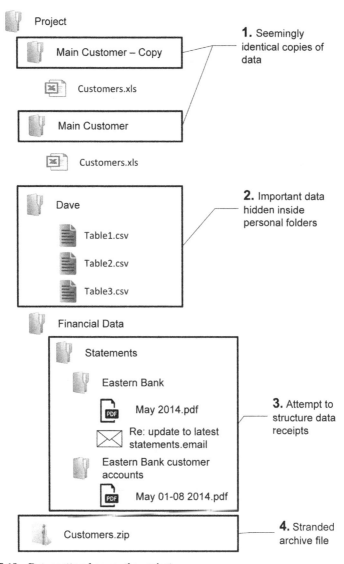

FIGURE 13   Data scattered across the project

5.3 PRACTICE TIP 7: HAVE A SINGLE LOCATION FOR ALL DATA RECEIVED

5.3.1 Guerrilla Analytics Environment

In a Guerrilla Analytics project, there will typically be data arriving from a wide variety of sources at a fairly high frequency. These sources may be different systems, third-party providers of data, data from other team members, and

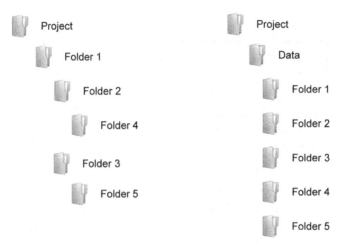

FIGURE 14   **A single data folder with a flat structure**

perhaps data from the customer themselves. Different versions of each data source may arise. In a project that does not have the time or resourcing to acquire data management software, the temptation is to try to classify all data received into a folder structure that is intended to help navigate and manage this complexity. Unfortunately, in a dynamic Guerrilla Analytics project, this understanding of the data structure will change and so the folder structure goes out of date or becomes overly complex. A better and simpler approach is needed.

5.3.2   Guerrilla Analytics Approach

Create a single location in the project for all received data. This single data location has a flat folder structure. Store all project data received by the team in this single location. Figure 14 shows how this could look. On the left is an approach with a hierarchical tree structure. On the right is the better Guerrilla Analytics flat structure.

5.3.3   Advantages

With a single location for data in place, much of the confusion around data receipt is reduced.

- **Ease of navigation:** Deep trees of folders are hard to navigate to find particular data drops. A simple flat folder structure avoids this problem. It is easier to search and count a list of 500 items than it is to search a tree of 500 items.
- **Easy to follow:** If there is a single location for all data received then there can be no confusion or unwanted team creativity about where received data is stored. When you need to find raw data, there is only one place to go.

- **One location for archiving:** A single data location is also beneficial for archiving and backup processes. Point these processes at one critical project folder and you know that all data your team received have been covered by your backup process.

5.4   PRACTICE TIP 8: CREATE UNIQUE IDENTIFIERS FOR RECEIVED DATA

5.4.1   Guerrilla Analytics Environment

Now that all data goes in one data location, how should you differentiate between different data deliveries and what are the most important ways to differentiate between them? A narrative label on each piece of data becomes cumbersome when team members are trying to communicate about data. A list of folders with arbitrary names is hard to use because every folder name has to be read and understood. What is really needed is a way to quickly locate any given data receipt.

5.4.2   Guerrilla Analytics Approach

Give each piece of received data its own folder in the project data location and its own unique identifier (UID).

5.4.3   Advantages

With a data UID in place, storage and search of received data is simplified. This has several advantages.

- **Related data is kept together:** With this approach you know that everything within a given data folder belongs to a particular data receipt and is therefore related somehow. You do not have to search a variety of locations to understand "this week's risk reports," for example.
- **Simplicity:** There is nothing complicated to remember when storing new received data – just put it in a folder with the next available data UID.
- **Data Receipt ordering is built in:** Very often we need to ask "where is the latest version of such a piece of data." By using an increasing data UID we can immediately infer the order in which data was received. Data with greater UIDs was received after data with smaller UIDs.
- **Decouple data from its metadata:** With a data UID, the data tracking and categorization details are separated from the data storage approach. Any amount of tracking and categorization information related to the data can be stored separately and referenced using the data UID. If tracking requirements change then you modify your data log but the simple structure of the data folder does not have to change.

These conventions remove a huge source of confusion in a Guerrilla Analytics project where a wide variety of data is being received by the team on an ongoing basis.

5.5 PRACTICE TIP 9: STORE DATA TRACKING INFORMATION IN A DATA LOG

5.5.1 Guerrilla Analytics Environment

It is important to store basic tracking information about data. At the very least, you need to control generation of data UIDs. Of course, in a Guerrilla Analytics environment where data provenance is key, you should also store tracking information such as who received the data and when.

5.5.2 Guerrilla Analytics Approach

A simple Guerrilla Analytics approach is to use a spreadsheet "data log" for storing tracking information about data receipts. If this log is stored in the root of the data folder, it is easy for busy analysts to find and maintain.

5.5.3 Advantages

A data log decouples data from the tracking metadata you wish to save. Knowing just the data UID, you can quickly look up additional information you have chosen to save, such as receipt date, receiver name, and provider name. There is no longer a need to try and categorize data with a folder structure.

5.6 PRACTICE TIP 10: NEVER MODIFY RAW DATA FILES

5.6.1 Guerrilla Analytics Environment

It is not unusual to receive data with weird and wonderful names. Spreadsheets are often named something like "Latest sales numbers FINAL v0.004.xls." Machine-generated files may have quite terse coded names like "TRS5.09." When it comes to storing this received data, there is a temptation to rename a file or save it in a different format for convenience. Unfortunately this only causes confusion. It breaks the link to how your customer relates to the data. For example, when the customer comes looking for "Latest sales numbers FINAL v0.004.xls," which is sitting in their email outbox, you won't be able to find that file in your analytics environment. When a system administrator asks if you are referring to the 9 table from the version 5 system, you will not be easily able to find the data received as file "TFS5.09."

5.6.2 Guerrilla Analytics Approach

Never modify raw data as it was received by the team. This means that the raw data files should not be renamed. They should not be opened and written over in another format. They certainly should not have their contents modified.

5.6.3   Advantages

Having an unmodified version of raw data is incredibly important for several reasons. As always, these reasons are related to data provenance.

- **Maintain the link between source data and data in the analytics environment:** Those who provided you with the data will refer to it by the names they provided for the data. Nonsensical dataset names are probably the dataset names that the system administrator recognizes and understands. Unusually named spreadsheets are names of the spreadsheets as they sit on the data provider's computer or email outbox. Renaming raw data breaks this critical link between how your provider references their data and how your team references the data.
- **Evidence of data errors:** The second advantage is somewhat defensive and a negative one. There will be occasions in your project when your analytics would be misunderstood or perhaps accused of being incorrect. That happens. But poor-quality data also happens. You need to be able to reproduce exactly the data you received, unmodified in any way. This allows you to dig into the cause of a problem all the way back to the original raw data as it was received by the team.

5.7   PRACTICE TIP 11: KEEP SUPPORTING MATERIAL NEAR THE DATA

5.7.1   Guerrilla Analytics Environment

We discussed how data is transferred to the team in many ways. Sometimes the data will be accompanied by documentation. There may be follow-up communications with the data provider to understand the data. It is important to capture any such supporting information relevant to the data. Supporting material takes many forms. It could be a data dictionary, a presentation file, or an email chain. As typical Guerrilla Analytics environments do not provide a proper data tracking or document management system, some projects try to keep a separate "documentation" folder for this type of information. This creates the same challenges as the problem of structuring the data folders. What folder layout, if any, should be used? How should the varied supporting information be managed?

5.7.2   Guerrilla Analytics Approach

Keep all data documentation and supporting information in the data folder, right beside the data it supports. A simple convention such as always using a subfolder called "supporting" or "documentation" makes it clear to all team members where they can find the supporting material under a given data UID. Some rifling through files still has to be done to locate documentation but knowing to begin the search in the "supporting" subfolder greatly accelerates your search.

5.7.3 Advantages

- **Simplicity:** When documentation shares the same folder as data, the team has one less project folder to maintain, communicate to one another, and to understand.
- **Not disruptive:** Analysts who are working on the data do not need to jump out of their workflow to find useful supporting information stored somewhere else in the project. The information about the data is right there for them in the data folder.
- **Coverage is evident:** If data has supporting information, there will be a "supporting" folder or similar in its data folder. You do not have to go searching some other documentation folder and trying to relate its structure back to the data folder to determine whether there is information available to help understand the data.

5.8 PRACTICE TIP 12: VERSION-CONTROL DATA RECEIVED

5.8.1 Guerrilla Analytics Environment

It is quite possible that the data is refreshed, replaced, and updated several times in a Guerrilla Analytics project. This happens because of errors, data goes out of date, etc., and so any data receipt process needs to be able to accommodate versions of data. It is critical that the team can easily distinguish between versions of data. It reflects poorly on the team when work products are not updated because of a lack of coordination on data versions.

5.8.2 Guerrilla Analytics Approach

There are two simple ways of version controlling data within the data UID framework already discussed.

- Create a completely new data UID for the new version of data received. Link this UID to the UID of the previous version of the data in the team's data log.
- Alternatively, store the new version of the data alongside its previous version under the same UID. Clearly label the different versions of the data.

5.8.3 Advantages

Having easily identifiable versions of received data is advantageous for several reasons.

- **Understand full history of data:** By having versions of data easily accessible, you are better able to understand the history of the data as it was made available to the team. This can help explain the evolution of work product versions and the impact of data refreshes. It also facilitates testing the consistency of data over time, which will be discussed in the book's testing Chapters 12, 13, 14 and 15.

- **Reduce confusion:** Versions of data are often delivered with exactly the same file names. By having a method to distinguish data versions, you mitigate the risk of data versions being confused or new versions overwriting older versions.

5.9   BRINGING IT ALL TOGETHER

This section brings together the data receipt tips from this chapter. Figure 15 illustrates a data receipt folder structure. The illustration covers a simple case of a team that has received two pieces of data. In practice, some projects will have hundreds of data receipts stored in this format.

- The first piece of data is the example spreadsheet from earlier in the chapter – the famous "Latest sales numbers FINAL v0.004.xls."
- The second data receipt is a set of three tables from a system extract.

The tables have been provided to the team in a CSV file format. After working with the system extract for a week, it was discovered that additional fields were needed from the system to be able to complete the required analysis. A second extract from the system was therefore issued and there are now two versions of this system data.

Let us now look at the characteristics of the folder structure and how this chapter's tips have been put into practice.

1. **Data folder:** There is a single "Data" folder in the project. All data received is stored under this folder and nowhere else.
2. **Data log:** In the root of the data folder there is a data log implemented in a spreadsheet called "Data log.xls." This is where all the tracking and categorization of information about a data receipt is stored. There are no complex data tracking forms like in the earlier war story.
   Data UID: Every data delivery has its own UID. Subfolders for storing the data are named by their UID. In this simple example, two pieces of data have been delivered to the team corresponding the UIDs D001 and D002.
3. **Supporting folder:** Within each data folder, there is a "supporting" subfolder. This subfolder contains all the additional information provided with the data. Looking at the subfolder of D001 we see there is some SQL code, presumably used to create the data extract. There is also an email with the subject line "explanation."
   For receipt D001, the raw data itself is the file called "Latest sales numbers FINAL v0.004.xls" in the root of D001.
4. **Raw data unmodified:** Moving on to subfolder D002, we see the system extract of three CSV files in the folder root. The file names seem to be system codes like "TR300M." These file names have not been modified as they are the original file names as received from the data provider.

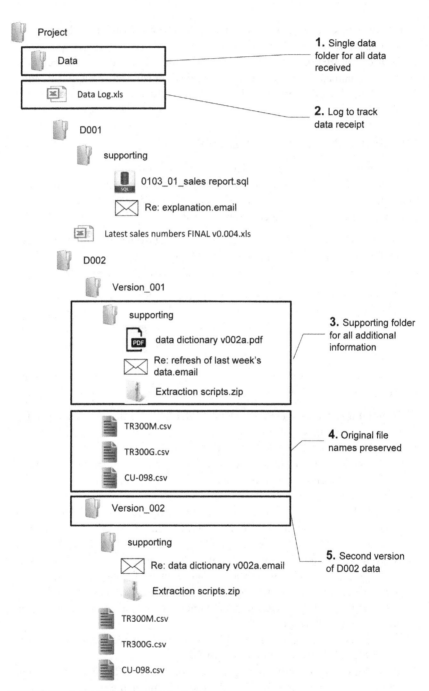

FIGURE 15 A simple data folder structure

5. **Version control:** As discussed in the introduction to this case study, the system extract D002 was delivered to the team twice. This explains the two subfolders called Version_001 and Version_002. There is little difference between the supporting information provided with both versions. The file names in both versions are identical because the data provider presumably tweaked their data extract scripts and then simply re-executed the extraction scripts.

The data folder structure described above implements all the tips discussed in this chapter. These conventions require a little bit of discipline and frequent reminders when they are first introduced to a team. However, because they have a clear visual pattern, it quickly becomes easy to see what was done before and to imitate that. If everybody else saves their customer emails in a folder called "supporting" then you probably should too or you will end up wasting time explaining your unique conventions to the rest of the team!

The conventions are easy to pick up, whatever the team member's experience level and they scale. On some projects we received several hundred data deliveries and had no problem identifying where every single piece of data was stored, who received the data, and identifying the original data files.

5.10 WRAP UP

This chapter has covered the Data Receipt stage of the Guerrilla Analytics workflow. You should now understand the following topics.

- Data Receipt as the second stage of the Guerrilla Analytics workflow. Data Receipt involves accepting data from a source provider and storing the data in the analytics environment.
- The main pitfalls and risks of data receipt are:
  - Data is lost on the file system.
  - Multiple versions of the data exist and cause confusion.
  - Local copies of the data are created.
  - Supporting information is lost.
  - Data is renamed.
- A number of practice tips were described that mitigate these risks. Specifically:
  - Have a single location for all data received.
  - Create unique data identifiers.
  - Store data tracking information in a data log.
  - Never modify raw data files.
  - Keep supporting material near the data.
  - Version-control data received.

Chapter 6

Stage 3: Data Load

6.1 GUERRILLA ANALYTICS WORKFLOW

Figure 16 shows the Guerrilla Analytics workflow. Data Load involves getting raw data from its storage location in the data folder on the file system into a Data Manipulation Environment (DME) so that it can be analyzed. This must be done in a way that is flexible and can cope with the variety of data types and DMEs the team may need to use. This must also be done while preserving data provenance by maintaining some link between data in the file system and the data as it is loaded into the DME.

6.1.1 Example Activities

There are several types of Data Load scenarios that you may have encountered.

- **A Relational Database Management System (RDBMS) extract:** A RDBMS system's data have been extracted into as many as several hundred text files, where each text file is an export of a data table in the source system. These text files must be loaded into the DME and the load must be checked to be complete and correct.
- **An unstructured extract:** A file share of thousands of scanned letters in PDF format has been made available for analysis. There is an intended meaning to the folder and subfolder structure in which these files are stored. For example, there may be a file year subfolder and within each file year subfolder there is a file month subfolder. Such a scenario is illustrated in Figure 17. You must run through this folder structure and load all files into a NoSQL document database (Sadalage and Fowler, 2012) while combining the loaded files with the "data" encoded in the subfolder locations and file names.
- **Semistructured data:** A customer has given you a spreadsheet workbook that contains 10 worksheets. Each worksheet has color-coded rows, where color is a Red–Amber–Green style indicator of importance. Some worksheets have hidden rows and columns that should not be used in any analysis. Some worksheets have embedded images that cannot be loaded. You must load this spreadsheet into the DME so it can be manipulated and integrated with other data.

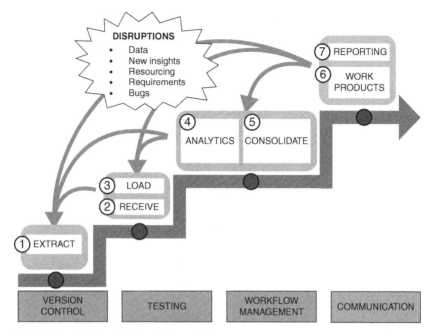

FIGURE 16   **The Guerrilla Analytics workflow**

- **Large files:** You have a single file of web log activity that is several giga-bytes in size and is time-consuming to load. The file contains a corruption that is preventing a successful load. The size of the file means you cannot open it in a text editor to determine where the fault is located in the file so you can assess and repair it manually.

These examples are hopefully somewhat familiar to you. There are some common themes to these examples that illustrate the variety of challenges faced at Data Load in a Guerrilla Analytics environment.

- **Preparatory work:** Some amount of preparatory work may have to be done on the data so that it loads into the DME correctly.
- **Need to peek at files:** There will be files that you cannot open using conventional text editors because they are corrupt or too large to load into memory. A method is needed to deal with these scenarios.
- **Validating a Data Load:** There will be a requirement to verify that the data has loaded correctly from the file system into the DME.
- **Chunking:** A single file may have to be broken into several files before it is loaded (as with spreadsheets containing multiple sheets).

This variety of data and associated challenges is increasingly common and must be dealt with using a reproducible approach that preserves data provenance.

FIGURE 17   **An unstructured data extract**

6.2   PITFALLS AND RISKS

The Data Load stage has several pitfalls and risks to bear in mind.

- **Data corruption:** As discussed in the data extraction stage, data can be corrupted as it go from a file system or source system into your DME. Data records can be dropped and data values can be corrupted. How do you gain confidence that this has not happened?
- **Data preparation:** Very often, raw data files have to be modified before they can be successfully loaded into the DME. The case of graphics and text embedded in spreadsheets has already been mentioned as an example of this scenario. If these "preparatory" modifications to data are not carefully controlled, then you lose data provenance. How much modification is appropriate and what are the best approaches to making these modifications clear and reproducible?
- **Where did the data go?** Loss of the link between data on the file system and loaded data in the DME breaks data provenance. Without clear team guidelines, loaded data can be located anywhere in the DME. It then becomes difficult to know which raw data file was the source of a particular dataset. When investigating a problem with your data, the trail then goes cold at Data Load.

This chapter now describes some tips to mitigate these risks in a Guerrilla Analytics project.

6.3   PRACTICE TIP 13: MINIMIZE MODIFICATIONS TO DATA BEFORE LOAD

6.3.1   Guerrilla Analytics Environment

As already discussed, loading data is difficult because of the variety of data formats, inconsistencies, and large volumes that are time-consuming to process. Inevitably, a raw data file may have to be modified so that it loads successfully into the DME. In other scenarios, there are explicit modifications that you absolutely should make to a raw file before loading to facilitate the maintenance of data provenance.

Think about spreadsheets as an example file format that is often encountered in analytics work. Spreadsheets can have hidden rows and columns. They can have embedded charts, graphics, and text boxes. Their columns can be derived from functions rather than hard coded data values. They may have "data" embedded in color-coding and formatting of content. They can be divided into separate tabs that are linked to one another. Spreadsheets are a particularly difficult example. Even a plain text file may have to have its line endings or its encodings changed.

Some changes need to be made to these files before they are loaded. But where do you draw the line? If you are going to extract spreadsheet tabs into individual files, why not also add an extra calculated column to save having to do it later within the DME? The danger is, the more changes you make outside the DME with ad-hoc manual processes, the less traceable data provenance becomes.

6.3.2   Guerrilla Analytics Approach

Minimize the modifications done to data before it is loaded into the DME. Modifications outside the DME are more difficult to track and reproduce, so try to do the bare minimum necessary to get a file to load successfully into the DME.

6.3.3   Advantages

There are several immediate Guerrilla Analytics advantages to minimizing data modifications outside the DME.

* **Traceability on the file system:** There is minimal difference between the raw data as it was received from the provider and the raw data that has been loaded into the DME. This means less documentation is required for other team members to reproduce the data preparation, should a load have to be redone.

- **Traceability in the DME:** The data that is loaded into the DME is as similar as possible to the raw data on the file system. This means that you can use program code in the DME to report on raw data characteristics rather than having to go back out onto the file system. For example, imagine a spreadsheet file that has been loaded into the DME. Only 3 of the 15 spreadsheet data columns are required for analysis, but you have followed this practice tip and loaded all columns. Your loaded data now has all the same data fields as the raw spreadsheet. This means you can easily run queries and report records from the loaded spreadsheet that the customer recognizes and can understand. Should more data columns come into scope, you do not have to revisit the data load.
- **Reproducibility of data modifications:** Since all analyses based on the raw data are done using program code in the DME, it is easier to understand exactly what those analyses were, and reproduce them if necessary. Again spreadsheets are a particularly troublesome file format here. If modifications have been done to raw data in a spreadsheet, it is quite likely that these modifications involved cutting and pasting data, dragging formulae, or calculating derived data fields with spreadsheet functions. All of these modifications are difficult to reproduce without detailed documentation. Program code modifications, by contrast are more succinct, easier to reproduce, and can be version controlled.

6.4 PRACTICE TIP 14: DO DATA LOAD PREPARATIONS ON A COPY OF RAW DATA FILES

6.4.1 Guerrilla Analytics Environment

On occasion you will have to modify raw data files so they can be loaded into the DME. Even though modifications are minimal, they are still a change to the raw data the customer provided. Questions could be raised over data provenance and whether your "minimal" modifications corrupted the provided data.

6.4.2 Guerrilla Analytics Approach

Any modifications to raw data should be done to a copy of the raw data file.

6.4.3 Advantages

The advantages of this tip are two-fold in a Guerrilla Analytics environment.

- **Data provenance is preserved:** There are two files, raw and modified, on the file system. If there are concerns raised about data loss or data corruption, these files can be compared and investigated.
- **Errors can be corrected:** In the event that a load has to be rerun because a file was inadequately prepared, there is an unmodified copy of the raw data that can be used to start from scratch.

6.5 PRACTICE TIP 15: ADD IDENTIFIERS TO RAW DATA BEFORE LOADING

6.5.1 Guerrilla Analytics Environment

Some data manipulation languages such as SQL do not preserve the ordering of rows in a data file as it is loaded into a dataset. For example, row 1413 in a raw text file will not necessarily be row 1413 in the equivalent loaded dataset. This causes problems for data provenance when data does not have unique identifiers, as is often the case with logs and spreadsheets, for example. If you encounter an issue with some of the data, you have a difficulty in identifying this record of data to the provider who gave you the original file. The row 1413 they refer to can only be identified by comparing all the data fields in the row, and this is time-consuming.

6.5.2 Guerrilla Analytics Approach

Before loading any data file, add a unique row number to the file. For text files, command line tools such as SED and AWK (Dougherty and Robbins, 1997) can easily run through large text files adding a row number column at the start of every row. For spreadsheets, it is a simple modification to create a row number column.

6.5.3 Advantages

When every row has a unique row number, there can be no ambiguities around identifying and communicating about a row of data. The row that the customer sees in their source file or spreadsheet is the dataset record with the same row number in your DME.

6.6 PRACTICE TIP 16: PREFER ONE-TO-ONE DATA LOADS

6.6.1 Guerrilla Analytics Environment

You will sometimes receive data that is scattered across a number of files. Perhaps the data has been chunked into files of a million records each to facilitate loading of the original source file incrementally. Perhaps a spreadsheet with many tabs needs to be broken out into individual files. You then have a choice. Do you load a large number of individual files into the DME? Alternatively, do you append those files together on the file system and do a single load of the concatenated file into the DME? The former approach is potentially more time-consuming but is better for data provenance because it preserves a clear one-to-one mapping between file system and DME. The latter approach is quicker, but requires documentation of the modifications that were done on the file system.

6.6.2   Guerrilla Analytics Approach

As far as possible, always load a single raw data file into a corresponding single dataset in the DME. Avoid appending files on the file system before loading unless these modifications can be easily understood and repeated.

6.6.3   Advantages

The motivation for this tip leads back to data provenance. If each file on the file system has a corresponding dataset in the DME, it is much easier to trace where a particular dataset came from. If 10 files on the file system become a single dataset in the DME, it is harder to follow this data flow back to the file system. This wastes time for the Guerrilla Analyst when trying to track down a bug in a Data Load or confirm a data receipt from the customer.

6.7   PRACTICE TIP 17: PRESERVE THE RAW FILE NAME AND DATA UID

6.7.1   Guerrilla Analytics Environment

A data file has to land somewhere when it is loaded into the DME. That somewhere is a dataset that has a name and a location. If it is difficult to determine where a particular file was loaded into the DME, time is wasted trying to track down the data.

6.7.2   Guerrilla Analytics Approach

As discussed in the Data Receipt stage, all received data files should be given a UID to help traceability. These files should be loaded into a dataset with a name containing the data UID in addition to the raw file name.

6.7.3   Advantages

The advantages of this tip are as follows:

- **Ease of identification:** By looking at a dataset name in the DME, you can immediately identify the raw file location in the data folder by virtue of the data UID and file name.
- **Ease of communication:** By using a dataset's name in the DME, you can immediately refer to it in terms that the customer understands from the data file they delivered to you.

These advantages are illustrated in Figure 18 for the example of a relational database DME. Which of the two data files in the data folders on the left are easier to identify in the DME on the right? The file "Marketing_Statement.xls" stored under data UID 096 can be found in DME name space 096 in a dataset

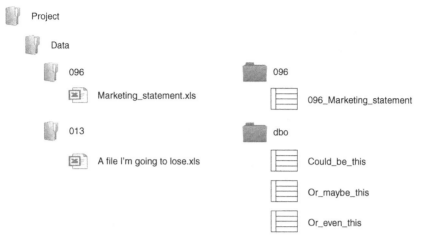

FIGURE 18   Preserve the raw file name and data UID

called "096_Marketing_Statement." The file under data UID 013 by contrast could be in any or none of the datasets scattered in the generic DME namespace "dbo."

A simple convention of preserving the raw file name and data UID makes communication and identification easier with no administrative overhead. This is critical for the Guerrilla Analyst who must stay up to speed with frequently changing data.

6.8   PRACTICE TIP 18: LOAD DATA AS PLAIN TEXT

6.8.1   Guerrilla Analytics Environment

It is possible in many DMEs to convert data into specific types as it is loaded. For example, you could specify that a numeric value gets loaded into a data field with a data type of integer. Alternatively, you could specify that the same numeric value gets loaded into a data field with a data type of floating point. With an unstructured document, you could enrich it as it is loaded, tagging entities such as people and business names. This changing of data at load should be avoided.

- **Brittle data loading:** Data type conversions at load time lead to a more brittle load process. There is nothing more frustrating than having a 1-hour load process fall over at its last data record because an unexpected value was encountered in the data. For example, a data loader encounters a text value when trying to load data into a numeric target field.
- **Less traceability:** Data Load utilities often give you less control of data type decisions. This makes load processes more difficult to trace and reproduce.

6.8.2   Guerrilla Analytics Approach

As far as possible, you should load all data in as generic and raw a format as possible. This usually means that all dates, numbers, currencies, etc. are loaded as text. Unstructured content is loaded as is without any enrichment. Conversion into more specific data types and enrichment can be done subsequently in program code.

6.8.3   Advantages

There are several advantages to loading data as plain text.

- **Robust loads:** Data Loads are less brittle because they use a simple data format that should work regardless of the contents of a data field. If numeric data is loaded into a text field, an occasional text value such as "Not applicable" will not cause the load to fail.
- **Better traceability:** In subsequent analytics workflow stages, loaded text data fields can be converted into more specific types using program code. This makes decisions on their type conversion clear and traceable.
- **Faster development times:** If a data conversion is incorrect, it can be quickly corrected in program code rather than having to undo and rerun a more time-consuming Data Load process.

Loading data as plain text speeds up the load and development process, so the Guerrilla Analyst can get on with the high value work of analyzing the data.

6.9   COMMON CHALLENGES

There is a lot to take in at the Data Load stage. Here are some common challenges encountered with teams and the possible resolutions when thinking about the Guerrilla Analytics principles.

6.9.1   Shouldn't My Data Preparation for Loading be Reproducible and Documented Too?

Ideally, yes it should. You have to keep in mind one of the overarching Guerrilla Analytics challenges, which is that of limited time. Your objective is always to preserve data provenance despite disruptions and constraints. The main occasion that would cause you to question your steps in preparation for Data Load is if you have discovered severely corrupted data that have to be extracted again or reprepared correctly. At this stage it matters little what the steps in the preparation were. All that matters is that something was broken when going from the raw file in your data folder to the prepared file in your data folder. Time to redo it!

6.9.2   If I'm Adding Metadata Such as Row Number Into My Loaded File, Should I also Add Receipt Date, Author, ... etc.?

The answer here is to think about what you most need for maintaining data provenance. Every piece of data has a UID and that UID is contained in the dataset name. The data log contains all the metadata you could possibly want. Include the metadata that will be useful in helping you preserve and report on data provenance. If there are likely to be questions around who provided various pieces of data, then perhaps it is helpful to make that answer available in the DME dataset. If these questions are not likely, then keep it simple and leave that information in the data log where it can be looked up with a small amount of effort. In general, including the data UID is enough to locate all the data tracking information you need.

6.9.3   Preserving these Crazy File Names is too Awkward. I Don't Want to Type Long Dataset Names When I Write Code

Unfortunately, losing track of the link between raw data files and loaded datasets is more time-consuming than typing an awkwardly named dataset. Most modern development environments can autocomplete dataset names. All things being equal, data provenance wins here.

6.10   WRAP UP

This chapter has discussed the Data Load stage of the Guerrilla Analytics workflow. Having read this chapter, you should now understand:

- The activities that take place during the Data Load stage of the workflow.
- The challenges of a Data Load.
- The common pitfalls and risks associated with data loading. These are:
  - Data loss through corruption and truncation.
  - Appropriate data preparation for load.
  - Location of loaded data in the DME.

You should now have some useful practice tips to help you address the pitfalls of Data Load. Specifically, you know to:

- Minimize data modifications in preparation for load into the DME.
- Prepare a copy of raw data files so that you never modify source data.
- Add identifiers to raw data records before load.
- Prefer Data Loads that map one file to one dataset.
- Preserve the raw file name and data UID in the loaded dataset name.
- Load data as plain text.

You should also be able to counter the common challenges to this chapter's tips.

Chapter 7

Stage 4: Analytics Coding for Ease of Review

7.1 GUERRILLA ANALYTICS WORKFLOW

At this stage in the Guerrilla Analytics workflow of Figure 19, data has been extracted from a source system and received by the analytics team. This data has been successfully loaded into the target DME. You have now reached a stage in the analytics workflow where you can do some actual analytics. This involves writing program code in your data analytics environment. Program code has several purposes in analytics work.

- **Manipulate data:** To manipulate data, changing it from one form and shape into another, and merging together datasets.
- **Derive data:** To create new data points that are derived from existing data points.
- **Test data:** To test and profile data so that defects in the data can be detected.
- **Build models:** To produce statistical models from the data.
- **Visualize insights:** To produce visualizations of the data.

The outputs of your program code will be one or more datasets and perhaps some graphical outputs. Keeping in mind the highly dynamic Guerrilla Analytics environment, you need to strive to write code that is easy to understand and review and that preserves the provenance of your data. You need to do this with minimal documentation and process overhead.

7.1.1 Example Activities

Here are some examples of analytics program code.

- A single SQL code file that connects to a relational database goes through a supplier address table and identifies the address country for each supplier by looking for recognized zip code patterns in the supplier address fields. This derived address country is added into the dataset as a new data field.
- A single R code file that reads a CSV data file, classifies its columns into variables, runs a statistical regression analysis on the variables, and then outputs the analysis results as tables and as plots to image files.

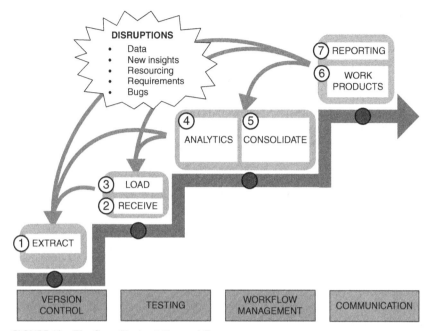

FIGURE 19   **The Guerrilla Analytics workflow**

- A Python script that runs through a directory of thousands of office documents, calls an external tool to convert these to XML format, and saves the
  XML file beside its original office document with the same name. This process is to prepare the data for further entity enrichment with another tool.
- Twenty code files are run in a particular order to manipulate and reshape
  data so it can be imported into a data-mining tool.
- A SQL code file that creates a predefined subset of data according to business rules and exports this subset of data into a spreadsheet with mark-up
  columns for the customer to review and complete.
- A collection of code files that incorporate spreadsheet inputs from users and
  build them into a data repository so they can be summarized for Management Information (MI) reporting and checked for inconsistencies.
- A direct export of a dataset in the DME so the customers can do their own
  work with the data.

There are of course many more examples. I have deliberately chosen these
examples to draw attention to some important Guerrilla Analytics themes.

- **Many languages:** A variety of data manipulation languages may be in use
  in the team either because of the functionality required or because they are
  familiar to particular team members. These languages will have code files
  with different structures because of the languages' designs.

- **Multiple code files:** Some work requires a single program code file while other work involves several code files that must be executed together in a particular order. It is the analyst's choice how the data flow is split into code files.
- **Multiple outputs and output formats:** Some work involves multiple outputs in a variety of formats such as data samples in spreadsheets and graphical charts in image files.
- **Multiple environments:** Some work is running on the file system and some work is running within a database or other DME.
- **Human-keyed inputs:** Some work is incorporating user inputs and mark-ups.
- **Tiny code:** Even the simplest code – extracting a copy of a dataset – is something that needs to be traceable to maintain data provenance.

7.2   PITFALLS AND RISKS

Analytics coding is a very wide area to cover as you have seen in the previous section's examples. This means that there are plenty of pitfalls and risks associated with coding. In essence, the challenge is that one or more code files is producing one or more outputs in one or more formats using one or more environments. Losing the mapping between the code files and these outputs runs the following risks for the team.

- **Lost data provenance:** Nobody is confident about where a particular dataset was generated and the DME becomes cluttered with datasets that cannot be deleted for fear that they cannot be reproduced.
- **Time wasted in review and development:** Review and debugging of code becomes awkward and time consuming. Since every code file produces its own outputs with no convention for what those outputs should be called, a reviewer has to read the code fully to find a reference to the output dataset name and location. Conversely, when a problem arises with a dataset, there is no quick way to determine which code file created that dataset and investigate the cause of the problem.
- **Reproducibility is impaired:** Work products that involve multiple code files are awkward to rerun and reproduce because it is difficult to determine the order in which files should be run. Work products that involve multiple program languages must be executed using different tools, have different structures, and may be located in different places.

    Work products cannot be rerun quickly because the code is cluttered with snippets and fragments of exploratory code that must be skipped over. Alternatively, work products cannot be rerun quickly because the code jumps between programming languages and so the user must jump between different code files and development environments.

An important theme across all these pitfalls is that of ease of reproducibility and review. The beauty and danger of program code is that you can get to an excellent and correct analytics result with a wide variety of approaches. At one end of the spectrum, you can write a hulking great single piece of code that must be stepped through and jumped in and out of by the person executing the code. Alternatively, at the other end of the spectrum, you can write a piece of modular code that flows through clearly defined steps. Both approaches will get you the right answer. Only the latter approach stands up to the dynamics and constraints of a Guerrilla Analytics project.

The subsequent sections detail tips for mitigating the risks associated with analytics coding.

7.3   PRACTICE TIP 19: USE ONE CODE FILE PER DATA OUTPUT

7.3.1   Guerrilla Analytics Environment

Recall that you are now writing code that manipulates data into a final output dataset. It is very easy and tempting to have a single code file produce many related outputs. But it is difficult to tie these multiple outputs back to their originating code file. You will need to do this when problems are identified with the dataset and when work needs to be handed over to another team member. Understanding a dataset is challenging when the code that is generated is hidden half way through an 800 line code file and depends on several other datasets that are equally well obscured.

7.3.2   Guerrilla Analytics Approach

It is best to structure code such that one code file produces one data output. Data outputs may be charts, images, and further datasets. If the name of the code file is included in the name of the output, this greatly helps traceability.

7.3.3   Advantages

One code file per data output has several advantages.

- **Ease of debugging:** When there is a problem with a dataset, your first place to go is a single code file of a similar name rather than having to trawl through the whole code base.
- **Ease of understanding:** When a dataset needs to be rebuilt, you have a single code file to understand and execute. This is much more difficult if a code file has to be executed starting somewhere in the middle of the file and finishing somewhere before the end of the code file.
- **Ease of knowledge sharing:** When work needs to be handed over or audited, you can easily identify the source code of a particular dataset.
- **Ease of testing and maintenance:** Code files tend to be smaller and therefore more manageable in terms of maintenance and testing of their functionality.

- **Ease of shared development:** Because code files are more granular and modular, it is easier for several analysts to work in the same code base without stepping on one another's toes. When your team has large code files, you can end up with analysts lining up to make changes to the file. This is of course inefficient.

7.4 PRACTICE TIP 20: PRODUCE CLEARLY IDENTIFIABLE DATA OUTPUTS

7.4.1 Guerrilla Analytics Environment

While a code file might produce a single data output, it probably also produces several intermediate outputs on its journey to a result. You may need to pull in other data sources and modify them. You may need to break down complex calculations into smaller steps and write out the results of those smaller steps into datasets. These intermediate datasets clog up the DME and make it difficult to find the result datasets.

7.4.2 Guerrilla Analytics Approach

Although intermediate datasets are important to understand the code file and data manipulations in detail, they are not essential to a quick understanding of the most important dataset – the code file's output. The code file's output should appear at the end of the code file (since it is the last thing the code file does) and should be clearly marked as the code file's output. A simple convention on dataset naming can achieve this. For example, conventions such as prefixing all intermediate dataset names with a character like "_" makes it clear that these datasets are less important to the overall results.

7.4.3 Advantages

When code file outputs are clearly identifiable, the advantages to the team and manager are as follows.

- You quickly identify the correct part of the code file where an output is produced so you can work backward and determine how the output was generated, step by step. This reduces code review and handover time.
- Intermediate datasets can be ignored until the full data flow needs to be understood or debugged. This helps team members to focus on the areas of code that matter most instead of wading through lots of preparatory code or even unrelated code.

Both of these advantages mean that less of the team's time is wasted in trying to locate and understand a result. This is critical in the Guerrilla Analytics environment.

7.5   PRACTICE TIP 21: WRITE CODE THAT RUNS FROM START TO FINISH

7.5.1   Guerrilla Analytics Environment

We have discussed how analytics by its nature leads to piece meal code. An analyst's workflow will typically include summarizing and profiling data to better understand it. They may trial several statistical models to determine the most appropriate one to use in the final work product. Exceptions and nuances in the data are discovered during analysis and have to be addressed with revised code. This exploratory code is necessary.

Problems arise if this exploratory code is left lying around in code files. Code files are then in a state where you cannot quickly execute them without tripping over all the exploratory code that is still in the file. Very often this exploratory code is old and breaks code execution. If nothing else, time and space are wasted executing code and creating data that is no longer needed.

7.5.2   Guerrilla Analytics Approach

In practice, many of the problems of creating understandable and well-integrated analytics code disappear if you insist on a simple rule – code files must always execute straight through from start to finish.

7.5.3   Advantages

With this rule in place, many of the following bugs and bad practice disappear.

- **Cleaner code:** Any code snippet that is not relevant to the final work product has either been deleted or commented out. This means it does not distract the reviewer, does not execute unnecessarily, and does not hang around going out of date and breaking code execution.
- **Stale data bugs are detected:** If a temporary dataset has disappeared or a dataset reference has changed then the code will fail. Lurking bugs of stale data references like these are quickly identified by making the code fail fast.

7.6   PRACTICE TIP 22: FAVOR CODE THAT IS NOT EMBEDDED IN PROPRIETARY FILE FORMATS

7.6.1   Guerrilla Analytics Environment

Broadly, we can identify two types of analytics tools.

- **Programmatic inputs:** These tools can be controlled via a command-line, can be configured with external nonproprietary configuration files and their data manipulations, and commands are executed through program code text files.

- **Proprietary graphical inputs:** These tools are controlled through a graphical interface. Their configuration, data manipulations, and execution are driven through a graphical interface, and their projects are often saved in proprietary binary file formats.

The latter tools make it difficult to automate data manipulation code and this slows down the Guerrilla Analyst.

7.6.2   Guerrilla Analytics Approach

Given the choice, prefer tools with programmatic inputs over those with graphical inputs. Note that I am not advocating avoiding tools with graphical inputs – these can be great time-savers and increase productivity on complex tasks. However, those same tools should have a programmatic interface that allows them to be deployed and executed outside the graphical interface when the design work is finished.

7.6.3   Advantages

Having programmatic control of analytics tools has huge advantages for productivity.

- **Automation, scheduling, and parameters:** If a tool can be controlled from a command-line, its work can be easily automated, scheduled, and parameterized. For example, you could write a script to open a PDF document (which you would pass into the script with a parameter) and then look up some domain-specific concepts used in the file such as office locations. Because you have a simple script that can be parameterized at the command line, you can now point that script at an arbitrary folder of millions of PDF documents and do the same work. This scale up and automation would have been difficult to execute inside of many graphical tools.
- **Complex configuration:** If configuration settings can be externalized into one or more configuration files, the analytics tool can easily be deployed in a variety of scenarios. Only the associated configuration file needs to change while the core analytics code can remain the same. This is typical of the approach taken in traditional software deployment scenarios. You would do development in a "development environment" against a development database. The associated location and connection settings for this development database would be in the development configuration file. In addition, you would have a production configuration file so that the same application could be pointed at a production database in a separate production location with different connection settings.
- **Version control:** Version control works best with text files. This is because version control software looks at files, detects differences between versions of the files, and tracks who made the edits that caused those differences. While this is easy to do with text format files, it is very difficult to do with

binary format files. If a tool can save its code in external text files then your work with that tool can be version controlled. However, if the tool saves your work in a large binary file there is little you can do to put robust version control around that file.

7.7 PRACTICE TIP 23: CLEARLY LABEL THE RUNNING ORDER OF CODE FILES

7.7.1 Guerrilla Analytics Environment

The practice tips covered so far allow you to quickly achieve the following.

- Locate the code file that created a dataset.
- Work backward through that code from the point at which its output dataset was created.
- Avoid the distraction of broken code snippets and stale data references.
- Execute code from start to finish to quickly reproduce an analysis.

However, complex analytics work products are often broken into several code files. You do this either to make them easier to understand or because a mixture of programming languages and technologies is being used. Without some convention, it is difficult to know which code files should be run in which order to reproduce a work product. There is nothing more frustrating than rummaging through a collection of code files to solve a run-order mystery.

7.7.2 Guerrilla Analytics Approach

In practice, the simplest and most lightweight way to highlight the running order of code files is to prefix their file name with their running order. This running order does not have to be numbered continuously. Indeed, it makes sense to space out the numbering so that you can easily insert a new file into the running order without having to rename all subsequent files.

Figure 20 shows a simple example for cleaning some data about crime rates. The data flow takes some crime data and attaches postcodes and zip codes to it. It then does some follow-up cleaning of the data file and plots the data by city using an R script. On the left, the order in which the code should be executed is unclear. On the right, files have been numbered in the order in which they should be executed. For little effort, a major source of confusion and wasted time has been removed.

7.7.3 Advantages

- **Efficiency:** Handovers and reviews do not necessitate a conversation around what files to run and in which order. It is immediately clear from how the files are named.

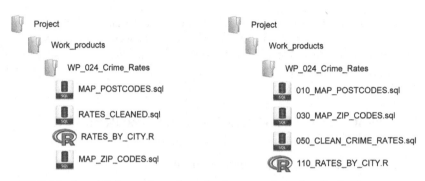

FIGURE 20 A muddled execution order and a clear execution order of code files

- **Provenance:** Work products can be reproduced quickly without having to understand the inputs and outputs of every code file in the code base. Take the code files as presented, run them in the order as presented and your work product should pop out at the end.
- **Automation:** Automation of code file execution is simplified. A script can list all code files in alphabetical order and then execute them in that order. Without this naming convention, script run orders would have to be maintained in a separate schedule. Under tight timelines, these external schedule files are difficult to maintain.

7.8 PRACTICE TIP 24: DROP ALL DATASETS AT THE START OF CODE EXECUTION

7.8.1 Guerrilla Analytics Environment

As analytics code is executed and then re-executed during development, it will try to create the same intermediate and output datasets that may already exist from a previous execution. This is easily detected when the analytics code halts and warns you that a desired output dataset already exists. However, failure to apply a drop and then create to all datasets related to a work product can hide a particularly nasty type of stale dataset bug. If there is a dataset that is not dropped and recreated on every run of the code, that dataset can linger in code references. Your code will happily run through without complaint but will be referencing an old and incorrect dataset.

7.8.2 Guerrilla Analytics Approach

Before running analytics code, drop all datasets produced by that analytics code if they already exist. Effectively this means cleaning out the target space into which the code is about to write its datasets.

War Story 7: The Haunting

Riley was working on a document classification problem for Cracken Inc., a research publishing house. The customer needed to automatically identify document subjects based on frequencies of words, keywords, and some other text analytics tricks. Riley was using a document database (Sadalage and Fowler, 2012) to classify this content. The classification was being implemented as a pipeline into the document database. At load time, documents were passed through this pipeline where they were parsed, checked for keywords, and tagged with properties describing their subject. For example, a document might be tagged as "North America" and "Oil and Gas."

In the development phase, Riley did not want to load all the content repeatedly into the database, so she instead re-executed the pipeline over already loaded content. She was puzzled by the result. The classifications being produced did not match the profile of expected document classifications. Checking with Cracken Inc., Riley confirmed that about 15% of the content should be reports and not the 40% she was seeing. After some investigation, it turned out that part of the pipeline had not been developed with "drop and create" in mind. Riley had been thinking of efficient document loading and so the classification routines assumed the documents being processed were vanilla raw data. An earlier development run of the pipeline had incorrectly classified some documents as "report." When Riley implemented a fix to classify some of these documents as "white paper", the old tag of "report" came back to haunt her. It wasn't that her fixed code was mysteriously classifying the document as a report. This was far less supernatural. The old "report" tag from earlier development efforts was still attached to the loaded data. The simple fix was to remember "drop and create." The first thing the pipeline should have done was to delete any existing document tags it detected. A quick "drop and create" routine for cleaning out existing tags and Riley was up and running with a working document classifier.

7.8.3 Advantages

The main advantage of the "drop and create" approach is that it quickly exposes stale dataset and stale data field bugs. Every execution of the code effectively rebuilds the intermediate and output datasets "from scratch." Dependencies on the existence of datasets are explicitly called out and necessary intermediate datasets have to be created by the code. Any breakages in data provenance are thus quickly detected.

7.9 PRACTICE TIP 25: BREAK UP DATA FLOWS INTO "DATA STEPS"

7.9.1 Guerrilla Analytics Environment

A "data step" is a small chunk of code that produces a dataset. You can think about a data analytics process as involving several data steps that make a series of manipulations to data until a final output dataset is produced. Even when code files are mapped one-to-one with datasets, it is still possible to have a lot of complex code within a single file. Many languages allow you to build up quite complex data manipulations in a single code segment. This makes code difficult to review and also obscures the impact on the data of individual data manipulations.

7.9.2 Guerrilla Analytics Approach

It is better to break down code into comprehensible data steps where possible.

7.9.3 Advantages

Coding with data steps is advantageous in several ways.

- **Debugging:** Code is easier to debug because the intermediate datasets after each data step can be inspected, tested, and understood. Any extra time spent in a slightly less efficient code execution is usually won back in the time saved trying to understand unnecessarily complex code.
- **Provenance:** The impact of data manipulations on the data is easier to quantify. Because significant data manipulations are broken out into individual data steps, it is easier to work through each data step and test, or report on its output as necessary.
- **Maintenance:** Code is easier to refactor in the future because there are more break points in the code where new rules and data sources can be introduced.

7.10 PRACTICE TIP 26: DON'T JUMP IN AND OUT OF A CODE FILE

7.10.1 Guerrilla Analytics Environment

In analytics work, it is common to have to apply a variety of programming languages to a work product. You may do heavy lifting of data in one language, statistical modeling in another language, and visualization in a third language. These languages generally do not work together in the same code files. You are therefore faced with having to jump between programming languages and associated code files. Without some simple conventions, executing code becomes a tangled mess of code jumps that are poorly documented and impossible to automate.

War Story 8: The Quantum Leap Handover

Poor Nick. He was new in his analytics job and wanted to impress. His first task was to take over a piece of work from a senior colleague. Unfortunately for Nick, he was about to experience quantum leap code that moved through space and time.

Nick sat with the senior developer to go through the code. The data flow began with loading data from a spreadsheet. The spreadsheet wasn't quite in the right format, so some modification and data manipulations had happened in the spreadsheet. Nick was told that this was just a quick and dirty fix instead of programming up a solution. Time was tight after all. These modifications were not documented, so Nick took careful notes.

The loaded spreadsheet dataset then went through some complex data manipulations in a single large code file. It seemed like some of these modifications were repetitions of what went before. Sections of code were old and "could be ignored," but there was no way for Nick to know that. They had not been removed from the code file of course. At this point, the senior developer is starting to think Nick is a bit slow on the uptake.

About half way through the code file, just as Nick was getting his head around it all, code execution had to stop. The intermediate dataset at that point in the data flow was exported from the DME into a spreadsheet. Jumping into this spreadsheet, further manipulations were performed to calculate a regression line on a separate worksheet. The slope of this line was noted and copied back into the large analytics code file. Execution of the analytics file then resumed with this regression line slope as an input typed into the code file. The final result was copied out of a dataset hidden in a mass of other intermediate datasets in the DME.

Including the explanation and follow up questions, the handover of this work product took several hours and dented Nick's confidence. Nick immediately went to work breaking the data flow into separate code files such as "up to the regression calculation" and "regression calculation onwards." He deleted the code that was no longer executed or needed. Finally he refactored the code into manageable data steps.

A day later, Nick was in a position to execute code that he understood and complete the handover from his colleague. Oh boy!

7.10.2 Guerrilla Analytics Approach

This tip says that a data flow should not jump out of a code file to execute another process and then jump back into that same code file to resume the data flow.

7.10.3 Advantages

The primary advantage of this tip is that you can preserve code that runs from start to finish. The advantages of end-to-end code were already discussed. Applying this tip helps extend that approach across multiple programming languages and tools typically required in Guerrilla Analytics.

7.11 PRACTICE TIP 27: LOG CODE EXECUTION

7.11.1 Guerrilla Analytics Environment

As the complexity and volume of code files increases, it becomes more difficult to monitor what the code is doing. If code execution is time consuming, you would like some indication of progress through the data flow so that you know the time remaining and whether data processing may have stalled for some reason. Having to manually inspect program outputs in a graphical development environment is time consuming and error prone.

7.11.2   Guerrilla Analytics Approach

Logging allows you to output log messages at various points in the execution of your code file. The richness of logging available to you depends on the programming languages and libraries you are using. In some cases, languages have comprehensive logging frameworks that output messages in a variety of formats and severity thresholds. In other languages you may be limited to simply printing messages to a text file.

Figure 21 shows a simple example of a log file containing the main features useful in Guerrilla Analytics. Every line contains a time stamp so you can see how the code is progressing. The log also mentions the file name in which the log is being stored. Every line contains the code file name from which the log is being printed. This is useful if an error is printed and needs to be followed up. Finally, the log reports how long it took to execute all files.

7.11.3   Advantages

With even the most basic logging in place, you can leverage the following advantages.

- **Execution progress:** You have feedback on the progress of code execution. If 10 of your code files have logged that they have completed, you know you are 10 files into your analytics run. Without this information, you have no idea whether the analytics code is 5% complete or 95% complete.

```
2005-10-30 10:45 Logging to 2005-10-30_1045.LOG
2005-10-30 10:45 Beginning code execution
2005-10-30 10:45 [SETUP.SQL] Tearing down all
datasets
2005-10-30 10:46 [POINTERS.SQL] Creating pointer
over latest web access log
2005-10-30 10:46 [POINTERS.SQL] Creating pointer
over latest HR file
2005-10-30 10:47 [PARSE.SQL] Parsing log file
2005-10-30 10:56 [ADD_HR.SQL] Joining HR info to
logs
2005-10-30 11:01 [INTERFACE.SQL] Creating interface
datasets
2005-10-30 11:03 Code completed
2005-10-30 11:03 Total run time was 18 mins
```

FIGURE 21   Example log output

- **Highlight inefficiencies:** After one code run, you can have a time stamp of how long each data step took and can easily identify pinch points and inefficiencies in the data flow. For example, if the fifth code file in your execution takes three times as long to complete as every other file, perhaps this is a good area for optimization. Perhaps the code could be better written or the data could be better constructed.
- **Find errors:** You can automatically check for errors by searching your log files rather than having to individually inspect and test outputs after every code run.
- **Audit:** You have a time-stamped record of the code that was run and what it produced. This can be important when tracing problems with work products and if there is an audit requirement to show that code was run without errors at a particular point in time.

7.12   COMMON CHALLENGES

Introducing some of the conventions of this chapter can be perceived as overbearing by some team members. People get used to their own way of working and are reluctant to change. Here are some common challenges you may encounter.

7.12.1   What about Graphical Analytics and ETL Tools?

There are many graphical tools for data manipulation and analytics work. By graphical tools we mean those tools that allow you to design and specify data flows and analyses by arranging graphical components. These tools are often touted because you "do not have to know how to code" and you get your documentation for free in the graphical interface. These tools struggle in a Guerrilla Analytics environment for the following reasons.

- The files describing the analytics cannot easily be version controlled as they are often in a binary file format.
- An analysis cannot be easily modified. The analyst has to drill down through the interface and navigate many wizards, check boxes, and dialogs.
- These tools can never be as flexible as raw analytics code. At best they will provide a "code component" in which you end up writing analytics code anyway.

These tools undoubtedly have their usefulness. However, they are not flexible enough for a Guerrilla Analytics environment.

7.12.2   This is Too Much; I Just Want to Write My Code!

The value of these simple code conventions becomes apparent to team members in two scenarios.

- **When work needs to be handed over between team members:** Have you ever seen situations where one analyst is on leave and the person covering for them needs to get up to speed? They spend most of their time trying to unravel spaghetti code files, versions of outputs, and datasets scattered throughout the DME. This is inefficient and looks bad in front of a customer. The simple conventions in this chapter avoid the major pain points in coordinating code between team members.
- **When you introduce peer review in the team:** If every code handover requires sitting down together with a detailed walk through, it quickly becomes a frustrating waste of time for team members. Having simple conventions that everybody follows will dramatically reduce this overhead. As far as possible, you want a team who can easily jump into one another's work with minimal overhead and documentation.

7.13 WRAP UP

This chapter covered the Analytics stage of the Guerrilla Analytics workflow, focusing on tips for producing reproducible and traceable analytics code files. In particular, you learned the following.

- The typical activities that take place in Guerrilla Analytics coding.
- The challenges to writing Guerrilla Analytics code that is traceable and reproducible.
- The pitfalls and risks of coding in a Guerrilla Analytics environment.
- Several tips that help your team produce high-quality code with minimal overhead that addresses the risks inherent in the Guerrilla Analytics environment.
- How to address the most common challenges to the tips presented in this chapter.

Chapter 8

Stage 4: Analytics Coding to Maintain Data Provenance

8.1 GUERRILLA ANALYTICS WORKFLOW

As in the previous chapter, we are still at the analytics workflow stage of writing program code to do data analytics. This is stage 4 in Figure 22. Data has been sourced, extracted, and loaded. You are now concerned with writing analytics code that preserves data provenance.

8.2 EXAMPLES

You can manipulate data in an almost infinite number of ways. Here are some typical examples encountered in an analytics project.

- **Casting:** Gather every dataset in a system extract and cast all its fields into a correct data type such as date, integer, or text.
- **De-duplicating:** Run through a large dataset of vendor details, identify duplicate vendors by name, and tag those duplicates in the vendor dataset.
- **Joining:** Take a year's product sales data and join customer information to it to produce an analytics dataset of what every customer purchased, and when they purchased it.
- **Filtering:** Step through a dataset of web log entries and remove all entries that occur before 8 am and are associated with the user id "SYSTEM."
- **Enriching:** Take a set of instant message conversations and enrich them by identifying entities such as people names, business names, and place names.
- **Deriving:** Add a new field to a dataset that is the sum of two fields that already exist in the dataset.
- **Cleaning:** Step through a set of names and remove any formatting characters such as apostrophes and quotes, remove multiple adjacent spaces, and convert the name to upper case.

You can probably think of further examples. In all cases, data is being changed. Depending on how this change is managed, data provenance can be maintained or lost.

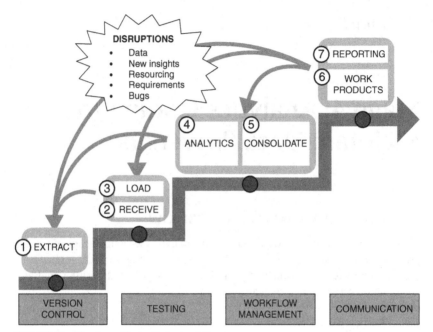

FIGURE 22   **The Guerrilla Analytics workflow**

8.3   PITFALLS AND RISKS

Since program code modifies data, there are many opportunities to make it difficult to maintain data provenance. In the worst case, you might break data provenance entirely. Here are examples of the pitfalls you will encounter.

- **Overwrites:** When cleaning a data field, the raw data is overwritten with the new clean data so the effect of the cleaning routine on that field can no longer be established.
- **Failure to distinguish derived data from original data:** Without some type of convention, it becomes difficult to know what data fields are derived by the analytics team, as opposed to being present in the original raw data.
- **Discarded records:** Data records can be directly deleted from data, perhaps because they are duplicates or because a business rule dictates their removal. However, there is then no way to assess the impact of the removal of these records, and no way to profile and test the removed records.
- **Difficulty in testing:** If modifications to data are not broken down into manageable data steps with intermediate datasets at the correct points in the data flow, then it becomes difficult to test that business rules were correctly applied to the data.
- **Loss of data record provenance:** If some type of record identifier is not carried through the data, it becomes difficult to trace a record back through the data flow to see where it came from and how it has been modified.

As always, a few simple Guerrilla Analytics practices and conventions go a long way toward mitigating these risks.

8.4   PRACTICE TIP 28: CLEAN DATA AT A MINIMUM OF LOCATIONS IN A DATA FLOW

8.4.1   Guerrilla Analytics Environment

In complex analytics data flows, there are numerous locations at which data cleaning can be performed. Regardless of whether you clean data early or late in the data flow, you should minimize the number of locations in which you do it.

War Story 9: You say tomato, I say TOMATO

Andrea was cleaning address data for mailing customers of Longwood Associates. The customer information came from several data sources, each with its own different format. A mistake was noticed in an output from the analytics team – a last name was inconsistently formatted and this was tracked back to Andrea's work. Some names were all upper case like "MAIN STREET" and some were all lower case like "main street." This was important both for presentation of the data, and for some of the data matching done earlier in the work product's data flow.

Andrea quickly introduced name cleaning in an early code file related to the offending dataset, making all its outputs upper case. After rerunning the data flow, there were still name inconsistencies present. Andrea chased down each of the offending data sources and added cleaning code to them separately, so that all their outputs were now upper case. Later in the project, a join in the middle of the data flow was not performing correctly because the join assumed lower case address details. Andrea was immediately on the case again (no pun intended). A quick cleaning step was introduced just before this join so that the data could be pushed through correctly as lower case.

After several of these ad-hoc types of changes, cleaning code had been scattered throughout the code base. It became very difficult for Andrea to know where particular data points were being modified. Effectively, data provenance was broken. The team paid the price in time wasted sifting through a code base scattered with ad-hoc cleaning and business rules.

If Andrea had been a Guerrilla Analyst, she would have identified one place in her data flow for cleaning. Early in the project, very little code might have been needed. As the project progressed and knowledge of the data improved, then she would have had that single data flow location for implementing additional cleaning rules. As new quirks in the data were discovered, these could be addressed in one place from which Andrea could report on the rules she had applied and assumptions she had made.

8.4.2   Guerrilla Analytics Approach

Whether data should be cleaned early in the data flow or later, is dependent on circumstances. Whichever decision is taken, ensure that data cleaning takes place in a minimum of locations in the data flow and is not scattered throughout the code.

8.4.3   Advantages

Performing cleaning in one location in the data flow makes cleaning routines easy to locate and maintain.

8.5   PRACTICE TIP 29: WHEN CLEANING A DATA FIELD, KEEP THE ORIGINAL RAW FIELD

8.5.1   Guerrilla Analytics Environment

Data always has quality issues or is not in a format that best suits an analysis. Data cleaning involves making changes to data to overcome these quality issues and to make the data amenable to analysis. Some examples include:

● Converting a data field to upper case for presentation purposes.
● Removing carriage returns and tab characters.
● Changing a coded system value into a meaningful business description. For example, "M" means "Male."

  Changing data in these ways affects data provenance.

8.5.2   Guerrilla Analytics Approach

When performing data cleaning, there are three things to keep in mind:

● **Copy:** Write the clean data field into its own new field rather than overwriting the original raw field.
● **Proximity:** Keep raw and clean fields close to one another so they can be easily compared.
● **Name:** Establish a naming convention so that cleaned data fields can be easily recognized and related back to their raw counterpart.

  Figure 23 shows an example of a dataset with clearly identified clean and raw columns for the phone number.

ID	NAME	PHONE	PHONE_CLN
1023	Joseph	+44 1456 981	+441456981
1024	Jane	00 5673 97346	00 567397346
1025	Michael	1	1
1026	Stephen	9999999999	9999999999
1027	Ciara	01207 956 333	01207956333

FIGURE 23   A dataset with clean and raw data fields

8.5.3   Advantages

The advantage of this approach to data cleaning is that data provenance is preserved. Cleaned data can be easily identified and compared to its raw source.

Looking at the example dataset in Figure 23, you see that the incorrect phone numbers for Michael and Stephen are due to poor raw data, as opposed to any error in the cleaning rules the team has implemented.

8.6   PRACTICE TIP 30: FILTER DATA WITH FLAGS, NOT DELETIONS

8.6.1   Guerrilla Analytics Environment

Sometimes records need to be removed from a dataset. The records may not be relevant to an analysis, or they may be poor quality data that should not be part of the analysis. Filtering is the data manipulation step of removing data records. But if records are removed, you lose the profile of the original data and the ability to try out combinations of filters to assess their impact on the data.

8.6.2   Guerrilla Analytics Approach

Instead of deleting filtered records, flag these records for removal. This is like a simple switch. When the filter switch is on, the record is not included in an analysis. When the filter switch is off, the record can be included in an analysis.

8.6.3   Advantages

The advantages of the flag approach to data filtering are as follows:

- **Assess impact:** You can profile the data by the various filters to see the effect on the population of using a particular filter or combination of filters.
- **Keep your options open:** Since records are not deleted but are instead flagged for filtering, you can easily discard a filter without having to worry about recovering deleted data from earlier in the data flow.

There is a trade-off here between flexibility of filtering and efficiency of data storage. Keeping Guerrilla Analytics principles in mind, it is best to use flags early in a project when data are poorly understood. Later in the project, when data understanding stabilizes, and if storage space is still a concern, records can then be removed from data instead of using flags.

War Story 10: Beginning to Flag

Chris was working on a large tranche of data for Shook Inc., a music company specializing in rock and roll artists. The aim of the project was to apply a complicated set of business rules to Shook's book with the aim of designing new royalty structures. The first challenge was to whittle down the data by a combination of rules that Chris was recommending from a clustering analysis, and that the customer needed to see for their own internal reasons. It was a big dataset of hundreds of artists' sales figures, record details, current contracts, and subgenres. This, in combination with Shook Inc.'s limited technology, meant that any rebuild of the data would take a couple of hours. Worse still, every time Chris would issue a segmentation, there would be disagreement and challenges from some of the client team. With even a small number of rules to consider, Chris was facing hundreds of potential rule combinations that may or may not have been acceptable to his client. This was wearing down Chris and frustrating his client.

Instead of taking a reactive approach, rebuilding data for every requested segmentation, Chris instead applied a set of flags to the dataset. Without wasting time on any filtering, Chris could now show the impact on the customer segmentations for any combination of flags. These candidate segmentations and their impact could be presented to Shook Inc. and Chris could quickly turn around new candidate rules that arose and were agreed. This meant Chris could remain agile in the face of changing requirements, respond to the project's growing data understanding, and explain the impact of various filter combinations without time-consuming data rebuilds. Rock "n" Roll Chris.

8.7 PRACTICE TIP 31: IDENTIFY FIELDS WITH METADATA

8.7.1 Guerrilla Analytics Environment

When cleaning data, you have already seen how it helps to keep the raw version of the data rather than overwrite it. However, it can still remain difficult in a dynamic environment to associate the raw data column with its clean counterpart.

Consider the example dataset in Figure 24. We cannot identify the raw and clean data fields because of a lack of consistency in naming fields. Is the PHONE field a raw field? Similarly the IN_SCOPE and ACTIVE? filters use different conventions. A query to switch on all filters would have to inspect and hard code every filter field from the data.

ID	CUSTOMER	ACTIVE?	PHONE	IN_SCOPE
205	Joseph	YES	+441456981	Y
206	Jane	NO	+567397346	Y
207	Michael	NO	1	N
208	Stephen	YES	9999999999	Y
209	Ciara	YES	01207956333	N

FIGURE 24 A dataset without any naming conventions

8.7.2 Guerrilla Analytics Approach

Imagine a typical office document such as a report. That report is a container of data. It contains sentences, paragraphs, appendices, tables, and figures. However, you can also use data to describe the document that contains this content. You can think of the whole document as having an author, a version, a publication date, and originating business department, for example. This "data about the data" is what is called metadata. What does this have to do with data manipulation?

If you name dataset fields according to a particular convention, then you can query and infer information from that field metadata.

8.7.3 Advantages

Figure 25 shows what the dataset now looks like after applying some simple conventions to field names and contents. Clean data field names are suffixed with "_CLN" and located beside their raw counterpart. Filter columns are prefixed with "IS_" and grouped together at the end of the dataset. This greatly improves clarity and data provenance.

In addition you can now do a lot with the data without specifying the exact structure of a dataset. For example, you could:

● Extract all clean fields from a dataset by looking for fields that have a name like "<something>_CLN."
● Switch on all filters by selecting data records where any fields called "IS_<something>" has a value of "YES."
● List all raw fields in a dataset by choosing fields that are not like "<something>_CLN" and not like "IS_<something>."

Simple conventions in clean field and filter field naming bring consistency to data fields, and also allow more powerful and flexible analytics that are not as dependent on a particular dataset structure.

ID	CUSTOMER	PHONE	PHONE_CLEAN	IS_IN_SCOPE	IS_ACTIVE
205	Joseph	+44 1456 981	+441456981	YES	YES
206	Jane	00 56 7397346	+567397346	YES	NO
207	Michael	1	1	NO	NO
208	Stephen	999 999 9999	9999999999	YES	YES
209	Ciara	01207956333	01207956333	NO	YES

FIGURE 25   A dataset with naming conventions

8.8   PRACTICE TIP 32: CREATE A UNIQUE IDENTIFIER FOR DATA RECORDS

8.8.1   Guerrilla Analytics Environment

In a data flow, raw data is manipulated by several data steps until an output is produced. In so far as possible, you would like to be able to trace individual data records through this data flow. This helps you debug and test program code, assess how each data record is being modified, and identify when data records are being dropped.

8.8.2   Guerrilla Analytics Approach

Creating a unique identifier (UID) for records helps maintain data provenance through a data flow. A good way to easily create a record UID is to apply a hash function to the full data record.

8.8.3   Advantages

Consider the simple data flow of joining two datasets as illustrated in Figure 26. The datasets have come from sources that did not have any primary key, so a UID has been added to both sources using a hash function. For any source record, it is simple to find where it ends up in the output of the data flow. The address dataset has a problem. One of its UIDs is repeated. When the datasets are joined on ADDR_ID, the resulting dataset has a repeated address for CUST ID 496. Using the address UID it is a simple matter to track down the offending record in the original address dataset. This is one simple example of how record UIDs are useful. The advantages of having a record UID are as follows:

- **Traceability:** If problems are encountered in a later dataset in a data flow, it is easy to trace problems back to the individual record at source without having to do complex dataset comparisons.

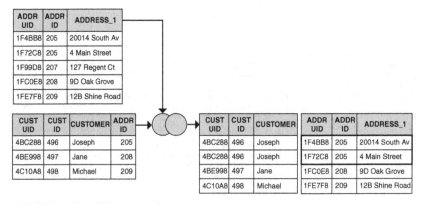

FIGURE 26   Data UID in a data flow

- **Finding dropped records:** If records are dropped from a join, it is simple to pull that population of dropped records out of the original source datasets by looking for missing UIDs.
- **Testability:** Much of testing becomes greatly simplified if there is a UID tracing a data record through a data flow. Testing will be discussed in detail in later chapters.
- **Duplicates:** If record UIDs are correctly calculated across an entire row of data, they are a quick way to compare and deduplicate rows without comparing every individual field.

8.9 PRACTICE TIP 33: RENAME DATA FIELDS WITH A FIELD MAPPING

8.9.1 Guerrilla Analytics Environment

In many scenarios, you are trying to bring together data from disparate systems. Because the data has different sources, it is unlikely to have the same format in each source. One system's CUSTOMER_ID field may be another system's CUST_ID field. Some fields will exist in only one of the systems and not the others. What is a flexible approach to appending data from disparate sources with different field names?

8.9.2 Guerrilla Analytics Approach

When different data sources must be appended together into a single data source, establish a data-field mapping to drive field renaming. A data-field mapping is simply a list of the field names in the disparate data sources, and the common destination field name in the unified output dataset.

Figure 27 shows an illustrative data mapping structure. The left "FROM" column is a listing of all raw field names that have to be renamed. The right "TO" column is a list of all field names that they get renamed to in the target dataset. If needed, a mapping dataset could also have columns to track sources of mappings, sign offs, and other important traceability information.

UID	FROM FIELD	TO FIELD
5GC298	CUSTOMER_ID	CUST_ID
3AE998	CUST_ID	CUST_ID
4C66A2	FNAME	FIRST_NAME
9H32B2	FIRST_NAME	FIRST_NAME

FIGURE 27   A field mapping dataset

8.9.3 Advantages

Taking a field mapping approach to field renaming has the following advantages.

- **Traceability:** The mapping dataset is a clear and traceable record of the business understanding of each field in the disparate sources. This can be important if there are misunderstandings later in the project.
- **Flexibility:** The mapping of fields exists in a separate dataset rather than being tightly embedded to program code. This makes changes to mappings more flexible. This is important as data understanding is evolving quickly.
- **Versioning:** If mappings change, versions of the mapping dataset can be maintained and compared with one another.

War Story 11: Field of Dreams/Nightmares

Sarah is a Guerrilla Analyst who has been drafted in to help Bean Enterprises with data integration and evaluation. Bean Enterprises sell healthy foods and snacks, and recently acquired another chain of similar stores called Lentil. As part of consolidating their product lines, Bean now want to look across their data store and Lentil's data store to get a single view of all products. The data stores are different. Bean uses a PRODUCT_IDENTIFIER field while Lentil have a PROD_ID field. Bean uses a CATEGORY field while Lentil uses something else. There isn't time or budget for a full data migration, so Sarah has to work quickly to get a reasonable view of the products across both data stores.

Her predecessor had made a start and began mapping each data field into a common field in program code. There are over 80 fields in 10 different tables, and no indication of who signed off any of the field mappings that have been completed so far. No wonder the analyst became overwhelmed and made a quick exit from this nightmare project.

Sarah's first step is to identify domain experts from Bean and Lentil who can help her understand the relevant product data fields from both data stores. She creates a big list of the in-scope fields from each data store and sets the domain experts to work agreeing where the fields are equivalent. This gives Sarah her data-field mapping. The data-field mapping is version controlled, and has clear sign off for every mapping. With even an early version of the mapping in place, Sarah can now apply it across all Bean and Lentil data and see what comes out. When the mapped field contents seem inconsistent, Sarah reports back to the domain experts and sets them investigating. When the mappings are good, Sarah can proceed with some early analytics for her customer.

After several weeks, all fields have a signed off mapping. Bean enterprises have benefited from incremental delivery of analytics instead of waiting months for a data migration exercise. In addition, they now have a valuable data asset should they wish to proceed with that data migration – a signed off mapping file for some of their critical data tables.

8.10   WRAP UP

This chapter has examined how to modify data in ways that preserve data provenance. In particular, you should now know the following.

- Code that changes data can cause loss of data provenance due to:
  - Overwrites of data.
  - Failure to distinguish derived data from original data.
  - Discarded records.
  - Difficulty in testing.
  - Loss of record provenance.
- Several simple practices can avoid these risks.
  - Clean data in a minimum of locations in a data-flow.
  - When cleaning data, keep a copy of the raw field.
  - Filter data with flags, not record deletions.
  - Identify clean fields and filter fields with metadata.
  - Create unique record identifiers.
  - Rename data fields with a data mapping rather than hard coding.

Chapter 9

Stage 6: Creating Work Products

9.1 GUERRILLA ANALYTICS WORKFLOW

Up to this point, we have discussed extracting data, loading that data, and writing code to manipulate and analyze that data. When analytics work is completed, there is something to deliver. The Work Products stage of the Guerrilla Analytics workflow is concerned with wrapping up analyses and other activities so they can be delivered either back to the team or to the customer. Furthermore, you must track those deliverables when they leave the team so that you can easily identify them should they return to the team for modification. You can see Work Products in the Guerrilla Analytics workflow of Figure 28. Note that we have skipped a stage called consolidate. We will come back to that in Chapter 12.

9.2 EXAMPLES

There is a multitude of work products that a Guerrilla Analytics team produces on a typical project. Here are just a few examples that you may recognize in your own work.

- **Data integration:** A data flow for taking a third party data source that is refreshed at some interval, cleaning and profiling this data source and joining it into the core project data for analysis.
- **Data profiling:** A summary of a new data source that has been loaded into the Data Manipulation Environment (DME). This is reported back to the team and customer on lessons learned about the data.
- **Data testing:** Checksums of some data received from the customer and a report on all checksums and exceptions.
- **Data analytics and visualization:** Code to extract a subset of sales data from a given year and identify all outliers by sales price and region. A visualization of these regional outliers using a box plot.
- **Third-party tools:** A data quality assessment of all data from a given system extract produced using a proprietary data quality tool.
- **Marked-up data:** An export of a financial data sample from the DME into a spreadsheet so that it can be reviewed and marked up. It is expected that these markups will be imported back into the DME and used in future analyses.

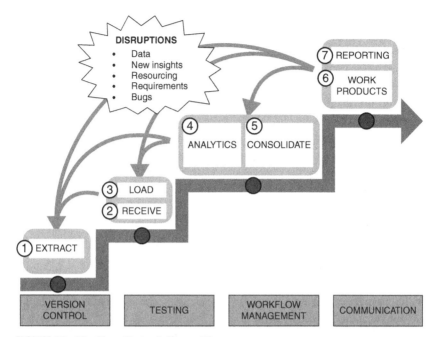

FIGURE 28 **The Guerrilla Analytics workflow**

- **Rework:** A modification of an existing work product from several weeks ago to add a new data feature to it. The new version of the work product is reissued back to the customer with a report on any implications of the new data feature.
- **Data sample:** An extract of the recently loaded address dataset so the client can confirm he delivered you the correct version of the data.

Looking through these work products examples, there are some common features to note.

- **Mix of programming languages:** You are sometimes using several programming languages in the creation of a work product.
- **Use of proprietary tools:** You will sometimes be using a proprietary tool that might have its own file formats, project files, and other ancillary materials.
- **More than just program code:** You are sometimes creating presentations, spreadsheets, and written reports. Not every work product involves program code.
- **Multiple iterations:** There are occasions where a work product is returned to the team for additions or corrections before being reissued to the customer. This raises the question of version control and impact assessments.
- **Complexity:** Some work products are complex data flows that will involve multiple code files and data steps. In many ways they are a significant piece of software in their own right and may take days to complete.

- **Simplicity:** Some work products are simply an extraction of an existing dataset – a single line of program code.
- **Data/people feedback loops:** There are occasions where data is leaving the data team, being modified in the broader team or by the customer, and then being returned into the data environment.
- **Multiple people involved:** Some work products may have multiple team members working on and reviewing them.

There is the potential for a lot of complexity here because of the wide range of activities engaged in by the Guerrilla Analytics team. Before going further it is worthwhile to define the concept of a work product.

9.3 THE ESSENCE OF A WORK PRODUCT

If we simplify things, there are three components to a work product.

- **Data Sources:** As you have seen in earlier chapters, data must be either raw data or data that the team derives from this raw data.
- **Generators:** These are the program code files and other data manipulation activities that create the work product from a data source.
- **Outputs:** These are the datasets, images, models, reports, and other derived materials that the generator creates from the data sources.

To preserve the provenance of a work product, you need the generators and their data sources. Apply the generators to the data sources and outputs should be rebuilt from scratch. Everything to do with preserving provenance in a data source is based on this simple structure. The next section discusses examples of how this structure is often broken.

9.4 PITFALLS AND RISKS

The main pitfalls to avoid when creating a work product are as follows.

- **Clutter of the DME and file system:** Where do you store all of these work products in the DME? Where do you store related work on the file system? Without guidelines, your DME and file system will be a cluttered mess.
- **Work product owner cannot be identified:** Without proper processes in place, a work product's creator and owner cannot be identified. This makes review and handover difficult and impedes your ability to manage the team's activities.
- **Work product versions confused or lost:** How do you identify versions of work products? In a cluttered DME, it becomes impossible to identify the latest version of a work product and compare it to previous versions. This is exacerbated when a work product is composed of many code files or has several outputs.

- **Work products deleted:** If you cannot identify the components of a work product on the DME and on the file system there is a higher risk that some critical component of the work product will be deleted or lost.
- **Knowledge is never consolidated:** If work products are developed in an ad-hoc fashion, it becomes difficult to identify common implementation and data needs. Team knowledge is never consolidated as every work product effectively starts from scratch. A customer can ask for a work product from one team member on one day and get a different answer from another team member on another day.
- **Team cannot identify its own work products:** Without work product tracking in place, a team cannot easily recognize a work product that is returned to the team and jump to that work product's outputs and code files for debugging or modification.

The following practice tips are guidelines to help mitigate these risks.

9.5   PRACTICE TIP 34: TRACK WORK PRODUCTS WITH A UNIQUE IDENTIFIER (UID)

9.5.1   Guerrilla Analytics Environment

The team is creating many work products and many of those work products are being delivered to the customer. Work products may be composed of multiple files including code files, images, dashboards, documents, and more. The customer will often modify the work product files they receive and perhaps return to the team to question and better understand the work product. Since these work products are leaving the team's data environment, the team has little control over their tracking and use (or abuse).

9.5.2   Guerrilla Analytics Approach

Every work product should be given its own UID. The best identifier is simply a number that increments with every new work product the team produces. With a UID established for a work product, the following should then be done.

- The UID should be embedded in the name of every work product file.
- Work product files should be saved in a folder, which also has this UID in the folder name.
- Work product activities in the DME should be stored in a location that also has the UID in its name.

Figure 29 summarizes these tips in a typical folder and DME structure. Work product 103 has its own folder on the file system and its own "folder" in the DME. Every generator and output in the file system has the UID in its file name. All intermediate and result datasets for the work product are stored in the "103" location in the DME so they are grouped together.

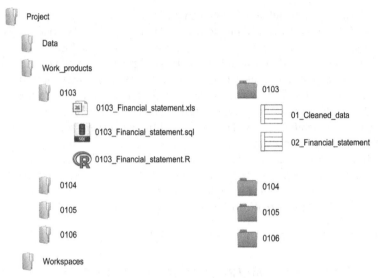

FIGURE 29 Work product UID in the file system and the DME

War Story 12: The Blame Game

Matt arrived onto a project to take over from another analytics manager. It was his second day in charge of the analytics team working in a wider project of about 50 analysts. The project was investigating the finances of a high-profile corporation that has been accused of fraud. There was a lot of pressure on the whole team with every result and report subject to scrutiny. The analytics team was overworked and being blamed for all project errors. With a project lead who didn't have an analytics background, it was difficult to gain their trust and understanding of complex analytics outputs. Matt was about to be a contestant in "The Blame Game."

He spent his first days getting familiar with work streams, the assigned data analysts, and the corresponding business analysts. All was going smoothly. Then Matt attended a meeting where a senior team member brandished an incorrect spreadsheet that they claimed to have received from the analytics team several months ago. Their accusation was that this incorrect spreadsheet had misled the wider team and almost caused the release of an incorrect report from the project. Analytics were to blame and they needed to take more care with their outputs. Diplomatically, Matt tried his best to reason with her and asked for some help tracing where exactly the spreadsheet had come from. His analytics team member claimed not to recognize it. Without an evidence chain and having only 2 days on the project, Matt was in a weak position. He took the offending spreadsheet back to his team and began looking into how the lapse in quality might have occurred.

After some "forensic" investigations of their own, Matt's team found the original spreadsheet and guess what? Somebody outside of the analytics team had changed its contents. The spreadsheet that left the team mailbox was correct. Matt's team wasn't to blame at all but had no way to back this up.

Matt immediately began a work product UID process where all files leaving the analytics team had this UID embedded in their file names. This was communicated to the wider project team. The simple process quickly put an end to blame games as there could be no doubt about what the analytics team had actually produced. It also made communication with the wider project team much easier. Instead of "spreadsheet from so-an-so.xls" the team could now talk about "work product 56." Within 2 months, work product UIDs were the standard vocabulary of the project and instrumental in planning and coordinating project phases. A simple Guerrilla Analytics tactic had protected the team and improved the wider project. Game over.

9.5.3   Advantages

The simple convention of work product UIDs has several advantages.

- **Communication:** By embedding the work product UID in the file names of work products, it is quite likely that the UID will be preserved. Better still, customers themselves will recognize the number. In projects where this is most successful, work product UIDs become part of the customers' vocabulary. They begin asking for a version of "work product 205" or ask you to send them a new version of "work product 500." This simple approach is surprisingly effective.
- **Location on the file system:** By creating a space on the file system that has the UID in its name, you can quickly locate a work product's files and know that every generator and output related to that work product must be somewhere within that file folder. You saw a similar approach with data UIDs.
- **Location in the DME:** By creating a location in the DME that has the UID in its name, you can quickly locate all datasets related to a work product and easily separate those datasets from other DME activities.

9.6   PRACTICE TIP 35: KEEP WORK PRODUCT GENERATORS AND OUTPUTS CLOSE TOGETHER

9.6.1   Guerrilla Analytics Environment

As mentioned earlier, every work product has three components.

- It has a data source.
- It has the program code and other data manipulation activities.
- It has some outputs created by the generators that are delivered to the customer or the team.

When a customer wants to discuss or modify a work product, he or she will return to the team with the work product output file. Both generators and outputs are critical to the reproducibility and data provenance of the work product since they encompass the data team's perspective and the customer's perspective, respectively.

9.6.2 Guerrilla Analytics Approach

Some teams will keep a separate folder for delivered work product files. This causes confusion. Keep work product generation code and work product outputs right beside one another in their work product folder.

Looking again at Figure 29, there are two analytics code files with the .SQL and .R extensions. There is also a spreadsheet file with the extension .XLS. The spreadsheet is a cut of data created by the analytics code files. All files are within the same work product folder and have the same file name so you know they belong together.

9.6.3 Advantages

The simple convention of keeping generators and outputs together offers several advantages.

- **Know what was issued to the customer:** Every work product has a definitive copy of what was sent to the customer. This helps resolve situations where the customer has modified a work product and there is a question over data provenance.
- **Traceability improves:** Debugging is now easy because everything that is needed to understand and reproduce a work product is located in one place. The analyst can first check the work product output file and confirm any problems. They can then follow up by examining the associated code files and DME datasets that generated the work product.

9.7 PRACTICE TIP 36: AVOID CLUTTER IN THE FILE SYSTEM

9.7.1 Guerrilla Analytics Environment

A work product has several components in terms of files that create the work product and perhaps versions of the work product. The work product's folder quickly becomes cluttered with files making it difficult to know what files to review and how to associate work product generators with work product outputs. Additional supporting materials such as emails and documentation are important but do not contribute to reproducing the work product output. How do you keep all relevant materials together but avoid accumulating confusing clutter?

9.7.2 Guerrilla Analytics Approach

A simple folder structure reduces clutter. The key insight here is that the latest version of the work product must be accessed easily and often. Older versions and supporting materials are rarely accessed and so can be filed away.

The minimal folder structure that serves the vast majority of work product scenarios is as follows.

- **Keep most recent materials in the root:** Keep only the most recent work product generator and outputs in the root of the work product folder. They are accessed most often.
- **Archive:** File away older versions of generators and outputs in a subfolder called "archive." The archiving approach need not be any more sophisticated than this as older materials are accessed less often.
- **Supporting:** File away supporting materials such as emails and documentation in a subfolder called "supporting."

Figure 30 illustrates a work product folder with this structure. Random supporting documents and emails are in the "supporting" subfolder. An older version 01 is in the "archive" subfolder.

FIGURE 30   **A simple work product folder structure**

9.7.3   Advantages

This simple filing tip offers these advantages.

- **Ease of debugging and modification:** On the majority of occasions a team will revisit a work product folder for two reasons. They want to grab the outputs so they can discuss them with the customer. Alternatively, they wish to delve into the work product code to understand how the work product was created, perhaps because it is incorrect or it is being handed over between team members. Knowing that only the latest relevant materials are in the root of the work product folder saves time sifting through older or unrelated files.
- **Versions are easily identified:** All older versions of generators and outputs are in one clearly labeled location – the "archive" subfolder.

9.8   PRACTICE TIP 37: AVOID CLUTTER IN THE DME

9.8.1   Guerrilla Analytics Environment

Much as files build up in the file system, datasets will build up in the DME. Trial analyses that were abandoned and multiple versions of a work product contribute to clutter. This clutter causes confusion and wastes time when reviewing work products and when trying to locate the source of a particular work product output file.

9.8.2   Guerrilla Analytics Approach

Two practices help with DME clutter, much like the approach taken with clutter in the file system.

- Establish a name space for a work product that is named with the work product UID.
- When a work product is executed, first clear out this name space and then rebuild all datasets generated by the work product code.

9.8.3   Advantages

This DME namespace approach combined with a tear down of all datasets has the following advantages.

- **Removes orphaned datasets:** Old orphaned datasets that are no longer part of the work product are cleared out. This makes it much easier to review and understand a work product because only relevant datasets are in the DME. Moreover, the risk of accidentally referencing an old dataset is eliminated.
- **Removes the risk of accidentally orphaning a dataset:** By requiring all derived datasets to be created when work code executes, temporary datasets that may be needed for reproducibility will be reliably present.

- **Easy location of work products:** Because the work product's datasets are located in a well-identified namespace, it is easy to find all datasets related to a given work product just by knowing its work product UID.

9.9   PRACTICE TIP 38: GIVE OUTPUT DATA RECORDS A UID

9.9.1   Guerrilla Analytics Environment

Placing a work product UID in work product file names helps identify the original output when it comes back to the team. However, what about data records within a work product file? Rows of data in a spreadsheet may be shuffled by the customer. Worse still, they may be modified or broken by the end user. Questions about dashboards and visualizations are hard to resolve when the underlying data cannot easily be referenced. Conversations with the customer are much easier if both parties have a way to precisely identify data records.

9.9.2   Guerrilla Analytics Approach

All data records in a work product output should be given a deterministic UID at the record level. As we have seen before, in the absence of primary keys, the best UID for a row of data is a hash of the entire row of data.

9.9.3   Advantages

Having a UID for each record offers the following advantages.

- **Comparison:** When a data record is returned to the team, the returned record can easily be identified and compared to the record that left the team originally.
- **Coordination:** When trying to collaborate on data, it is risky to talk about the "fifth" record or the record for "person named James Smith." If you have a record UID there can be no doubt about the record you and the customer are referring to.
- **Reintegration of data:** If data from a work product needs to be reintegrated into the DME and joined into data already in the DME, having a UID greatly helps this process.

9.10   PRACTICE TIP 39: VERSION CONTROL WORK PRODUCTS

9.10.1   Guerrilla Analytics Environment

It is inevitable that work products will go through several iterations with the customer or peer review within the team. This will happen either because requirements change as the customer explores the data with the team or it may happen because of mistakes in the work product. How should the team deal with these circumstances?

9.10.2 Guerrilla Analytics Approach

Establish a version-control process such that there are clearly identified versions of the work product generators and corresponding clearly identified versions of the work product outputs. Retain all versions of generators and outputs.

Figure 31 shows a simple example of how this can be done. On the left, files have a version number embedded in their file name. This example has a version 01 and a version 02. In the DME on the right, a version 01 and version 02 schema give name space separation to the datasets associated with each version.

9.10.3 Advantages

With a version-control process in place, much of the confusion of the Guerrilla Analytics environment is avoided. In particular, the team can show a customer the impact of changes to the work product by comparing the latest version to some previous version. The inevitable question of "why have the numbers changed" is easily answered by comparing versions of output datasets.

Second, the latest version of the work product is easily identified from the file naming and dataset namespace.

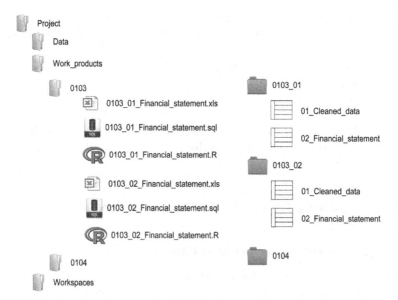

FIGURE 31   **Simple version control in the file system and DME**

9.11 PRACTICE TIP 40: USE A CONVENTION TO NAME COMPLEX OUTPUTS

9.11.1 Guerrilla Analytics Environment

Work products are composed of one or more code files and produce one or more outputs. There may be code files that only manipulate data in the DME. There might be other code files that take data from the DME and generate several plot files. There may be code files that create multiple data samples that are delivered to the customer in spreadsheets for further analysis. Without putting some type of process in place there is no easy way to know where an output came from. This situation is made worse when one generator creates several outputs.

9.11.2 Guerrilla Analytics Approach

An output should have the same name as the code that generates the output. If the code generates multiple outputs then the code file name should prefix those multiple output file names. Table 1 illustrates some examples.

- In scenario 1, there is a clear one-to-one mapping between the generator file and the output file as implied by their having the same names.
- In scenario 2, one generator is producing two output files. Since they all share the same file name prefix, it is clear where the generated files came from.
- Scenario 3 is a mix of scenarios 1 and 2. From the naming convention we can easily see that D300_data_prep.SQL generates the CSV file output. Separately D300_plotting.R generates the other two outputs.

9.11.3 Advantages

This simple naming convention has the following advantages.

- **Speed of debugging:** The code that generated one or more output files is easily identified in the work product folder.
- **Data provenance:** The link between the DME and the work product is maintained with no documentation overhead.

TABLE 1 Example Scenarios and Naming Convention for Complex Outputs

	Scenario	Generator file name	Output file name(s)
1	One code file and one output	D050_03.SQL	D050_03.XLS
2	One code file and multiple outputs	D009_01.py	**D009_01**_customers.XLS **D009_01**_addresses.XLS
	Multiple code files and multiple outputs	D300_data_prep.SQL D300_plotting.R	D300_data_prep.CSV **D300_plotting**_Bar.PNG **D300_plotting**_Scatter.PNG

9.12 PRACTICE TIP 41: LOG ALL WORK PRODUCTS

9.12.1 Guerrilla Analytics Environment

It is always useful to store some additional information about a work product. For example, it would be good to know which team member did the work as well as which customer it was delivered to. Some basic management information (MI) on date of request and date of delivery helps determine bottlenecks in delivery. What is the best way to track this type of information?

9.12.2 Guerrilla Analytics Approach

Similar to data tracking, the simple Guerrilla Analytics approach is to have a work product log in the root of the work products folder. Entries in this log use the work product UID for tracking and the team completes whatever information about the work product is deemed useful for data provenance and tracking.

9.12.3 Advantages

It is not unusual for a Guerrilla Analytics team working in a fast-paced environment to deliver hundreds of work products over several months. Having a log of who worked on what is helpful when old work products come back to haunt you or when you need to locate the most appropriate team member for a particular piece of work. The log also enables the team to clearly articulate their efforts to the customer and identify the major drivers of customer demand.

9.13 WRAP UP

This chapter has discussed creating and tracking work products in a Guerrilla Analytics environment. Having read this chapter you should now know the following.

- The risks associated with poor management of work products on the file system and in the DME. Specifically:
  - Clutter of the DME and file system.
  - Work product owner cannot be identified.
  - Work product versions confused or lost.
  - Work products deleted.
  - Knowledge is never consolidated.
  - The team cannot identify its own work products.
- Some simple practices and conventions greatly mitigate these risks. These primarily involve:
  - Giving every work product a UID.
  - Giving every data record in a work product its own UID.
  - Using sensible file naming conventions to identify versions of work product files.

- Avoiding clutter in the file system by having an archive process for older or irrelevant materials.
- Using a name space in the DME to group together all datasets related to a version of a work product.
- Versioning work products so that the impact of changes can be understood and quantified.

Chapter 10

Stage 7: Reporting

10.1 GUERRILLA ANALYTICS WORKFLOW

Reporting is one of the types of analytics team outputs. It therefore happens at the end of the Guerrilla Analytics Workflow as illustrated in Figure 32. Given how late reporting happens in the workflow, any disruptions encountered at this stage can be very expensive. Mistakes in the underlying build, work products, or data introduce mistakes into the report. Refreshing data will require revisiting all analytics feeding into the report to make sure its analytics components are up to date, consistent, and correct.

10.2 WHAT IS A REPORT?

The previous chapter discussed how to produce work products and how this is something the Guerrilla Analytics team does from the very beginning of the project. Since much effort is devoted to exploring and understanding the data in collaboration with business users and customers, you would expect there to be many work products and iterations of those work products. This is the case and several chapters of this book have been devoted to coping with the disruptions of this highly iterative and dynamic cycle.

On many projects, there will be occasions where a weightier deliverable also needs to be produced. This is typically a written document or presentation that is communicating key project findings to project stakeholders and sponsors. The document is often produced at milestones in a project or to summarize a project's findings at the end of the project. The format is predominantly text, which is then interleaved with numbers, figures, tables, and analyses. Some of these will have been produced by the Guerrilla Analytics team but it is possible that others will have been produced by members of the broader project team. Here are some examples.

- In a forensic investigation, a report is a key deliverable that details the results of the investigation. Its contents may be presented in a court of law or used in a firm's internal HR process. The report may draw heavily on data "evidence" produced by the analytics team.
- In management consulting projects, the report may deliver key recommendations for a customer or shareholder. Examples include decisions on a firm's strategy, a decision to pursue a merger, the launch of a new service, etc.

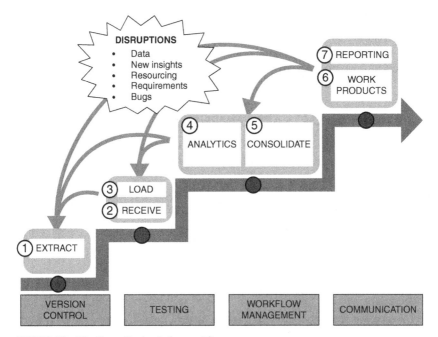

FIGURE 32 The Guerrilla Analytics workflow

- In a transformation project, the report may summarize current customers, potential for churn and recommend a new strategy, product and marketing to counteract this churn. These report recommendations could feed into significant investment decisions for the business.
- A banking conduct risk project will describe the types of risk models created and the assumptions and data on which these models were built. Many scenarios may be modeled and commented on with recommendations for operational changes in the bank.
- A well written scientific paper must be reproducible with clear conclusions for it to pass peer review and be published.
- A well-archived Guerrilla Analytics project will have a closing document that describes the data analyzed, how it was sourced, assumptions made, analyses, and recommendations.

The list of reporting examples goes on but hopefully you have the idea. Work products are the day to day evolving analytics that represent the team and customer's growing understanding of the data. Reports are set-in-stone work products that absolutely have to be correct, traceable, tested, etc. Once delivered, there is little scope for retraction, iteration, and corrections.

Reports have other significant inputs beyond analytics work products. Writing a report means combining some form of write-up and commentary with analytics results from the team. These results might be a single number embedded in a larger paragraph of text. Results might also be relatively clear-cut figures or tables taken directly from data analytics work products. A more difficult scenario is when the analytics team's result goes to another team member or a business analyst who then modifies the work product further before it contributes to the report. Clearly this presents a particularly difficult challenge for the traceability and data provenance of the Guerrilla Analytics team's outputs.

10.3   WHY REPORTS ARE COMPLICATED

There are some clear risks in report writing in addition to the general risks around work products that were discussed in the previous chapter. Let us first look at a typical report example.

Figure 33 shows a page from a report. This is a completely fabricated example and is deliberately simplistic. However, it has many of the features you see in a typical report and therefore nicely illustrates many of the sources of lost data provenance for the Guerrilla Analytics team.

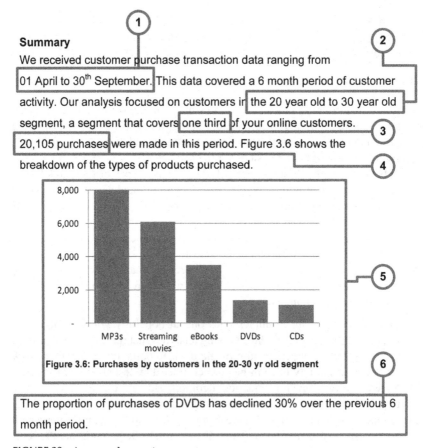

FIGURE 33   An example report

The report contains a small paragraph of text. Several numbers are mentioned in this paragraph. There is also a simple figure, which is referenced from the paragraph. Such a report presents a number of challenges for traceability as highlighted in Figure 33.

- **A date range for the data is quoted.** Who sourced this date range and is it correct? Is there a particular date field in the data that could reproduce this date range?
- **A customer segment is quoted.** Again who sourced this and is it correct? How was this segment determined from the data? Was it already in the data or was some segmentation performed?
- **It is stated that this customer segment is one-third of the total customer population.** Was this calculated from the same data used in the previous quotes? Do the authors mean one-third in numbers or in sales value or by some other metric?
- **A total number of purchases for the customer segment in this date range are quoted.** Again who calculated this total? Are we sure it was calculated from the exact same data as provided by the other quoted numbers?

Even if the above challenges on accurately specifying data populations are overcome, there remain challenges around consistency of components of the report.

- **There is a figure summarizing purchase types.** Do the totals and breakdown in this figure tie out to the numbers quoted in the preceding paragraph?
- **The data are compared to a previous date range to make a claim about a decline in sales.** Where was this number sourced from or is it an anecdotal reference?

This simple example illustrates how one paragraph of text and a summary figure can generate many questions around data provenance, correctness, and consistency.

10.4 REPORT COMPONENTS

It is helpful when discussing reports to think if them as having the components illustrated in Figure 34. The components are divided into written components and analytical components.

- **Written components:** These are the concern of the report authors. They consist of the usual report sections such as scope, introduction, comments, conclusions, recommendations that are part of any analytical report. They are not directly dependent on data.
- **Analytical components:** These are the concern of any teams doing analysis work, including the Guerrilla Analytics team. The types of analytical components are figures, tables of data, text that references these figures and tables, and text that references data in general.

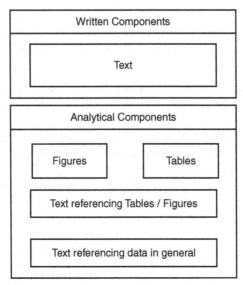

FIGURE 34 Components of a report

Have a look through the example report at the start of this chapter and see if you can identify each of these components.

10.5 PITFALLS AND RISKS

Thinking about the questions raised by the sample report of the earlier section, we can identify the following risks for the Guerrilla Analytics team. Broadly these fall into two categories.

10.5.1 Data Provenance

These risks relate to recognizing a particular analytics component in a report and being able to trace its origins.

- **Data modified after leaving the team:** The data that leaves the analytics team can be further modified by somebody outside the team before it enters the report. This is done for two reasons: the data needs to be modified for presentation purposes or somebody wants to do their own analysis before putting a final work product into the report. The latter could happen when an analytical domain expert such as an insurance actuary needs to perform his/her own analysis.
- **A data team's work products cannot be identified:** Not all numbers in a report will have come from the analytics team. In bigger projects there may be business analysts, accountants, scientists, and other domain experts who are perfectly capable of generating their own data and outputs. Alternatively, a single number quoted deep in some paragraph may be a complex analytics team work product of several code files that evolved over several versions.

10.5.2 Consistency

Consistency relates to the risk of components of the report not agreeing with one another.

- **Consistency with the analytics team:** Are the components used in the report consistent with what the analytics team would produce?
- **Self-consistency:** Are components within the report consistent with one another? Components can become inconsistent if they come from separate sources or are modified in inconsistent ways. In our illustrative example, the figure may have come from the analytics team while the summary comments on the figure may have been written by a different team and calculated from an analytics data sample. They all involved the same data, however, so they had better all be consistent with one another.

10.5.3 Implications

These risks have several implications for the Guerrilla Analytics team.

- First, without a proper process in place there can be disagreement over which components came from the analytics team and which came from some other part of the project.
- Second, if a component cannot be identified, there is no way to reproduce the given component.
- Third, and perhaps most seriously, there is a lot of scope for an incorrect report.

Let us now look at the key ways to mitigate these risks.

War Story 13: The Quick Fix

Claire was managing the analytics team working on a project which involved writing formal reports for a client every 6–8 weeks. The report writers would hide themselves away for a week, writing up their findings with data they had received from Claire's analytics team in a variety of work products over the course of the previous 6 weeks. Timelines were always extremely tight and all of this happened without bringing analytics onto the reporting team. The report would be reviewed internally and then published. This was how things went until somebody raised the question of the provenance of all numbers used in the reports. Panic!

The quick fix was to revisit all possible analytics components in the report and check that they could be reproduced. A dump of figures, spreadsheets, and data came back to Claire's team with a copy of the published report. Some of the data contained recognizable analytics work products (Claire was using a work product UID in the team's file names). Some of the data seemed to have been modified or even had nothing to do with the analytics team at all.

Claire had to sideline several analytics team members for a week as they went through the 60 page report writing analytics queries that would reproduce report numbers and highlighting numbers that did not involve her team at all.

Imagine how painful this was. Think of the number of ways to filter and pivot a dataset to turn it into a report table. Think of having to reproduce a single number quoted in the middle of a paragraph of text with little or no analytics context. Much effort could have been saved by involving Claire's analytics team with the report writers at the time of writing and agreeing a process for maintaining data provenance in the report.

10.6 PRACTICE TIP 42: LIAISE WITH REPORT WRITERS

10.6.1 Guerrilla Analytics Environment

Very often, the person writing the report is not from the analytics team. There may be more than one writer and some or none of those people may be from the analytics team. How can you maintain data provenance if you do not have visibility of how analytics work products are being used?

10.6.2 Guerrilla Analytics Approach

Whenever a report is being produced, an analytics team member should be part of the report writing team. Their job is to liaise with the report writing team and do the following key things.

- Have an overview of the report content.
- Identify when new analytics work products are required and when existing work products are being used.
- Ensure that every analytics work product used in the report can be traced back to its work product UID.

10.6.3 Advantages

The main advantage of a mixed team of Guerrilla Analytics and report writers is that data provenance of report content is maintained. If this tip is applied successfully, every analytics output in a report should be identifiable by a work product UID. This ensures full reproducibility of the report content.

10.7 PRACTICE TIP 43: CREATE ONE WORK PRODUCT PER REPORT COMPONENT

10.7.1 Guerrilla Analytics Environment

We know that some of the Guerrilla Analytics team's outputs will appear in a report as an individual number, a statement about another component, a table or a figure. It is difficult for the analytics team to know in advance the context in which their work product will be used. It would therefore be very useful to be able to easily reproduce any given analytical component that appears in a report. You would rather avoid having to do an excessive amount of searching through a history of analytics work product, some of which may have to be reworked.

10.7.2   Guerrilla Analytics Approach

Every report component from the Guerrilla Analytics team should be a work product with its own work product UID. This should happen regardless of how simple or complex the component in the report is.

Consider a simple example where the report must have a sentence such as "Data was analysed from April to September." "April to September" should be a simple work product with its own UID. In practice this may be a one line query to calculate the earliest and latest month from the data. Nevertheless, there would now be a definitive traceable record of the date field and dataset from which the quoted date range was generated.

10.7.3   Advantages

The advantages of this tip are as follows.

- **Data Provenance:** Any analytics component of the report can be identified and reproduced quickly without rework or reinterpretation.
- **Efficiency:** Time is saved in trying to ensure that a report has the latest numbers and that those numbers are consistent with one another. Every report component from the analytics team has full data provenance so you know how it was produced in code and the version of the data it was based on.
- **Explaining Changing Numbers:** Because report components are based on actual work products, they have an identifiable version. Future project reports can explain why their quoted numbers and analyses may differ from previous reports.

10.8   PRACTICE TIP 44: MAKE PRESENTATION QUALITY WORK PRODUCTS

10.8.1   Guerrilla Analytics Environment

The Guerrilla Analytics team will often produce work products that are further modified by other team members or the report writers themselves. For example, a fairly raw dataset may be filtered or aggregated to produce a summary table appropriate for a report. The more an analytics component is modified outside the analytics environment, the more difficult it is to reproduce it at a later date and so these types of modifications need to be discouraged somehow.

10.8.2   Guerrilla Analytics Approach

Analytics work products for a report component should be tailored to be as close as possible to the format required in the report. For example, if a report table should have certain headings and row labels, then you should produce those headings and row labels in the analytics work product rather than leaving it to the report writer. If a figure should have certain axis labels and limits then you should set those axis limits and labels in the work product code, not after the figure has been handed over for inclusion in the report.

10.8.3 Advantages

This tip eliminates the need for report writers or nonanalytics team members to modify work products and break data provenance. As far as possible, if they have everything they need in the format in which they need it then everybody's life will be a lot easier.

10.9 EXTREME REPORTING

You may be reading this chapter and thinking it all seems a little brittle. Have an analyst sit with report authors identifying work products? Make work products presentation ready so a link isn't broken between the analytics team and its work products? Surely there is a better toolset for doing this? There are some options worth mentioning.

10.9.1 In-Line Documentation

Much of what was discussed in this chapter involved simple processes for bringing the analytics into the report. That is, a report document exists in a word processor application and we want to embed analytics work products into the word processor document.

In-line documentation turns this approach on its head and takes the report into the analytics. A large "code" file is written that generates all the required outputs such as numbers, tables, and figures. This same code file contains the text for the report. When in-line documentation tools are run on this "code file" it typesets the text and generates the latest versions of the analytics components to produce a final document. This is the approach taken by tools such as Sweave (Leisch, 2002).

There are some challenges to this approach when used in a Guerrilla Analytics project.

- **Programming language variety:** The reality is that Guerrilla Analytics involves analyses with a wide variety of tools and datasets. There is no one size fits all analytics language that covers all the team's needs.
- **Need for iterative reviews:** Many of the team's analyses are iterative and require skilled interpretation before they can be used. You cannot just click "go" and trust that the outputs are ready to go straight into a report.
- **Incompatibility with office software:** Many report writers prefer to use office suites that do not look like "program code."

So unfortunately, while in-line documentation seems like a promising approach, the opportunity to use it in Guerrilla Analytics projects is rare. Only projects with short analytics execution times and a small number of report writers are appropriate.

10.9.2   A Simple Alternative

A simple alternative is to provide a word processor add-in with the following functionality.

- **Tagging:** Can tag analytics components (numbers, text, figures, and tables) with a work product UID.
- **Listing:** Can create a report listing all work product UIDs used in a document.

Then the only change to a team's approach to report writing would be to teach report writers to tag all analytics components with the work product UID they received from the analytics team. When a report needs to be reproduced, the relevant work products UIDs can be easily listed.

10.10   WRAP UP

This chapter has discussed report writing in Guerrilla Analytics projects. You have learned.

- **What a report is:** A report is a formal document that is a combination of written content and analytics work products. Unlike a typical work product that may be iterative and collaborative, a report is generally a complex document perhaps with multiple authors and many components both from analytics and from other teams.
- **Report components:** Regardless of how complex or lengthy a report is, it fundamentally consists of written components and analytical components. The analytical components are tables, figures, text that references both tables and figures and finally, text that references data in general.
- **Risks in reporting:** The nature of reporting where the report writers often take analytics outputs for inclusion in the report raises the following risks.
  - Data modified after leaving the team.
  - The team's work products cannot be identified.
  - Consistency of report components with the analytics team outputs.
  - Consistency of report components with one another within the report.
- Simple practice tips mitigate the risks in reporting.
  - Stay close to the report writers and liaise with them.
  - One work product per report component.
  - Make presentation quality work products.

Chapter 11

Stage 5: Consolidating Knowledge in Builds

11.1 INTRODUCTION

As analytics code is written by the team to produce work products, common patterns of data manipulation will begin to emerge. Here are some examples.

- **Repeated cleaning:** Every time a dataset is used, it must be prepared by cleaning data fields. For example, for a dataset of country names, the team may have to remember to produce one common version of UK, U.K., United Kingdom, and variants such as GBR and Britain.
- **Repeated joining:** Some datasets will have to be joined together. For example, every time a particular view of department and spend is required, the department and spend data sources must be joined together. This may have to be done while remembering particular rules about the join. For example, perhaps older decommissioned departments no longer have any spend data and so drop out of joins.
- **Customer inputs:** The customer or a nonanalytics team member will have inputs into the data through human keyed datasets. For example, a vendor master dataset contains 10 approximate duplicates that the customer has reviewed and identified in a list. The customer always wants these duplicates removed from analyses when counting the total number of vendors.
- **Consistent cleaning:** Imagine that as a team, you have agreed a convention of always using upper case names. For example, "Mahony" always becomes "MAHONY." This type of rule is sometimes needed for presentation purposes or to comply with algorithm inputs. The team must remember to do this consistently on appropriate fields only.
- **Need for functionality:** The need for certain code functionality will arise again and again. For example, if the team is testing data completeness they will need generic code that converts and checksums fields in datasets. If one team member has gone to the trouble of writing this code, the other team members should be able to benefit from this effort.

There are some common themes here. Both the Guerrilla Analytics team and the customer are growing their understanding of the data and this understanding of the data needs to be captured in everything the team does for consistency.

When discoveries are made in the data they need to be communicated to everybody in the analytics team. High-profile work products delivered to a customer must include the rules the customer has agreed with the team. It reflects poorly on the team if their outputs are inconsistent or previous lessons learned appear to be forgotten at a later date.

The team will develop code to solve common data problems and this code should be reused as far as is possible. There is no point in every team member reinventing the wheel.

11.2   PITFALLS AND RISKS

Failing to maintain a consistent data understanding presents some risks to the analytics team's outputs and efficiency.

- **Copy and paste code:** Because every work product is built from scratch, there is a temptation to copy and paste code from previous work products so they can quickly be reused in the current work product. This is particularly the case when work product code is complex. Copy and paste code is inefficient in terms of the size of the team's code base and the necessary reviews. It also means that many bugs are spread through many work products. There is also a risk that old copy and pasted code does not capture the latest data and business rules.
- **Inconsistent work products:** With each team member taking their own approach to implementing manipulations of the data, there is a lack of consistency in approaches. For example, one team member's cleaning routine may remove £$%^ from text strings. Another team member's cleaning routine may remove £$%^ and in addition the symbol *. Even this simple example could result in two team members giving inconsistent counts of unique strings. If that difference translates into a difference in a material value then there are serious implications for the project.
- **Reduced efficiency from lack of abstraction:** Every team member potentially needs to know every dataset quirk and join to be able to create work products. There is no core collection of datasets that the team can trust and use without needing a full understanding of how to derive those datasets from scratch. In effect, there is no abstraction of data understanding.
- **Reduced efficiency from repeatedly building data from scratch:** Let us say it takes a significant number of data manipulations to get to a particular view of the data. Some of these data manipulations may be time consuming to run. Now, every time a work product is created that depends on that dataset, those time-consuming data manipulations must be rerun. This wastes the team's time and computational resources.

• **Data populations are not explainable to the customer:** Because every team member is producing every work product "from scratch," there is not one true view of the data that can be explained to the customer and signed off.

Clearly something needs to be done to address a lack of centralized team knowledge in a Guerrilla Analytics environment.

11.3   EXAMPLE: THE CUSTOMER ADDRESS PROBLEM

To understand the problem of evolving data understanding, it helps to visualize what is happening to the data. Figures 35 and 36 illustrate the situation for the example of a customer address problem.

The raw data consist of a customer details dataset and an address history dataset. This particular analytics job requires only the latest address for a customer. However, there are some inconsistencies and duplicates in the customer address dataset. These have been identified and manually reviewed by the broader team on two occasions and this knowledge has been captured in two duplicate review datasets. Two work products have also been created from the data on two separate occasions by two different analysts.

Figure 35 shows the approach taken by one analyst for the work product with UID 314. This analyst used the manual duplicate markups from 2nd February and immediately deduplicated the addresses. The latest address was then calculated and combined with customer details to produce a customer address dataset. At this point, some problems in customer names were noticed and so cleaning was applied to the customer address dataset to produce the final work product dataset.

Now, consider Figure 36 that is a later work product with UID 320, which was produced from the same data but by a different analyst. This analyst used

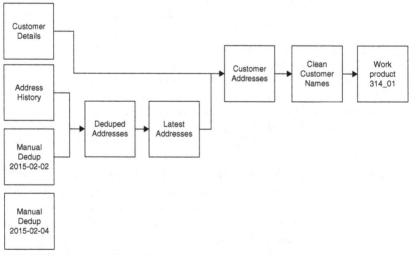

FIGURE 35   Data flow (Option 1)

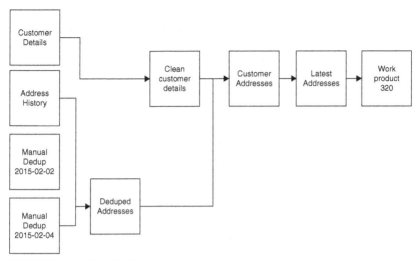

FIGURE 36   Data flow (Option 2)

a later manual deduplication file from 4th February, so the results are probably different from the previous work product 314. In addition, this second analyst has made some different design choices. They noticed issues with the customer details dataset and applied some cleaning to it. They produced a customer address dataset before calculating the latest address and then output the result into work product 320.

These two approaches to the same problem illustrate the challenge of data consistency in a very dynamic environment. The analysts have manipulated data in different orders, using slightly different inputs and perhaps different customer cleaning rules. Trying to communicate within the team the myriad ways of doing the same analyses is challenging. When larger teams are producing many work products, achieving any kind of consistency is impossible. What is needed is a way to control and version the evolving data understanding.

11.4   SOURCES OF VARIATION

If you want to control evolving data understanding, you must first identify what causes data understanding to change. Earlier in the book, we examined sources of variation in work product outputs. As a recap, these sources of variation are the following.

- **Changes in raw data:** All work products are derived from raw data provided to the team. Modify the raw data and all work products using that data are affected. You saw in the customer address example where a new deduplication mark-up changed the total number of customers identified in the population.

- **Changes to code:** A work product is created by using program code to manipulate data. That code is a reflection of both the creator's design decisions and the project's business rules that are applied to the data. If this code changes, it is very likely that the data resulting from the code will also change. You saw this in the customer address example where one analyst noticed issues with the customer details dataset and applied some custom code to fix these issues.
- **Changes to common libraries, languages, and services:** Program code will draw on libraries of common routines and services. Examples include analytics libraries, fuzzy matching libraries, and data-enrichment services. If these are changed then the data manipulation code is effectively changed too.
- **Changes to input parameters:** Some data manipulations have input parameters that change their behavior. For example, a fuzzy matching algorithm might have a threshold similarity of matched words for inclusion as a match. A machine-learning algorithm for clustering may require that a starting number of clusters be specified. Running these algorithms with different input parameters effectively changes their behavior and therefore their data outputs.
- **Nondeterministic code:** In some scenarios it is possible to write nondeterministic code. That is, code that executes differently on every execution. A typical cause of nondeterministic code is the use of random number generators. Without careful use, a random number generator in code (for example, to randomly choose a sample population) could create data that cannot ever be reproduced in the future.

To achieve consistency in the consolidated knowledge from the team and customer, you need to remove or control these sources of variation. This is achieved using something called a build. The rest of this chapter will now discuss builds. Note that this is probably the technically most challenging chapter of the book. It is worth the investment of your time as builds are by far the most significant contributor to maintaining data provenance in Guerrilla Analytics.

11.5 DEFINITION OF A BUILD

A build is centralized and version-controlled program code and data that captures the team and customer's evolving knowledge. Such knowledge about the data includes the following.

- **Rules:** The business rules and cleaning rules that must be applied to the data.
- **Convenience datasets:** The common useful views of the data that facilitate work product creation.
- **Fixes:** The agreed and signed off fixes for known data quality issues.
- **Common code:** The useful centralized code libraries that the team can use to reduce their development efforts and promote consistency.

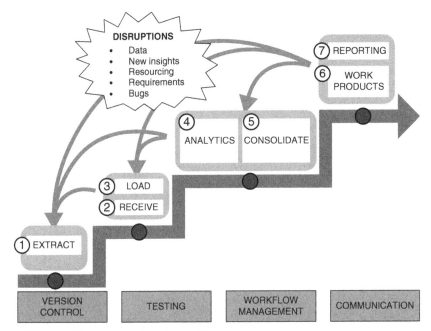

FIGURE 37   **The Guerrilla Analytics workflow**

• **Reference data:** The lookup datasets such as data mappings, filters, and mark-ups that feed into manipulations of other data.

Consolidation into a Build happens in Stage 5 of the Guerrilla Analytics workflow (Figure 37). We avoided discussing this stage so far as I first wanted you to understand what the full workflow looks like. Builds are best illustrated with an example, so we will now revisit the customer address problem with a build approach.

11.6   THE CUSTOMER ADDRESS EXAMPLE USING A BUILD

Consider the customer address example again. Figure 38 shows a better approach to achieving consistency by using a build. In essence, raw data is manipulated through several intermediate datasets to produce a single "official" customer address interface that is used by both work products. Here are the steps in the build.

• The first step is to create a pointer over the latest version of each type of raw dataset. This removes the problem of different analysts choosing different versions of the manual deduplication review.
• All datasets are then passed through a cleaning step. This removes the problem of inconsistent ad-hoc cleaning that could affect the outputs of the duplicate detection. While the need for cleaning may be minimal, having a

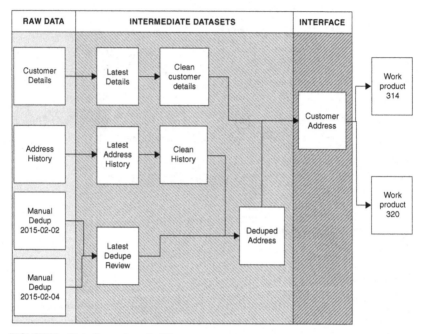

FIGURE 38 Data flow using a build

clearly defined location for cleaning in the data flow avoids ad-hoc modifications to the data throughout the data flow.

- Finally, a customer address dataset is created in an interface layer. It is this interface layer dataset that is used by all work products. This means the work products do not have to worry about the complexity of producing the customer address dataset and can instead rely on a consistent view of customer addresses.

The intermediate datasets and interface dataset in this example are a Data Build. They are produced by version-controlled code and can be completely reproduced by executing this code against the underlying raw data.

The following section discusses Data Builds and how to architect them.

11.7 DATA BUILDS

There are several points to note about how data is now flowing in the customer address Data Build.

- **The Build can be completely regenerated from raw data and Build code alone:** Build datasets are derived from the raw data using program code and that program code alone. There are no ad-hoc manual steps in the process as these steps cannot be version controlled and cannot be easily reproduced.

- **Data flows out of raw, never into raw:** No process (work product or build code) is writing back into the raw layer. Remember that a core Guerrilla Analytics principle is that raw data is never modified.
- **Some work products draw from the Build interface:** Work products that need the convenience of these Build datasets draw on them in their specific work product code.
- **Some work products still draw from raw:** There will always be work products that need to draw directly from raw datasets because these raw datasets are not yet part of any build. This is to be expected. A good build process will monitor these types of work products and include their features in the build as necessary over time.
- **Not all data is used in a build:** There are some raw datasets that are not part of any build. They might be stand alone datasets that bear no relation to anything in the build. They might be datasets that are not in frequent enough demand by the project to merit inclusion in a build.

You can now see how this Data Build promotes consistency and efficiency in the team. A work product that uses a build dataset has a head start since much of the hard work in manipulating the data into a necessary shape has been done in the build. All work products drawing on a build dataset do not need to worry about consistency as the build datasets are provided in one central and version-controlled location.

11.7.1   The Structure of a Data Build

How do you make a Data Build happen in practice? There are several components to put in place.

- **Raw data location:** There must be a Data Manipulation Environment (DME) location where raw data is stored and read by the build code. Build processes can never write into this location.
- **Intermediate and Interface data location:** This is a DME location where the build code can create and delete its intermediate and interface datasets
- **Temporary dataset location:** To avoid clutter in the DME, it is useful to have a location for temporary datasets created during the build process but not needed as a final intermediate or interface dataset.
- **Version-controlled build code:** This is a location where build program code can be stored and version controlled.

This is illustrated in Figure 39. The program code files manipulate the raw data through a data flow, turning it into several intermediate and temporary datasets until one or more interface datasets are produced. The intermediate datasets are primarily available for debugging and explaining data provenance. The rest of the team mostly uses the build datasets at the published interface. These are the datasets they use in their work product development, testing, and audit.

11.7.2   Practice Tip 45: Decouple Raw Data from Build Data

In the discussion of data flow and in the description of the Data Build structure, you saw how the starting point of any build is raw data. Using just the build program code and raw data, every dataset in the build could be generated from the raw data. You also know that a Guerrilla Analytics project is going to present the team with frequent raw data refreshes, replacements, and additions. If any of these refresh datasets contribute to the Data Build, then the build must be rerun to generate up-to-date build datasets. It would be convenient to minimize raw data references in build code so that there are minimal changes to make to the code when new data arrives.

The first stage of any build should create a pointer to the latest raw data. It is this pointer that is then referenced in the subsequent build code rather than any direct referencing of the raw data.

When new data arrives, only the pointer to the raw data needs to be changed and the rest of the build code should still execute.

Figure 39 shows pointers in the intermediate dataset layer immediately above the raw data layer.

11.7.3   Practice Tip 46: Generate Data Builds with Version-controlled Code

You have seen how new data arrives and you can decouple build code from that new data so that the build code changes required by the new data are minimized. However, your data provenance alarms should be sounding. You have changed the raw data and therefore have changed the Data Build datasets. Any work products that depend on these datasets are now broken and cannot be reproduced. You need a way to version control the creation of Data Builds so that

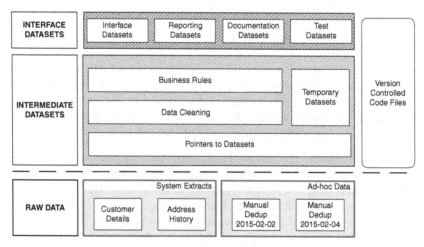

FIGURE 39   Structure of a Data Build for the customer address example

earlier versions can be recreated if necessary and the use of a particular build version can be easily identified in a work product.

Recall that every Data Build reads from raw data but never writes back to raw data. Everything flows from raw datasets through to interface datasets. This means that if you have Data Build program code and your raw data is still available, you can completely regenerate every dataset in the Data Build. With version-controlled build code, you always have a means to regenerate earlier builds as new builds evolve.

11.7.4   Practice Tip 47: Embed the Build Version in the Build Dataset Names

Over time, many versions of a Data Build will be created. Some Guerrilla Analytics projects will have over 20 versions of a build and several build projects. Work products will be derived from all of those build versions. It would save the team a lot of effort if they could easily determine the particular version of a build they are working with. A simple way to do this is to embed the Data Build version in the namespace of the build datasets.

Figure 40 shows a set of build code versions on the file system and the associated build datasets they have produced in the DME.

- Each Data Build project has its own code folder.
- You can see that each version of the build code is located in a subfolder named with the version number. In this case there are two versions of the build.
- Each build dataset has the same build name and version number embedded in its schema.

Note that this relational database example uses schemas for namespace separation. Other namespace separations are possible in non-relational DMEs.

Work product SQL code that uses this build's datasets from version 2 would look like the following.

```
Select CUSTOMER_NAME
FROM CUSTOMER_ADDRESSES_002.CUSTOMER_ADDRESS
```

Without any documentation overhead, a reader of the code can tell which build (customer addresses) and which version (version 002) were used. If necessary, the correct version of the build code to recreate the dataset can be found on the file system under a folder with the build project name and build project version number.

11.7.5   Practice Tip 48: Tear Down and Rebuild Often

For each version of the build, you now have a specific destination namespace for the generated build datasets. Builds can become time consuming to execute

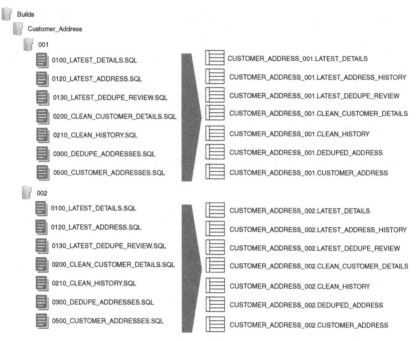

FIGURE 40 A basic version control system for a Data Build

since they are doing a lot of the "heavy lifting" for the convenience of work products. The temptation is to rerun subsets of the build's data flow and avoid regenerating all intermediate datasets. This gives rise to the legacy dataset bug, where old and out of date datasets continue to be referenced in the build code. Build code continues to execute without problems but is referencing an older incorrect dataset. Here is a simple example of how this could happen in the customer address data flow from Figure 38.

Imagine that the cleaning of the latest datasets is time consuming. The team is focusing its efforts on the deduplication code as this is more difficult to implement. The customer details dataset is refreshed so code is written to point to this latest dataset and the build is executed. This new data however, has a previously unseen quirk that requires an addition to the cleaning rules that create CLEAN_ CUSTOMER_DETAILS. If this rule is not implemented, the total customers will be over counted. An analyst codes up this rule and writes the results into a new dataset called CLEAN_CUSTOMER_DETAILS_ADVANCED. However, there is now a problem. All subsequent build codes are still referencing the original CLEAN_CUSTOMER_DETAILS. This code will probably continue to execute without problems. The stale data reference may go unnoticed and the interface datasets will not reflect the advanced customer detail cleaning logic.

The simple solution to discovering and eliminating these bugs is for the build code to clear out its destination of all datasets before every execution run of the build code. In the customer address example, a tear-down approach would have deleted all datasets including the old CLEAN_CUSTOMER_DETAILS. Subsequent code that still used references to this dataset would then have failed to execute and the stale data reference would have been spotted quickly.

11.7.6   Practice Tip 49: Automate the Execution of Build Code

Builds capture a lot of team knowledge. They can therefore grow to become significant code bases in their own right. The analytics coding chapter advised having one code file per data output. This makes it easy to find and test the program code that produced a particular dataset. In the case of build code, there will be one code file for every intermediate and interface dataset. This is potentially a large number of code files to open up and execute every time a build needs to be torn down and recreated. Executing build code should be quick and easy as this encourages the team to tear down and recreate builds often, as recommended in the previous tip. Additionally, being able to easily execute the entire build code base or some subset of it helps accelerate the development of the build.

   In practice, this automation can be as sophisticated as available time and tooling permit. A simple shell script that recursively executes all code in a build folder is sufficient for some projects. Other projects use dedicated scheduling software that can execute code files in parallel where appropriate. Popular build tools from traditional software development such as Apache Ant (Moodie, 2012) can be appropriated for data analytics needs. Regardless of the approach however, a build cannot be automated if some of its data flow relies on technologies that cannot be executed programmatically from a script. This is another good reason why there is a Guerrilla Analytics principle to prefer program code over graphical tools.

11.7.7   Practice Tip 50: Embed Testing in the Build's Data Flow

Following the practice tips introduced so far, you should now have a version-controlled Data Build that tears down all datasets in its target namespace, and then automatically executes all the program code files necessary to produce its build datasets. As the build grows to incorporate team knowledge, it will become complex. This means you will need a quick way to know that its code has executed correctly and to report and summarize what the build code has done to the data. A critical component of the build process then is to create clearly labeled test datasets. These test scripts should execute during the build process so that a build can "fail fast" if it is not passing tests of its expected output.

   Figure 41 shows the now familiar customer address example with the addition to two test datasets. The first test dataset checks that all postcodes in the cleaned address dataset are valid. The second test dataset checks that all customers from the raw data are still present in the final interface dataset of customer addresses.

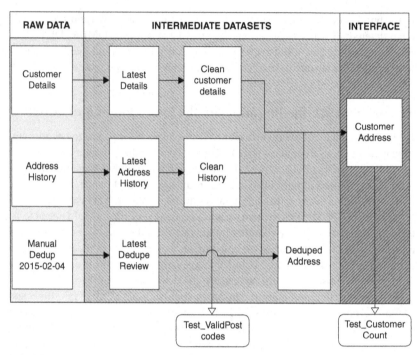

FIGURE 41   A build data flow with embedded tests

These are simple examples to illustrate the point. It is difficult to anticipate how analytics code will change the data and interact with the data flow. You should test to make sure your expectations about the build are being met. Testing is a huge area that is covered in its own part of the book. The point to emphasize here is that testing occurs during and beside the build process. There is no point in waiting until the end of a 2-hour build to discover that data records were corrupted in the very first data step.

11.7.8   Practice Tip 51: Embed Reporting in the Build

Much like testing, you would like to know what your build is doing to the data at key points in its data flow. That is, you would like to know the impact your build code has on data populations such as number of records, number of duplicates, date ranges, and so on at critical points in the build process. For example, a customer will often ask for the impact of applying certain business rules to the data. It makes sense then to incorporate this reporting of summary statistics into the Data Build process much as was done with testing. This has the following advantages.

- **Report on impact:** When a build completes, important reporting information about the build is already available. A team can easily say to their customer that "the new population number is such a value". "The impact of the revised business rules is the following."

- **Quantify differences between build versions:** Having summary reporting information available as dedicated build datasets helps comparison of versions of a build. This makes it easy to demonstrate how critical project numbers might have changed between versions of the build.
- **Drive a modular build design:** When reporting is part of the build, it tends to drive a build design that is clear, modular, and traceable in terms of critical numbers derived from the data. If a report is needed on particular data steps in the build process then this drives the creation of intermediate datasets for easily creating those reports. This leads to a clearer and more modular build design that can be audited, reviewed, and tested without reworking intermediate datasets.

11.7.9   Practice Tip 52: Builds do not Produce Work Products

A danger when teams enthusiastically undertake builds is that they then try to create a build that anticipates all possible work product needs. In an ideal world, they imagine a build interface that has all possible datasets ready for use and work products simply export interface datasets for delivery to the customer. This is a mistake. The complexity of maintaining and running the build process will typically exceed any advantage of this design, even if all possible interface dataset needs could ever be anticipated anyway.

Work product and therefore customer needs should drive the build design not an attempt at anticipating all possible dataset needs. If patterns of repetition are seen in work products, then it is time to consider incorporating new functionality into the build interface.

11.7.10   Practice Tip 53: Create Documentation Datasets

As builds become more complex, it can become difficult for team members to remember exactly what every interface dataset represents and how it should be used? Where did that data field come from? Which build dataset do I go to for a particular data sample?

A traditional approach here would call for a data dictionary document to be maintained so that the team can look it up and understand how best to use build datasets. A Guerrilla Analytics project rarely has time for this approach. Analysts have to stop their analytics work to go off and find documentation and read and understand it. The documentation has to be maintained separately from the build code which risks its going out of date. It would be much better if the documentation sat right beside the code and data where analysts could easily find it when they need it. There is a simple Guerrilla Analytics solution here that creates a dataset that contains documentation. Table 2 is an example documentation dataset for some retail sales data that contains two interface datasets.

TABLE 2 An Example Documentation Dataset

Dataset	Purpose
PRODUCTS_SOLD	This dataset is a list of all products sold by day. Fields describe day of week, week number, year, and date.
PRODUCT_RANKING	This dataset lists all products sold and their rankings within various categories.

The advantages are as follows.

- **Version control:** The documentation is under version control (it is written in the build code after all).
- **Accessibility:** The documentation is easily accessible. It is right there in the interface datasets where the analysts are working and not buried in some folder on a file server.
- **Export for reporting:** The documentation itself can be queried and summarized if needed for reporting. With documentation datasets in the build interface, it is a simple matter to export these descriptions of the data and include them in work products when relevant.

Only simple written notes about datasets should be included in the build in this way. If build documentation really requires figures or software engineering tools then more traditional methods need to be used.

11.7.11   Practice Tip 54: Develop Layered Build Code

If you think about the build data flow, you can see how it takes code through several "layers." This was suggested in the structure of a Data Build illustrated in Figure 39. A build should always begin with pointers over raw data as discussed earlier. It almost always follows with data cleaning. Then there will be some type of joining or enrichment of various data sources. Then there will be a phase of applying business rules and doing analytics.

The intermediate datasets in the early "layers" have two important characteristics.

- **Low rate of change:** Unless data is refreshed or significant data quality issues are discovered, this lower layer build code does not need to change very often and the associated intermediate datasets therefore do not change.
- **Lower layers involve more data:** As the build data flow progresses, there may be some filtering of data so that the higher layers manipulate smaller datasets.

Looking at these characteristics of build layers, we see that lower layers are more time consuming to execute (there is more data), but change infrequently so rarely need to be re-executed. Architecting builds to have clearly defined layers

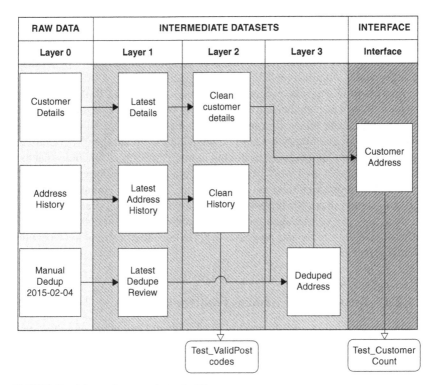

FIGURE 42   **A layered approach to a build**

allows these layers to be run independently rather than having to execute the entire build. This is very useful at development time as execution can focus on higher layers where the complex business logic is implemented. This of course does not mean that you should discontinue frequent tear down and rebuilds from scratch. Rather this makes code easier to maintain and to execute incrementally.

Figure 42 shows the customer address build with layers now identified.

- **Layer 0:** This is the raw data layer. This data is never modified.
- **Layer 1:** This is the pointer over the latest raw datasets. As discussed, this decouples raw data from the build data flow.
- **Layer 2:** This is the data-cleaning layer. This is the only place that cleaning rules are applied to the data.
- **Layer 3:** This is where business rules are applied. In the example shown, our business rule is the tagging of signed-off duplicate addresses.
- **Interface:** This layer contains interface datasets that are published to the team for use in their work products.

Note that more or fewer layers can be used as required but there should always be a Layer 0 for raw data and an interface layer. Layering can be included in the dataset namespaces to help identify datasets.

11.8 SERVICE BUILDS

Until now, this chapter has focused on Data Builds. Data Builds are convenience version-controlled *datasets* made available to the team so that work product development is simplified and consistency is facilitated.

Service Builds are the program code equivalent of Data Builds. They are common pieces of *code* made available to the whole team to avoid repetition and promote consistency. In a relational database, a Service Build may be a stored procedure or library loaded into the database. In another programming language, a Service Build may be a set of common macros or functions that the team can call on in their work product and Data Build code. Regardless of the team's chosen programming language, Service Builds are common code that the team should share. Since Services builds are stand-alone code, independent of data, they can be managed much like traditional program code using software engineering tools and processes with minor modifications for Guerrilla Analytics needs.

11.8.1 The Customer Address Problem Revisited

Earlier in this chapter, we discussed Data Builds in the context of a customer address-cleaning problem. Revisiting this problem, there are at least three areas that might benefit from a Service Build.

- In cleaning customer addresses and testing those addresses, it is useful to have some type of postcode or zip code validation. That is, rather than having complex pattern checking logic buried in the main Data Build code, it might be better to extract this logic into a validation function that could be used in several locations in the Data Build's cleaning layer. In addition, you might want to develop several functions for United Kingdom, United States, and other countries that each have their own address systems.
- The team might also notice that remembering the project's name cleaning rule of "remove all punctuation and numbers and upper case" is a little tiresome. They decide to also create a function for cleaning a given data field that captures this simple cleaning rule.
- Finally, the team decides to have date cleaning code. This code takes a given date field and steps through various dates, reformats them into a standard format, and then converts them to a date type in the DME. This saves having to remember a myriad of date conversion functions for every date type encountered.

These three function types for postcode validation, name cleaning, and date cleaning are example components of a Service Build. Over time, these functions will be modified by the team. For example, a postcode that had not been previously encountered may appear in a dataset refresh and the postcode validation function will have to be updated to accommodate this.

The customer address codebase now has two types of code files. It has the Data Build code files previously discussed. These manipulate data and apply business rules to create build datasets. Also, there is now Service Build code. This is version-controlled convenience code that can be called on from the rest of the code base. The following sections look at how best to create and manage Service Build code.

11.8.2   Practice Tip 55: Generate Service Builds with Version-controlled Code

Service Builds will undoubtedly evolve during the course of a project and between projects. New features will be required. Bugs will be uncovered and will have to be fixed. But what does this mean for the team's data provenance when the Service Build in question has already been put into "production" and been used in creating work products or Data Builds? Simply replacing the Service Build code will destroy the reproducibility of past work products and Data Builds.

The best approach is to version control all Service Build code. Older versions remain deployed and available to the team so that older work products and Data Builds can always be reproduced. Newer Service Builds get written and deployed as distinct new versions in the DME. Figure 43 illustrates a basic version control system for two Service Build functions and their deployment on the DME (in this case a relational database).

You can see that there have been two released versions of the postcode validation Service Build. These are numbered with a simple versioning scheme. Looking at the DME, you can see that both versions of the Service Build are loaded and deployed. Once again, this emphasizes the idea of maintaining a clear visual link between file system (where the code is developed) and the DME (where the code is deployed). If you find bugs in version 2 of the US postcode validation function say, or just want to better understand it, you know where to find its code quickly.

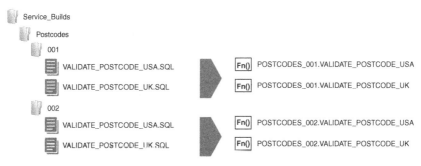

FIGURE 43   A basic version control system for a Service Build

Sample work product or Data Build code that uses this function could look like the following in SQL.

```
SELECT POSTCODES_002.VALIDATE_POSTCODE_US(PSCD) AS
PSCD_VALIDATED
FROM CUSTOMER_ADDRESS_002.ADDRESSES
```

As we saw with the Data Build, it is immediately clear which version of the Service Build for postcode validation is being used. Note also that this example shows a particular version of a Service Build being applied to a particular version of a Data Build.

11.8.3   Practice Tip 56: Embed the Service Build Version in Service Names

You will notice from the previous tip's example that the Service Build's version number is embedded in the DME relational schema name. In a Guerrilla Analytics project, you should always focus on maintaining data provenance with as little overhead as possible. A traditional software approach might deploy code so it overwrites previous versions of the function. No code dependent on this function would break and this would maintain backward compatibility of the code base. In the Guerrilla Analytics environment, your primary goal is maintaining data provenance. This means that all versions of code and data have to be maintained for reproducing historical results.

There are two advantages.

- By embedding the version somewhere in the Service Build's path, it is explicit which version of the Service Build is being used in a given piece of analytics code.
- By using a namespace for Service Build deployment, multiple versions of the Service Build can exist in the DME at the same time.

11.8.4   Practice Tip 57: Locate and Deploy Services Consistently

You are probably going to have multiple versions of several Service Builds in use at the same time on a project. The code files for these services need to be stored somewhere and the services need to be deployed somewhere. Without consistency in storage and deployment, it becomes difficult to maintain data provenance and services will accidentally be deployed to multiple locations.

- **Code location:** Locate all code libraries under one of the project's code folders. This lets the team find them easily and time is not wasted on conflicting code versions.

- **DME deployment location:** Deploy all services to one easily located place in the DME so the team can quickly determine what is available in the DME and what might be missing. Having to search the DME to determine whether a function has been deployed or not is time consuming.

11.8.5   Practice Tip 58: Tear Down and Rebuild Services

For development efficiency and ease of deployment, Services builds should have a method to tear down everything in their target deployment destination. Similar to Data Builds, there is a risk that incorrect versions of services are left lying around in the DME and that a team member then uses them on the assumption that they are correct. The first step in any Service Build process should be to tear down everything in its deployment destination location. In the relational database example already illustrated in Figure 43, the postcode Service Build was being deployed into the schema named POSTCODES_002. The first step in this Service Build's code should be to delete all existing functions within this schema. That way, only the services defined in the latest version of the Service Build code get deployed to the DME and no legacy functions are left lying around in the location POSTCODES_002.

11.8.6   Practice Tip 59: Automate Service Deployment

Similar to Data Builds, Service Builds may involve many program code files. In the postcode validation example, there are two code files to define the USA and UK validation functions. You would also need a preparatory code file to tear down any existing functions in the deployment schema as discussed in the previous tip. For other programming languages and analytics DMEs, some code files may have to go through preparatory steps such as compilation or packaging. The file or files for deployment then have to be moved to some deployment location.

This process should be automated with a build tool. Without automation, the manual deployment process is error prone. Developers have to remember the deployment location. Developers under time pressure will be tempted to edit functions as they are deployed on the DME rather doing development of the source code and redeploying and changes. As with Data Builds, a simple shell script may be sufficient for automating a Service Build.

11.8.7   Practice Tip 60: Services Builds
do not Produce Work Products

As the name suggests, Service Builds provide services. That is, they provide convenience code that helps promote the team's efficiency and consistency. There may be a temptation to wrap up work product code in a Service Build because the work product is frequently requested by the customer. You would then have centrally deployed code with a very specific purpose. If services are needed as part of a single work product, they should sit with that work product code rather than being shared with the team in a Service Build.

11.9 WHEN TO START A BUILD

When should you set up builds on your project? Do you wait until the team knowledge and data are complicated enough that they merit being stored in a build? How much time should be devoted to a build and its maintenance rather than direct delivery using work products?

You should start a build on the first day of a project, even for the simplest code and datasets. The following steps should be followed.

- **Build file:** Get a basic build framework in place with a build file for automation. This means that adding to the build will be easy should the requirement arise under tight timelines.
- **Assign a build master:** Assign at least one team member as the build master. Their job is to maintain the build and add new features to it as needed by the team.

11.10 WRAP UP

This chapter has discussed consolidating knowledge in Data Builds and Service Builds. Having read this chapter you should now know the following.

- **Why both Data Builds and Service Builds are needed:** Builds consolidate knowledge about the data and code functionality in a centralized location. This promotes consistency of work products that use builds and saves time redoing the same programming and data manipulation from scratch for every work product.
- **What causes data provenance to break:** Changes in code, libraries, and raw data affect any work products that use that code, library, or data. Controlling your evolving data knowledge involves controlling these three sources of provenance breakage.
- **Definition of a Data Build:** A Data Build is a collection of version-controlled convenience datasets that capture knowledge about the project data in a single central location for the convenience of the team.
- **Definition of a Service Build:** Service Builds are coded and version-controlled functionality that is made available to the team in a single central location. Typical Service Builds provide data-cleaning services and advanced functionality such as pattern matching and fuzzy matching.
- **How to version control Service Builds and Data Builds:** The key is to have a deployment namespace that includes the build name and version number. This allows multiple versions of the builds to exist at the same time in the DME.

Part 3

Testing

Chapter 12

Introduction to Testing

12.1 GUERRILLA ANALYTICS WORKFLOW

Figure 44 shows the now familiar Guerrilla Analytics workflow. In this figure you can see that testing is one of the fundamental building blocks on which all workflow activities are based. Ideally, testing should happen at every stage from Data Extraction all the way through to delivery of work products and reports. The nature of this testing will depend on the stage of the workflow in question. Before exploring this in subsequent chapters, let us clarify what it means to test in an analytics context.

12.2 WHAT IS TESTING?

The main purpose of testing in general is to detect defects so that they may be corrected. In the context of data analytics, defects can include incorrectly programmed data manipulations, incorrectly interpreted and implemented business rules, and incorrect choice of models. Because of the immense variety of conditions in which Guerrilla Analytics work is undertaken, testing cannot establish that everything functions properly under all conditions. Rather you can only establish that it *does not* function under *specific* tested conditions. This is an important, if subtle, distinction. It means that it is very difficult to say that something is 100% correct in all conditions. However, by testing as many combinations of conditions as possible you increase confidence in the correctness of tested work products.

12.3 WHY DO TESTING?

Testing and the resulting discovery of defects have several benefits in Guerrilla Analytics work.

- Increases confidence in the correctness of work products.
- Validates that specific business rules have been implemented as agreed with the customer.
- Validates that visualizations, reports, and other presentations are usable by the customer and give the customer the insights they require.
- Increases confidence in the capability of the team's program code to handle a variety and volume of data.

149

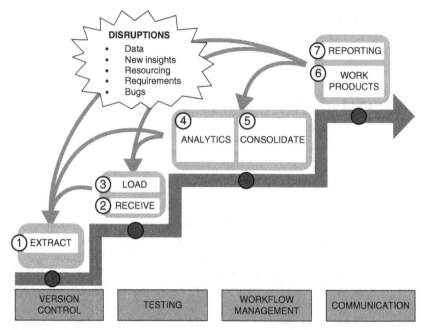

FIGURE 44   The Guerrilla Analytics workflow

- Supports the team's development of analytics code by confirming that the code's performance is as designed.
- Increases confidence that a machine learning or statistical model will perform well on new and as yet unseen data.
- Helps identify failures in nonfunctional requirements such as testability, scalability, maintainability, usability, performance, and security.

Testing is well established as a necessary part of traditional software development work. In fact, some software development methodologies even advocate that tests be specified and written before the core product code is written (Beck, 2002). Perhaps because data analytics involves people from a variety of disciplines other than software engineering, there seems to be little awareness or appreciation of the importance of testing in data analytics. Furthermore, the nature of data analytics, being tightly coupled to datasets that are often large, requires a different approach to testing than traditional software development may only involve program code.

12.4   AREAS OF TESTING

There are three overarching areas of testing that need to be done in a Guerrilla Analytics environment. In the order in which they are typically encountered you have:

- **Testing data:** This is testing of raw data to produce a measure of its data quality. Data testing analyzes data to find defects such as corruption of data values, truncation of records, and unexpected ranges of field values. It is all too easy for data to be "broken" as it is extracted from one system and loaded into another system. Data testing increases confidence that this transfer process was executed correctly. Even if data is not officially broken, it may contain features that could trip up subsequent analytics work and so it is useful to detect these features as early as possible.

- **Testing code:** This is the testing that is done to check that analytics program code manipulates data correctly and produces expected data outputs that are sensible and correct. This type of testing is probably closest to software engineering testing as it involves checking the logically correct implementation of analytics program code. However, code testing in Guerrilla Analytics has two major differences to software engineering. First, the data contains flaws that can change with every data refresh and the program code must change to accommodate this. Second, the business rules that are being interpreted and applied in program code are being discovered and evolve with the project.
- **Testing statistical models:** This is the testing that is done to check that a statistical model is well built and a good model of the real world. In some fields, this type of testing is called model validation. There is little point in developing a model if it cannot be used to make decisions about the real world and if the practical and statistical assumptions on which the model is built are not valid.

12.5 COMPARING EXPECTED AND ACTUAL

There are several points to note about the areas of testing described above. Fundamentally, to frame a test you need to do two things.

- **Define expectations:** Specify some system's expected output for a given input.
- **Compare:** Compare the system's expected output to its actual output.

Here is what that looks like for some typical examples.

- For some raw data, you might expect it to have 5000 records and no NULL values.
- You might have an expectation from the customer that the data covers some date range.
- You might expect only two values of a particular business domain flag such as customer gender.
- For some simple program code, you might expect it to, say, rank all offices by total spend.

12.5.1 Example

Consider the example data in Figure 45. Customers have been sorted in order of descending total spend. What happens when we apply ranking code to this data? Depending on our choice of ranking function, you may expect several

ID	CUSTOMER	TOTAL SPEND	DENSE_RANK	RANK
1205	Acme Widgets	150,000	1	1
671	Joe's bikes	89,000	2	2
1703	Jane's trikes	89,000	2	2
1809	Wheelies	50,000	3	4
20	Tyresome	30,000	4	5

FIGURE 45   Comparing expected and actual

outcomes. Do you want tied customers to have the same ranking value? What should the next ranking be after these tied customers? The answer depends on the business rule and conversations with the customer. Regardless, you would like to test the code and make sure that it is applying the agreed business rule as expected.

These types of tests become important when you consider what your answer would be if you were asked for the top four customers by spend. Even a simple example like this can raise many questions about expected outputs. This becomes much more complex when dealing with bigger data flows, datasets, and multiple business rules.

12.6   THE CHALLENGE OF TESTING GUERRILLA ANALYTICS

Testing presents many challenges in a Guerrilla Analytics environment.

- **Wide variety of expertise:** Testing of data is familiar to data quality engineers and data governance practitioners. Testing the correctness of program code is familiar to software developers. Testing models is standard practice for statisticians. However, a Guerrilla Analyst needs to be familiar with testing approaches in all of these domains if they are to have confidence in their work.
- **Unknown data:** Since analytics projects usually aim to quantify and understand data in some way, how can we declare expectations about the data? How can you be sure that your estimation of 5% fraud in an insurance claims dataset is realistic and correct? How can you verify that 1000 of your 3 million vendors in a vendor master dataset are duplicates? Increasing confidence in your answers to these types of questions involves some careful thought about data, program code, and business rules.
- **Scale:** The largest software code bases take hours to compile and execute their suites of tests. In data analytics, even a simple sorting of data can take hours to run. Faced with this obstacle of scale and therefore time constraints on code execution time, how do you run sufficient tests to gain confidence in code?

- **Completeness:** In software development, it is possible to clearly specify the input conditions to a program code unit. Techniques such as object-oriented programming (Gamma et al., 1994) help control data and changes in state as they are passed around program code. With data analytics, every record of data is potentially a unique input condition for program code. It is entirely possible for data analytics code to perform as expected on 999,999 records of data in a 1 million record dataset and then fall over on the very last record. How do you design tests that cover this variety of input conditions?

Subsequent chapters will address these challenges. Before diving into these distinct types of testing, there are some considerations that are common across all testing areas.

12.7   PRACTICE TIP 61: ESTABLISH A TESTING CULTURE

People and culture are the first things to get right when testing. Testing is often seen as a "necessary evil" or something that is handed over to a "testing team" to worry about. Testers are then second-class citizens who play catch up with the rock star developers and if bugs sneak through then it's the testers' fault. If such old-fashioned attitudes to testing are allowed to establish themselves then the team will struggle with sentiments such as the following.

- I (a data scientist) cannot test my own code as I know how the code works and am biased. Testing is for a test team.
- We cannot test yet as the data build is not ready. We're too busy adding features and fixing problems. We will test it all at the end.
- I don't have to test my code as it is not customer-facing work so it is ok if there are some small mistakes.
- I don't have to test my code as it is a simple data sample. What could go wrong?!
- I (a developer) am not going to work closely with a test team. Let them read the documentation and figure out what to test.

And so on. You might think this could not happen in your high-performing team but believe me it does. Much of this misunderstanding and unhealthy approach to testing stems from a lack of understanding of testing. You would be surprised how many data analysts have never read anything on testing or heard of testing frameworks. Of course, the lack of good literature specifically targeted at testing data analytics does not help.

The first thing to do is to establish the following in the Guerrilla Analytics team.

- **Everybody who writes code is also a tester.** The burden of quality rests with all those who write analytics code.
- **Testing is about the quality of the team's work products.** Team members need to lose any negative mind-set about testing and being "caught out."

- **Quality is not a distinct function in a team.** Quality is achieved by having development and testing work so closely together as to be indistinguishable from one another.

It is difficult to implement this tip because it is cultural as opposed to being a functional process. The best way to establish an appreciation for testing is through education, feedback, and establishing buy-in from senior analysts who lead and coach others. If you encounter resistance to a test-driven culture it is worth asking whether the individual is so valuable to the team that you can afford to have them waste others' time in understanding and checking their work.

12.8 PRACTICE TIP 62: TEST EARLY

12.8.1 Guerrilla Analytics Environment

There is a temptation to postpone testing under tight timelines and other project pressures and disruptions. "We have important analysis to do, we'll confirm that the data is good once those deadlines are met." This can only lead to trouble. If data is not tested early then the team runs the risk of wasting time producing work products that are not usable because they are based on incorrect data.

12.8.2 Guerrilla Analytics Approach

The Guerrilla Analytics approach is to test early in the development cycle. Of the three testing types, testing data is the most critical and should not be postponed. Testing code can arguably be done after heavily caveated work products have been delivered. Again testing models is critical to the validity of the model. If a model makes poor predictions than it is irresponsible and even dangerous to release it to a customer.

12.8.3 Advantages

The longer testing is postponed, the more expensive uncovered defects become. For example, imagine discovering that a sophisticated statistical model must be scrapped because the data on which it was based was corrupted way back at data import. All the time spent trying out various models and validating them would have been wasted. Testing early helps shape development and reduces future costs of defects.

12.9 PRACTICE TIP 63: TEST OFTEN

12.9.1 Guerrilla Analytics Environment

In the dynamic Guerrilla Analytics environment, data is changing frequently and so the build is changing frequently to incorporate new understanding about this data. Tests can fail to keep pace with build development, meaning they are less useful at guiding development and defects are not detected early enough to be of use.

12.9.2   Guerrilla Analytics Approach

Tests should ideally be run as often as development code changes. A developer should not be changing build code without running the associated tests that cover that code. New features should not be added to the build without sufficient testing. Simply testing around a particular code/data segment is often not enough to know that a build is performing properly. Data flows interact in many complex ways with many dependencies. Ideally, the whole test suite should be run as often as possible on a freshly executed build.

12.9.3   Advantages

Testing often has the following advantages:

- When you identify problems early and often they are much cheaper to fix. This is primarily because fewer work products have been issued that depend on the flawed build.
- Frequent testing discourages the accumulation of "technical debt." That is, testing identifies and highlights defects that need to be fixed for the build to be complete. If these defects are allowed to remain in the code base, they become more difficult to fix over time as the build grows and its interdependencies become more complex.

12.10   PRACTICE TIP 64: GIVE TESTS UNIQUE IDENTIFIERS

12.10.1   Guerrilla Analytics Environment

Tests will incorporate some type of logic and comparisons and so it is difficult to describe them with a short label. Without a better way to refer to tests, it becomes difficult to maintain and understand all tests in the project.

12.10.2   Guerrilla Analytics Approach

Unique identifiers (UIDs) are the best way to identify tests. The UID can be accompanied by as much metadata as is needed by the project. For example, a business description will certainly be helpful. A classification of small, medium, and large is also useful when filtering and searching tests. Tests could also be associated with a particular build layer such as cleaning or business logic.

12.10.3 Advantages

As we saw with data tracking (Section 5.4) and work product tracking (Section 9.5), the advantages of a UID are as follows:

- **Simplicity.** There is a simple and clear way to identify every single test.
- **Tracking.** Every test can be tracked in the file system and in the data manipulation environment (DME).

12.11 PRACTICE TIP 65: ORGANIZE TEST DATA BY TEST UID

12.11.1 Guerrilla Analytics Environment

Test data needs to evolve with test code. This raises the question of how and where test data should be stored and how versions of test data should be recorded. If test data is not managed, it clutters the DME and the file system and distracts the team from the real work of delivery.

12.11.2 Guerrilla Analytics Approach

Test data can be organized in much the same way as ordinary project data. Create a dedicated test data folder for the project. Within this, have a subfolder for each test UID. In each test folder, store clearly marked versions of test data files.

As with ordinary project data, each test file gets loaded into a DME area that can be easily linked back to the test data folder. A good approach in a relational database is a schema named after the test UID, for example.

Figure 46 shows how test data storage could look. The file system on the left contains folders named by Test UID. The DME on the right is almost a mirror

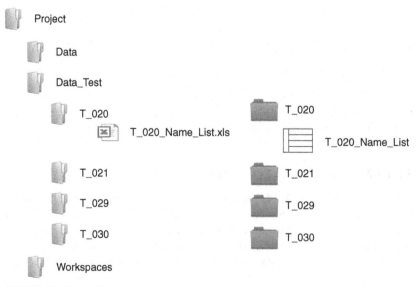

FIGURE 46 Example test data storage

image of the file system. There is a schema for each test UID and a dataset for each test data file. Some tests do not need to call on external data and so are not represented. Some tests may have multiple external datasets and versions of datasets.

12.11.3 Advantages

As you can see from the example of Figure 46, it is very easy to locate data on the file system and DME for a particular test. Clutter is avoided and versions of test data are also accommodated.

12.12 NEXT CHAPTERS ON TESTING

The next chapters in this part of the book will cover the following areas of testing in Guerrilla Analytics.

- **Data testing.** This will cover how to test data that the team receives.
- **Testing builds.** This will cover how to test build code and build datasets.
- **Testing work products.** This will cover how to test the work products produced by the team.

Testing statistical models is a large field in itself that is already well covered in the statistics and machine-learning literature.

12.13 WRAP UP

This chapter was a short introduction to Guerrilla Analytics testing. In this chapter you learned:

- **How testing is fundamental to all aspects of the Guerrilla Analytics workflow.** Testing should be done at data extraction, data import, creation of work products, creation of builds, and model validation.
- **What testing means in the context of data analytics.** Testing is about comparing expected outcomes to actual outcomes to identify defects. Although you cannot cover every possible scenario, increased testing increases your confidence in the correctness of our work.
- **Why testing is done.** At a high level, you want to increase confidence in the correctness of (1) the data the team receives, (2) the program code it uses to manipulate that data, and (3) any statistical models that are applied to the data.
- **How testing analytics presents a variety of challenges.** Expertise is required in a variety of domains. The data is often unknown or poorly understood. The scale of data restricts the amount and coverage of tests that can be executed. The variety of data presents a large number of possible scenarios that must be tested.

- **An appropriate supportive culture must be established to implement testing successfully in a team.** Testing and development must be indistinguishable from one another and destructive attitudes of "them and us" (analysts and testers) must not be permitted.
- **Testing as early as possible in the Guerrilla Analytics workflow saves costs and time.** In the worst case, a statistical model or report that was time-consuming to develop may have to be scrapped because of defects in the data that arose at data extraction and were not identified at any point in the Guerrilla Analytics workflow.

Chapter 13

Testing Data

13.1 GUERRILLA ANALYTICS WORKFLOW

Figure 47 shows the Guerrilla Analytics workflow. Data testing happens at steps 1, 2, and 3 of this workflow. This is because data testing is about increasing confidence in the data received by the analytics team.

The journey of data as it makes its way to the analytics team follows three key stages.

- **Extraction from "source":** Data begins in some "system" which we will refer to as its source. This might be a system in the familiar sense such as a warehouse, a database, a file share, or a content management system. It may also be some type of online web page or application from which data is "scraped." Even data created by manual data entry is a type of source. Data needs to be taken out of these sources so analytics can be applied to it. It is assumed that there has been a previous exercise with the customer to identify the most appropriate data for the project.
- **Transfer to the analytics team:** Next, the data needs to be transferred to the analytics team. The complexity of this step varies. If the analytics team is doing web scraping, for example, then the "transfer" is simply the downloading of scraped web pages. However, it is also possible for customers to run their own data extractions from their systems and provide this data to the team. These extracts of data need to be transferred to the analytics team, logged, and stored in a way that data provenance is preserved.
- **Loading into the "target" analytics environment:** The analytics team then needs to do something with this data. Generally this means loading data into some type of analytics tool where the data can be manipulated and analyzed. The place this data gets loaded into is the "target."

Data can be corrupted or lost at every stage of the journey from source to target. Even if corruption or loss does not occur, accountability and traceability of the data must be maintained from source to target.

13.2 THE FIVE C'S OF TESTING DATA

The book "Bad Data Handbook" (McCallum, 2012) has a very insightful chapter called "Data Quality Analysis Demystified." Gleason and McCallum

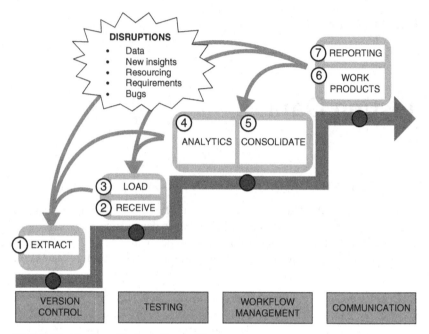

FIGURE 47   The Guerrilla Analytics workflow

introduce their 4 C framework of data quality analysis. This chapter borrows their four Cs of Completeness, Coherence, Correctness, and aCcountability and adds a fifth C of Consistency. This section will also expand on the five Cs with specific test details and practice tips as appropriate in a Guerrilla Analytics project.

At a high level, the five Cs can be summarized as follows.

- **Completeness:** Do I actually have all the data I expect to have?
- **Correctness:** Does the data actually reflect the business rules and domain knowledge we expect it to reflect?
- **Consistency:** Are refreshes of the data consistent and is the data consistent when it is viewed over some time period?
- **Coherence:** Does the data "fit together" in terms of its expected relationships?
- **ACcountability:** Can we trace the data to tell where the data came from, who delivered it, where it is stored in the DME, and other information useful for its traceability?

These are quite straightforward concepts at a high level. You will soon see the variations and subtleties that arise when you try to wrap tests around these concepts and specify expected values for your tests. The subsequent sections now examine the five Cs.

13.3   TESTING DATA COMPLETENESS

Data Completeness can be thought of as knowing whether you really have all of the data you expect to have. This raises the question of where expectations about the data come from and what they might be. You may be wondering how it could arise that data is not as described. Extracting data from a system is simply a matter of running a query against a database table, right? Actually, loss of data at extraction and at load time can happen for many reasons in real-world scenarios.

The team who extracted the data from the source system may have made a mistake in their extraction code. This has the result that the expected range of data is wrong or particular data fields and tables are missing or corrupted. Database administrators are more used to stuffing data into databases and maintaining database performance. It is rarely their role to pull data out of databases into text files and other file formats.

Even when the correct ranges of data and the correct data fields are present, the fields may not have been populated correctly. Formats of dates and numbers can be corrupted at extraction or inconsistent with expectations. Long text values can end up being cut short. Records can be wrapped and incorrectly delimited. Extraction from other sources such as web pages and file shares is quite ad-hoc as these sources vary so much. How does your team know that all of the source data has been extracted?

The approaches to testing data completeness for structured and unstructured data are slightly different and so we will now deal with them separately.

13.3.1   Approach to Structured Data

The approach to testing completeness of structured data involves two checks.

- **Width:** Establish and agree the data fields that are to be provided.
- **Length:** Establish and agree a checksum for each of the data fields of concern.

The first of these tests is straightforward. The data provider communicates the data fields they are going to provide and the data receiver (the analytics team) checks that all those fields are in the delivered data.

The second test is a little more involved. Before discussing the process though, we need to first understand a "checksum." A checksum is some type of sum or calculation that is performed across every record of a given data field. This effectively summarizes a collection of values from a data field into a single number.

Figure 48 shows a simple checksum for two data fields, a customer name, and a number of visits. The number of visits field, being a number, has simply been summed down the entire data field to give a total of 105. The customer name field, being text, is treated slightly differently. Here the *length* of each word is summed down the entire data field. Churchill (length 9), Athens (length 6), and so on are summed to give a total of 27.

ROW	CUSTOMER	Visits
1	Churchill	10
2	Athens	32
3	Pompeii	8
4	Faust	55
	27	105

FIGURE 48   A checksum example

The process for checking data completeness is then the following.

- The data provider calculates checksums as per an agreed definition on their source system.
- The data provider then extracts the data from the source system.
- Data is transferred to the analytics team and loaded onto the target system.
- The analytics team calculates the same checksums as per the agreed definition on their target system.
- The checksums from the source system and the target system are compared to see if there is any difference. A difference in checksums means that the data has changed during its journey from source to target system.

The following sections provide some tips on testing structured data completeness according to this process.

13.3.2   Practice Tip 66: Capture Checksums Before Data Extraction

Even when teams do perform checksum calculations, they often slip up on the timing of the calculation. Think about the process that is being followed. Data is being extracted from a source system. The source system is probably live and so new data is being added to it all the time. The checksums calculated on the source system today could be very different to the checksums calculated tomorrow or even an hour later.

It is important that checksums are calculated on the source system at the time of data extraction. This ensures that there is a baseline checksum for comparison against when the data is imported into the target system. Going back to the source system at a later date and trying to retrieve checksums for the data extract is usually difficult. The data will have moved on significantly and there is increased disruption for the customer.

13.3.3   Practice Tip 67: Agree an Approach to Blank Data

Blank data is different from NULL data. While a NULL field will not contribute to a checksum, a blank value might make a contribution depending on how the teams agree to handle blanks.

For example, if a text field contains nothing except 4 blank characters, should its length be reported as 4 or as 0? If a text field has leading or trailing blanks, do they contribute to the field length calculation?

Make sure that the checksum definitions explicitly define how blank and NULL data should be handled.

13.3.4   Practice Tip 68: Allow a Threshold Difference for Some Checksums

Some checksums such as the length of a text field can be calculated precisely. They should not differ between source and target system provided that the checksum is well defined. However, other data types such as floating point numbers can be expected to differ between systems. In practice, you will find that checksums for these data types will differ by a very small amount.

A sensible approach is to agree an allowed threshold for the difference in checksums for data types that vary between source and target systems.

13.3.5   Approach to Unstructured Data

When dealing with unstructured data, the concepts of tables and fields no longer apply. A paragraph of text with embedded tables and perhaps other formatting does not lend itself to a typical checksum. However, it is still important to test that the data has not been modified between extraction and receipt.

Here, the best approach is to create a hash of each dataset. A hash function takes a block of data of arbitrary length and converts it into a number of fixed length. In practice, this means that a file of unstructured data can be summarized by a single number calculated by a *hash function*. If the contents of the data file change in any way, the number generated by the hash function also changes and you know the data has been modified.

13.3.6   Practice Tip 69: Agree and Test the Hash Function

There are many available hash functions and versions of hash functions. A quick search will yield common functions such as MD5 and SHA as well as their variants such as SHA-1, SHA-2, etc. The implementation of these algorithms should be standardized so that they perform consistently between *implementations* in various programming languages. If hashes are being calculated by two different teams, it is prudent to agree the specific hash function being used and test that both teams' implementations are the same.

13.3.7   Why Not Use Hashes in Checksum Calculations?

In the earlier discussion of checksums for structured data, we went to some length to emphasize the importance of defining a checksum for a given data type and how this checksum must then be calculated for all important data fields. You may wonder why we would not recommend using a hash function for a data field or indeed using a hash function for an entire dataset. There are several good reasons for using checksums rather than hashes.

- **Hash functions depend on data order:** A hash function's output is dependent on the order of the data that is fed into the function. This means that checksums of data fields using a hash function would have to be careful to order the rows of data consistently in the source and target system. A checksum using a straight forward total does not depend on the order of data rows.
- **Hash function implementations may differ between systems:** Despite standardizations of hash functions, there is still a good chance that implementations of hash functions may differ between systems or that a particular hash function is not available in one of the source or target systems. Simple sum calculations do not have this limitation.
- **Hash functions take longer to compute:** A hash function is designed with additional characteristics. Without going into the involved mathematical details, hash functions are designed to produce outputs with a very high probability of uniqueness and certain distribution characteristics. This adds to their computational complexity and execution time. This can be significant when calculating hashes for a large number of data fields in large datasets.
- **Hash functions are less informative:** A hash function produces a single number as its output. If two data fields differ, two different hash numbers will be produced. However, the difference between these numbers is no indication of how different the data fields are because of how hash functions are designed to work. By contrast, using sums gives a rough measure of how different two compared data fields are.

13.4   TESTING DATA CORRECTNESS

Data correctness can be thought of as knowing whether the data actually describes the expected business rules. As with completeness, you may wonder how incorrect data could get into a system in the first place. Unfortunately, the all too common reality is that most real-world data contains some amount of incorrectness and so we must test around this to try and detect and quantify it.

Humans enter incorrect data into systems. For example, you may see all sorts of variations for an unknown value such as "N/A," "UNKNOWN," "Not Known." Data fields sometimes get reappropriated for another purpose because of insufficient IT budget or business appetite to reengineer the existing database. Poor application interface design can lead to inappropriate data entry and misuse of data fields. I recently encountered a user "Testy McTestPerson" in some data. Apologies Testy if you are a real person.

War Story 14: Those Dummy Employees

Maggie is an in-house data analyst working for Grattan Drugs, a pharmaceutical manufacturer. Grattan are regulated so they have to demonstrate that they tightly control access to buildings, data, and IT systems. Over the past year, Grattan has grown significantly and had to rely on many contract staff. Now there is a question over how many contractors and employees still have active accounts in Grattan's various systems.

Maggie is given the single largest system to look at as a priority. She dives into the data and begins profiling employee user accounts with their names, roles, and last login dates. Excited by her progress, Maggie begins reporting to her stakeholder on active users and accounts that need to be closed.

Unfortunately for Maggie, she hadn't done any data testing or worked to understand the business domain. The first report of active accounts she submits to IT has several flaws that her stakeholder immediately spots. The particular IT system originally did not have an ability to delete accounts. The administrators instead had a work around of adding the letters "ZZZ" to the start of these account IDs so they could be easily identified as dummy users and ignored. Several test accounts, all with the user name of "Tester," were also created for the system upgrade and Maggie had also listed these as active accounts.

It was a bad delivery of results for Maggie. If she had taken the time to profile the data she received from IT, she would have spotted these patterns and gone back to her customer with follow-up questions. Maggie was the only dummy in this data.

Testing data correctness amounts to profiling data fields. That is, you create measures of characteristics about the data field contents. The most relevant types of tests for Guerrilla Analytics come from the field of data quality (Sebastian-Coleman, 2013). These can be categorized as follows.

- **Metadata characteristics:** These are descriptions of the data itself. There is one piece of metadata that is of most importance in Guerrilla Analytics.
  - **Data Types:** These are the types of data stored in fields such as dates, integers, text, bits, and so on.
- **Field Content Characteristics**
  - Lists of values/labels allowed in a field.
  - Formats such as number of decimal places or ordering of day, month, and year in a date.
  - Statistics describing the distribution of contents of a data field.
- **Dataset Combination Characteristics**
  - Cross-Column Rules look at combinations of field values in a single record.

The following sections will now discuss these tests in further detail.

13.4.1   Metadata Correctness Tests

Metadata is simply "data about data." In the case of all DMEs, metadata about a dataset includes the names and types of data fields that are present in a dataset.

Most DMEs allow metadata to be queried. It is therefore a simple query to extract the metadata for all datasets and compare it to expectations.

For example, you would expect a date field to have a type of DateTime, Date or some other recognized data type. You would expect a count field to have a type of integer. Occasionally, these expected types are well described in the source system documentation but this should not be assumed to be correct in a Guerrilla Analytics environment.

This type of data correctness information can be compared to documented specifications and validated with business domain experts to test how closely the data matches expectations.

13.4.2 Field Content Correctness Tests

Field content correctness tests, as the name suggests, test the contents of data fields. The scope of testing here is as varied as the data that can be stored in data fields. The following sections describe some of the key types of tests a Guerrilla Analytics team needs to be familiar with.

13.4.2.1 Date Data

Most problems associated with date data can be identified by profiling the distribution of dates in a field.

- **Default values:** These often show up as the earliest or latest date in the field and stand out because they are significantly different from the rest of the genuine data. For example, 1st January 1900 should be conspicuous if all other data begins in 2013.
- **Typos:** Confusion about various date formats is common in data entry. For example, a United States user would read 12/10/2014 as December 10th, whereas a British user would read this as 12th of October.
- **Sense checks:** A dataset of last year's financial data should not have dates from 10 years ago. A dataset of young adult social media habits should have birth dates from about 15 to 25 years ago.
- **Sequences:** Working with dates and times suggests the idea of sequences of events. This can be used to assess data correctness. For example, a customer on-boarding date is expected to be earlier than any customer purchase dates.

13.4.2.2 Invalid Values

Some data fields are used to store a particular set of values. A survey question's answer field may be designed to hold the values "Yes" or "No" but not "Y" or "N." There is, therefore, an expectation about the contents of these fields that you should test.

- **Allowed values:** A field to store a RAG value (Red, Amber, Green) should not contain Blue or any other value.

- **Invalid values:** You will very often find values such as TEST or DO NOT USE, as happened to Maggie in the previous war story 14.
- **Invalid ranges:** For fields that are a continuous number (as opposed to a list of labels) there may be an allowed range of values that the field can have. For example, a negative payment might not be permitted. A person's age over 120 would be unusual.

13.4.2.3   Profiling

Even if a field is populated entirely with allowed values, the distribution of those values may not be correct. This is where profiling is important. Calculating distributions of each variable value within a field reveals the frequency of each unique value in the field. Having calculated a distribution, the following analyses can then be applied.

- **High-Frequency Values and Low-Frequency Values:** The highest and lowest frequency values may be incorrect and should be investigated. After dismissing such outliers, the distribution should be checked to ensure that high and low frequency values are expected from a business perspective. For example, in a distribution of supermarket check-out receipts, you would expect the highest frequency values to be distributed around the average supermarket shop as opposed to small convenience store type purchases.
- **Fields with only one value:** You will sometimes encounter a field that contains only a single value. This raises the question of what the purpose of the field is. There will be sensible explanations. For example, the field may contain the data processing date or perhaps you are working with a subset of data from a single business region. As with many of these checks, common sense and conversation with the data provider are required.
- **Blank fields:** A special case of a field with only one value is that where a field is completely NULL or blank. Sometimes fields are deprecated. But sometimes data extraction procedures break and fail to populate a field. When entirely blank fields are detected in testing they should be reported to confirm they are correct.
- **Fields with an unexpected number of values:** The expectation of high or low numbers of values depends on the purpose of the field. A gender column should only contain male, female, and perhaps unspecified. A column of business products should contain no more values than the total products sold by the business. Variations in the expected number of values can be a sign of incorrect data. For example, three types of values in a field describing activity of an account may lead us to discover correct values of "ACTIVE" and "INACTIVE" as well as an incorrect value such as "NOT ACTIVE."

13.4.3   Data Combination Correctness Tests

The correctness tests discuss so far have focused on a dataset being set up correctly (metadata correctness) and individual data fields being populated correctly (field content correctness). Within a given dataset, there is another important way in which data may be considered incorrect, even when the metadata and field content tests have passed. You can consider incorrect combinations of values across data fields. Some examples of combinations of exclusive field values follow.

- A medical test particular to male patients should not appear in combination with a patient gender of female.
- A customer purchase order date should not appear in combination with a later customer on-boarding date.
- A customer billing address in the United States should not appear in combination with a customer country identifier of Ireland.

There are also obligatory combinations where the presence of one value necessitates the presence of another value.

- A given postcode/zip code requires a given county in an address.

Needless to say, there are many scenarios here as they depend on the business domain and how it is modeled in the data.

13.4.3.1 Testing Data Combinations

The best way to test for data combination problems is simply to look at all combinations of the data fields in question. The output can then be reviewed to find unexpected and disallowed combinations of data field values.

13.5 TESTING CONSISTENCY

The tests described so far have helped establish confidence in the completeness and correctness of data as a static snapshot. Data consistency can be understood as similarity with characteristics previously observed in the data. Consistency therefore incorporates a time dimension. For example, if the current dataset of website visits has 20,000 hits per day, then an earlier dataset would be expected to a have a similar order of hits per day. The question of data consistency arises in two scenarios encountered in Guerrilla Analytics projects.

- **Data refreshes:** Data is refreshed during the project because data goes out of date or because additions and changes to the data such as new fields need to be included in an analysis.
- **Long time ranges:** When a date range for some data stretches over a significant time span, there is a greater chance that business processes might have changed during the course of the data generation. For example, new products were introduced, regional offices were shut down, and significant economic events such as a January sale changed the patterns of data observed.

Consistency testing is about comparing more recent data to that which was seen in the past to detect if patterns in the data have changed over time. The basis of this comparison is similar to many of the tests previously discussed. However, the fact that we are usually comparing data over different time periods forces us to frame these tests slightly differently. Here are the comparisons that can be considered when testing data consistency.

- **Consistent field types:** If a dataset is refreshed, does it have the same data types as encountered previously? Perhaps text field lengths or numeric types have changed? This issue arises very often in projects where different team members perform the data extraction on separate occasions and do not share the format of the data extracts with one another.
- **Consistent rates of activity:** Data from an earlier and later time period will obviously have different date values. However, you might expect the rate of activities such as sales or logins to be consistent in both datasets. You could also look for consistency in periodic activities. For example, does account closing always happen within the last 2 days of a month? Is a salary payment always executed on the last Thursday of a month?
- **Consistent content:** Do fields have the same distribution of values or the same sets of allowed values? For example, a count of the distinct number of staff represented in human resource data should change in line with the business. Unless there has been a dramatic business event, such as an acquisition or rationalization, there should not be significant changes in total staff over time.
- **Consistent ratios/proportions:** Are the proportions of some combinations of data fields consistent? For example, the number of financial trades per trader or the number of system logins per user per day.
- **Consistent summary statistics:** Do the sum, range, average, etc. of certain fields remain consistent over particular ranges?

Again, there is potential for much variety in these tests. The intention here is to outline what should be considered. You must then prioritize as appropriate for the given Guerrilla Analytics project.

13.6   TESTING DATA COHERENCE

Data coherence (sometimes called referential integrity) describes the degree to which data relationships are correct and as expected.

In a relational database, each table should have a primary key that uniquely identifies a row of data in that table. The table may also have one or more foreign keys. Foreign keys are a reference to primary keys in other tables. By joining a foreign key to its parent table, a relationship is established between two tables.

Consider the illustrated example in Figure 49. The customer table on the left contains a primary key called CUST_ID that uniquely identifies every customer. It also contains a foreign key called CITY_ID. The CITY_ID is a primary key in its own parent table on the right. These two tables have an expected relationship that every customer lives in only one city.

CUST_ID	CUSTOMER
1	Morgan
2	Richardson
3	Collins
4	Newton

CITY_ID	CUST_ID	CITY
1	2	London
2	1	Galway
3	4	New York
4	3	Sao Paulo

FIGURE 49   Testing data coherence

Testing data coherence is about establishing (1) whether these table relationships are complete, and (2) whether these relationships are as expected.

13.6.1   Testing Incomplete Relationships

It is expected that any value present in the foreign key column will also be present in the table for which it is the primary key. In the example from Figure 49, every CITY_ID present in the customer table as a foreign key must be present in the city table also. If the value is not present on the parent table then something is wrong with data coherence.

Incomplete relationships can occur for many reasons including problems in data extraction, bugs in the source system, and data purges and archiving processes in the source system. Testing relationships identifies these problems.

13.6.2   Relationships Different from Expectations

There are three basic types of relationships in data that has a relational model.

- **One-to-one:** An entity in one table is related to only one entity in another table. For example, a given customer can only register one email address with an online shopping site.
- **One-to-many:** An entity in one table is related to one or more entities in another table. Instances in the other table cannot be related back to other instances in the first table. In effect, the relationship is a hierarchy. A classic example is that of a family tree. A father can have more than one daughter but the daughter cannot have more than one biological father.
- **Many-to-many:** An entity in one table can be related to many entities in another table and this relationship works in both directions. For example, a supermarket customer can purchase several product types. Each of those product types can also be purchased by many other customers. From a customer perspective, we can say "this customer bought the following products." Conversely, from the product perspective we can say "this product was bought by all the following customers."

These types of relationship are sometimes referred to as the "cardinality" of the relationship. Cardinality can easily be tested by joining and counting foreign key to primary key relationships and comparing results to the expected data model.

13.7   TESTING ACCOUNTABILITY

Finally we arrive at data accountability. This is about tracking where data came from. This is more an operational issue in the team's project management rather than something that is inherent in the data model or data content. To properly track the data you need to be able to say at least the following about it.

- **How?**
  - What queries and process were used to produce the extracted data and are these queries and process repeatable?
- **Who produced the data?**
- **When was the data extract produced?**
- **What data was produced?**
  - What source was the data extracted from? This could be a system, file share, email archive, web site, third party, or other data provider.
  - What was the scope of the extraction in terms of time, products, customers, regions, or some other business domain boundary?
  - What list of datasets was provided in the extract?
- **Where are the raw unmodified datasets stored now?**

Since accountability is more to do with data management process than data characteristics, it is more difficult to specify automated tests of accountability. You should put in place frequent audits to check completeness of accountability information and consider making a team member responsible for this.

13.7.1   Practice Tip 70: Use a Data Log

Data tracking information for accountability is best stored in a data log which describes the contents of an accompanying data folder. Lightweight methods for tracking data extraction, data receipt, and loading were discussed in an earlier chapter on Data Receipt. At its most basic, a data log can be implemented in a spreadsheet. If available, workflow management tools (Doar, 2011) can also be customized to track data and make individuals accountable for data provenance.

13.7.2   Practice Tip 71: Keep it Simple

Sometimes, the temptation is to try to capture everything you can about the data. Remember the over-arching Guerrilla Analytics principle of simplicity. In a highly dynamic project, there often will not be time or need to capture everything about the data. Focus on the key descriptors that help preserve data provenance.

13.8   IMPLEMENTING DATA TESTING

13.8.1   Overview

So far in this chapter, we have discussed the five Cs of data testing and the various types of tests that can be executed. We have not gone into any details of how these tests would be implemented.

You may have noticed that data testing at a high level amounts to checksums and data profiling. These activities are applied to entire datasets and also fields within datasets and are generally sums, counts, ranges, and other aggregates of datasets and fields.

This section now summarizes some tips for implementing these data tests in a Guerrilla Analytics environment.

13.8.2   Practice Tip 72: Limit Data Test Scope and Prioritize Sensibly

There is a huge scope of tests that can be performed when testing completeness, correctness, coherence, consistency and accountability. You could profile every data field, enumerate the contents of every field and test every dataset join. Bear in mind that tests are like all code and so have a maintenance cost. Tests have to be maintained and then rerun and reviewed as frequently as the data changes. There is a judgment call to make on the balance between testing every aspect of your data and exhausting project resources versus doing enough testing to cover critical defects. The Guerrilla Analytics environment often limits the sophistication of data profiling tools available, if any, and the time you can use in data testing. To help prioritize data testing, ask questions such as the following.

- Which data joins are critical in rebuilding any relational data?
- Which fields are used in business rules and so influence calculations and filtering?
- Which fields appear in customer outputs and so must be correct?
- Which datasets are being refreshed and are expected to remain consistent across refreshes?

Keeping agility in mind, the critical tests can be built first and additional tests added as resourcing and project requirements dictate. This leads to the next testing tip.

13.8.3   Practice Tip 73: Design Tests with Automation in Mind

Data refreshes of even moderate size and complexity can contain hundreds of datasets. Manually running tests for each of these datasets is not practical. The latest results have to be inspected in addition to a comparison with the results of the previous test run. The best approach is to automate test execution, as is done with test harnesses in traditional software engineering (Tahchiev et al., 2010).

A strategy for test automation requires the following automation features.

- **Test scripts can be easily identified and executed:** Test scripts can then be automatically picked up and executed with a command line script or scripting language.
- **Test results are written to a consistent location with a consistent format:** Test results can then be inspected and reported on automatically.

Setting aside project time to program this automation greatly diminishes the testing burden and thereby encourages the team to run critical tests frequently rather than postpone them. The team need only inspect test outputs when tests fail. This frees them up to either refine tests, increase test coverage, or do other analytics work.

13.8.4   Practice Tip 74: Store Test Results Near the Data

Data testing is a critical activity. If errors are discovered in test results, and mistakes in business rules are ruled out as a cause of error then the data itself will come under scrutiny. Even though the analytics team does not generate the raw data, there is a responsibility on them as domain experts to test the data they receive and avoid wasting time on analyses that cannot be used. Despite this responsibility, teams very often run data tests in an ad-hoc fashion, manually inspecting results, and then discarding results.

Test results should be stored in a way that the tests done on a particular dataset can easily be located without the overhead of unnecessary documentation. One method is to place test results in a dataset with a similar name to the dataset being tested. For example, checksums on a dataset called FX_TRADES could be stored in a dataset called FX_TRADES_TEST. You may wish to locate these test result datasets in the same namespace as their target datasets or you may want to file test results in another location. The key here is to have a team convention that makes test results for a given dataset or field easy to locate, ideally with minimal documentation overhead.

The main advantage of storing test results in the DME is that the team can quickly inspect, query, and report on test results without having to leave the DME. This is useful for quickly preparing data quality reports and for reporting on any differences between data refreshes.

13.8.5   Practice Tip 75: Structure Data Test Results in a Consistent Format

If the team is following the good practice of keeping all test results in test datasets, it would also be beneficial to structure these tests results in a similar format.

Establish a dataset of test metric definitions. This should contain at least a metric ID, metric name, and metric description. Each test result dataset should then contain some of the following fields.

- **Metric ID:** This is a reference to the metric definition table.
- **Dataset name:** This is the dataset being tested.
- **Dataset source:** This is a reference to the dataset source. This may be needed if the source cannot be identified from the dataset name.
- **Expected value:** For the given test metric, this lists the expected value of the test.
- **Actual value:** For the given test execution, this records the actual value that was calculated by the test.
- **Timestamp:** This records when the particular test was run and the result was recorded.
- **Pass/fail:** This records whether a particular test run passed or failed.
- **Reason:** This is a short business description of why a test failed.

The exact format may differ between types of tests. For example, a coherence test would need to list both the dataset on the left of the join and the dataset on the right of the join.

If test datasets have a common format then automated reporting across test datasets is far easier. This saves precious time in a Guerrilla Analytics project.

13.8.6 Practice Tip 76: Develop a Suite of Test Routines

Data testing does not need to occur at a daily or even weekly frequency. Since data testing is about finding defects in data that comes to the team, these tests need only be run once when new data is delivered to the team. Furthermore, there is a lot of repetition within tests. You always look at aspects of the data such as:

- Comparisons of primary and foreign keys.
- Distribution of values.
- Lists of allowed data values.
- Grouping of combinations of multiple fields.

These common patterns cry out for some common team code for running these types of tests. Such code could have the following types of functionality.

- Given a dataset and foreign key field and another dataset in which that foreign key is the primary key, do a comparison of the values in the foreign key and primary key field.
- Given a field of data, list all unique values and compare to a list of expected values.
- Given a date, numeric, or text field, calculate an appropriate checksum.

There are sophisticated data profiling tools that will do all of this and more. Again, in a Guerrilla Analytics project you should expect that available tool sets will be limited and so you need to think about the priority test functionality that can be automated by your team with minimal overhead.

13.9   WRAP UP

This chapter has described testing of data. In this chapter you have learned the following.

- The five Cs of data testing which are Completeness, Correctness, Consistency, Coherence, and aCcountability.
- Completeness testing checks whether the team has received the expected data fields and that the data as it left the source system is unchanged from the data that was loaded into the team's target DME.
- Correctness testing covers the following.
  - Metadata testing checks whether data fields are of the expected data types such as date, numeric, and text.
  - Field content testing asks whether data fields have expected content.
  - Combination tests check whether expected combinations of values in multiple fields occur together.
- Consistency tests check whether the characteristics of the data have changed significantly over some period of time and one or more data refreshes.
- Coherence or Referential Integrity tests check that table relationships are correct. Foreign keys must exist as primary keys in some table and the expected cardinality of data relationships must be respected.
- Accountability tests check that all the relevant detail is present to track where data came from.
- Recommended data structures and locations for storing test results were discussed. In particular, it was emphasized that test results should be stored near the datasets they test and should be structured in a consistent format.
- Automating test execution means that tests can easily be repeated with data refreshes. Removing the manual process of running tests reduces the temptation to postpone testing and reduces the risk of omitting tests when running a large number of test scripts.

Chapter 14

Testing Builds

14.1 STRUCTURE OF A DATA BUILD

The structure of a build is illustrated in Figure 50. A detailed treatment of data builds can be found in Chapter 12, but here is a brief summary. A raw data layer contains unaltered data, exactly as it was received from the customer. There are both system extract data sources and ad-hoc data sources that have been created as part of ongoing project work. Version-controlled code files then create one or more intermediate datasets as data is cleaned, enriched, and business rules are applied. The final layer is the interface layer. This contains the convenience datasets that are exposed to the analytics team to promote consistency in their work products.

14.2 AN ILLUSTRATIVE EXAMPLE

It will be helpful throughout this chapter to consider an illustrative data build. Figure 51 shows the build process from raw data through to build datasets. The example project involves analyzing the user permissions in a collection of IT systems so that we can determine duplicate users, missing user IDs, decommissioned users, and HR leavers who have not had their system accounts deactivated. This is a typical problem encountered in the area of Identity Access Management (IAM). To keep things simple and illustrative, we will imagine there are three systems involved in this project and we will name them "System 1," "System 2," and "System 3." There is an extract from each system that lists the user ID, user name, and last login date. We will also consider an HR system extract that conveniently lists all leavers by their company-wide user ID and the date they left the company.

Throughout this project, our wider team who specialize in security audit will need our support in providing details on specific systems and users, as well as views on the rate of closure of leaver accounts and the health of the systems under investigation. Once proper data checks have been done and data has been loaded, the next step is to create a data build where this evolving knowledge can be maintained. The details of the build layers are described in the following sections.

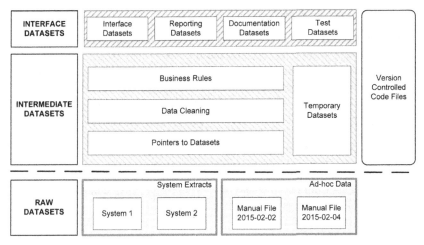

FIGURE 50   Structure of a build

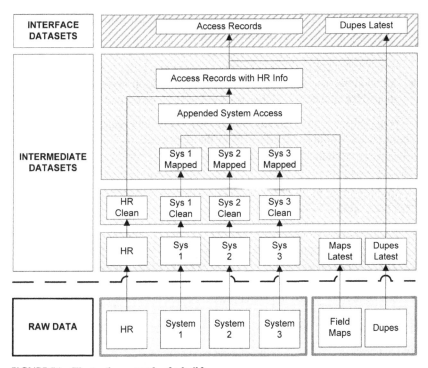

FIGURE 51   Illustrative example of a build

14.2.1   Layer 0: Raw

This is the storage area for all raw data received. It contains both the access permission extracts from three systems and the HR system extract. There are also ad-hoc extracts of duplicate reviews and system field mappings. All of these data extracts could be refreshed during the course of the project. In a live environment, IT staff will continue to add and remove users to the systems, and people will join and leave the company. This is typical of a Guerrilla Analytics project.

14.2.2   Layer 1: Pointers

As discussed in the earlier builds chapter, this is a simple pointer layer to decouple raw data from intermediate build datasets and ensure that the latest version of any data extract is always being used.

14.2.3   Layer 2: Cleaning

This layer takes each raw dataset and applies cleaning rules. The typical cleaning rules are as follows.

- Convert every user name to upper case.
- Break out names into first name and last name fields. Some system extracts have done that for us. Others are in first name, last name format, and still others are in last name, first name format.
- In one system, some User ID fields contain a blank or just some dud characters. All of these fields are identified and set to NULL.
- A coherence test that joins the HR data onto each system file shows that about 10% of the system data does not have a corresponding HR record.

Hopefully you have already spotted how these data issues were identified? These issues would have arisen from the data correctness and completeness tests discussed in the previous chapter 13.

14.2.4   Layer 3: Rules

This layer applies business rules to the cleaned data.

- Each system extract's fields are mapped into a common format using the agreed field mapping that has been worked out with the customer.
- The mapped extracts are appended into a single dataset that contains a source system identifier, a user ID, a user name, and a last login date.
- HR details are added to this dataset.

14.2.5   Layer 4: Interface Datasets

Two datasets are exposed in the interface.

- A single dataset of all system access records across all systems tagged with HR information and recognized duplicates.

- The latest duplicate markup file is exposed in the interface so it can be included with work products and used in reporting. This helps customers understand where duplicates are coming from, and work with the Guerrilla Analytics team to sign off or correct any duplicates they have identified.

The next sections will describe the types of tests you can implement to find defects in this simple data build.

14.3   TYPES OF BUILD TESTS

Testing is a huge field in its own right. Reading the software engineering literature you will find mention of many types of tests and many approaches to testing. There is also ample technology support for developing, maintaining, and executing tests. Many test types and much of the literature are focused on traditional software development and are only partially suitable for Guerrilla Analytics work. Before going any further, it helps to narrow down the types of tests that need to be considered when testing an analytics build in the constraints of a Guerrilla Analytics environment.

Whittaker et al. (2012) provide a good and simple classification of test types used at Google. Their approach emphasizes scope of testing rather than the form of testing. They define the following three types of test.

- **Small tests.** These tests cover a single unit of code in a completely mocked up environment. In traditional testing circles these tests might be called unit tests.
- **Medium tests.** These tests cover multiple and interacting units of code in a faked or real environment. Again, in traditional testing circles, these tests might be called component tests (several code files that together form a service) or integration tests.
- **Large tests.** These tests cover any number of units of code in the actual production environment with real resources. These tests are about performance at scale and on real production data.

Whittaker et al. (2012) are of course writing from the perspective of software development. These three types of test go a long way toward increasing confidence in an analytics build also. The next sections will describe these tests from the perspective of testing a Guerrilla analytics data build.

14.3.1   Small Tests

Small tests cover a single unit of code (generally a single program code file). In traditional software engineering and testing, these tests would have been called "unit tests" or perhaps "component tests." But what exactly is a unit or component in a build?

A program unit in a data build is a clearly identified data step or set of data steps that perform a significant data manipulation, and result in a significant intermediate or interface dataset. Here is a small test scenario from the illustrative build example of Figure 51.

The team is concerned that some of their Layer 2 data cleaning may be a little over zealous. They have used a function that strips all dud characters from a user name field in each of the system permission extracts. Characters such as -, $, %, # are removed. The first version of this cleaning code included apostrophes in its list of dud characters as these had been seen to occur in unusual places in users' names. However, the team later notice that some Irish and Scottish user names are badly affected by this cleaning. A valid name like "O' Malley" is being cleaned to "O Malley."

Having created a fix in a new version of the cleaning code, the team now wants to write a test to make sure this problem does not arise the next time the cleaning rule is adjusted. This test will ensure the cleaning code is not making this apostrophe replacement when apostrophes come after a standalone letter "O" between a first and a last name. Here is a high-level small test script.

- Run through data records in the raw user dataset from "System 1" and using a regular expression count the occurrences of "O" followed by an optional one or two spaces followed by an apostrophe. This is the test's expected number of names with the O apostrophe characteristic, and we expect that these should not be cleaned out of the raw data.
- Run through the cleaned user data from "System 1" and using a regular expression to perform the same count. This is the test's actual number.
- Compare the expected number and actual number.
- If the expected and actual differ, write a test result file that lists test details such as run time, tested dataset, expected value, actual value, and a result of "FAIL."

What the team have done here is wrap some expectations around a single code file to check that it does not "over clean" the data feature of user name. As other problematic cleaning features are discovered, the team will add further tests to capture those additional functionalities. Here are a few suggestions.

- Some fields may have trailing spaces because of file format differences. These, while often invisible to the developer and user, can cause problems when matching field contents. The field "Joe Bloggs   " is not the same as "Joe Bloggs." A test could check that all trailing spaces and multiple adjacent spaces within fields have been removed.
- Often blank fields need to be converted to NULL. A test could check that no blank fields remain after cleaning.
- Date fields should be within a sensible range. A test could check there are no dates before some business relevant point in time.

There are many possible tests depending on what is expected of the cleaned datasets. The main point to take away here is that small tests wrap around a single code file and modular functionality.

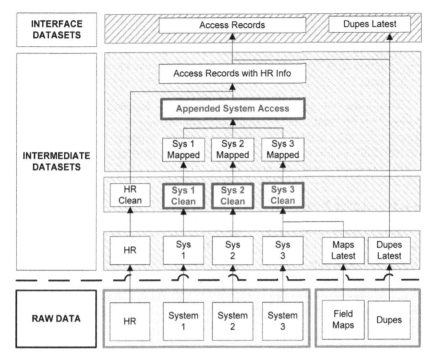

FIGURE 52   **An illustration of a medium test**

14.3.2   Medium Tests

Medium tests cover several code units that work together to produce an interme-diate or interface dataset. Let us look at a medium test from the illustrative build example. The build data flow is reproduced in Figure 52 with the datasets from the relevant data segment highlighted.

Several datasets interact to produce the "Appended System Access" interme-diate dataset. The relevant code files are as follows.

- "Sys 1 Clean," "Sys 2 Clean," and "Sys 3 Clean" are passed through the mapping dataset to produce equivalent mapped datasets where fields have been renamed to a common agreed set of field names.
- Once the system extracts have a common format, "Appended System Access" unions together the mapped datasets to produce the dataset "Appended System Access."

One key feature requiring a medium test is whether fields have been cor-rectly renamed given the definitions of field mappings. A priority field to test would be the user name field. A medium test (covering the interacting code files above) could look like the following.

- Find the distinct list of IDs and user names in the Appended System Access dataset.

- Find the distinct list of user IDs and user names in the three clean system extract datasets.
- Check that all ID and username combinations are the same in the "Appended System Access" dataset as they are in the individual cleaned system access datasets.

This medium test is very similar in principle to the small test. An expected value of user ID and name is calculated from the input system access files. An actual value after mapping is calculated from the "Appended System Access" dataset. Both are compared to test that the mapping application did not break the combinations of user IDs and user names.

14.3.3   Large Tests

Large tests are run against significant marker points in the build datasets, ignoring all the intermediate datasets and code units between those marker points. They are really a type of end-to-end test.

Returning to the illustrative build one last time, a large test could look like the following, illustrated in Figure 53. The aim is to test that no users are dropped at any point in the build's data flow.

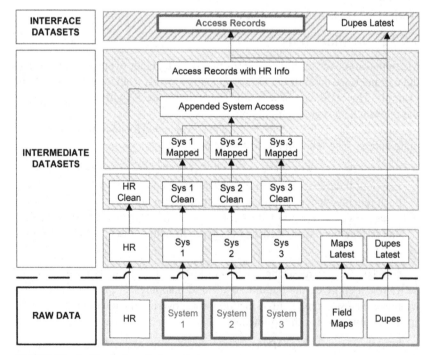

FIGURE 53   An illustration of a large test

- Append together all user IDs from the raw data files. This is the expected list of user IDs in the population.
- Compare this list to the user IDs in a build interface dataset. This is the actual list of user IDs.

As you can see from this example, there is no reference to or concern with any intermediate datasets and data steps on the journey from raw to interface. Also, this test is run at scale across the entire data population as opposed to a data segment or intermediate dataset.

14.4   TEST CODE DEVELOPMENT

Implementing a test involves writing a test code file. There are several tips and tricks to make this code easy to understand and share amongst the Guerrilla Analytics team.

14.4.1   Practice Tip 77: Use a Common Layout in Test Code Files

14.4.1.1   Guerrilla Analytics Environment

Test code files are no different from analytics code files. They can become complex and they require maintenance. Without a proper strategy for developing test code, the Guerrilla Analytics team can end up overwhelmed by a large number of poorly understood test scripts that are more trouble than the code they are supposed to be testing.

14.4.1.2   Guerrilla Analytics Approach

We have seen how all tests follow a similar pattern.

- **Setup.** Gather an expected dataset or calculate an expected value from the data.
- **Test.** Compare the expected value to the actual value in the data.
- **Store results.** Write a test result dataset.
- **Report failures.** If the test fails, write a test fail details dataset to help investigate and understand the failure.

This pattern is needed regardless of the details of the test, which can vary significantly.

More established software engineering test frameworks help a developer by having clear methods for setup, teardown, messaging, assertion, and failure code (Tahchiev et al., 2010). Guerrilla Analytics borrows from these fields. Within a test code file, the layout of setup, test, and result should be clearly visible from the test code layout and comments.

14.4.1.3 Advantages

The advantages of a clear test code layout in a Guerrilla Analytics environment are the following.

- Code is easier to understand, review, and share between team members. This is important to avoid the potential chaos of a dynamic Guerrilla Analytics project.
- Common code functionality for setting up and tearing down tests can be developed and used across the test suite. This saves the effort of reinventing the wheel for every test and so gives precious time back to the Guerrilla Analysts.
- Maintenance of test code is easier when all test code files are similar in form. This helps when the provenance of test results is challenged and when tests begin to fail.

14.4.2 Practice Tip 78: Create a Common Test Results Dataset Structure

14.4.2.1 Guerrilla Analytics Environment

Similar to when testing data, build tests will also write a test results dataset to record the outcome of every test execution. If this results dataset is different for every test, then it becomes time-consuming and error prone to inspect results and determine which tests are failing. In a Guerrilla Analytics project where code should be executed and tested often, this can result in delays in the publication of new builds that the team need for their work products.

14.4.2.2 Guerrilla Analytics Approach

Test result datasets should be developed with a structure that is common across all tests. Figure 54 shows a suggested test result structure. This provides information such as:

- **Test unique identifier (UID):** This is the UID of the test.
- **Description:** This is a simple reporting level description of what the test does.
- **Test type:** This simply states whether the test is small, medium, or large.

TEST ID	DESCRIPTION	TYPE	DATASETS	TIME	RESULT
50	Appended system access mapping	MEDIUM	APPENDED_SYSTEM_A CCESS, SYS X CLEAN...	2014-04-17 10:03	FAIL
50	Appended system access mapping	MEDIUM	APPENDED_SYSTEM_A CCESS, SYS X CLEAN...	2014-04-16 11:49	PASS
34	Dud character removal	SMALL	SYS_1_CLEAN	2014-04-16 11:47	PASS
49	Deduplication of names	MEDIUM	ACCESS_RECORDS, DUPES LATEST	2014-04-16 11:46	PASS
20	Trailing space removal	SMALL	SYS_3_CLEAN, HR...	2014-04-16 11:46	PASS

FIGURE 54 A test result dataset structure

- **Datasets:** This is a list of the dataset or datasets being tested.
- **Time:** This records when the particular test was run and the result was recorded.
- **Result:** This records whether a particular test run passed or failed.

While this is a suboptimal data model, remember that these datasets will be inspected by users to understand test failures and so there is a compromise between efficiency of data model and user friendliness.

14.4.2.3   Advantages

If the test results dataset has a common structure, then it becomes very easy to write further code across the test suite to provide functionality such as the following.

- Collect and report on the latest test result from every test result dataset.
- Create summary statistics across all tests or some subset of tests to show coverage, last execution time, total run time, etc.

14.4.3   Practice Tip 79: Develop Modular Build Code to Help Testing

14.4.3.1   Guerrilla Analytics Environment

The temptation in a pressurized Guerrilla Analytics environment is often to write code that performs several key data manipulations at once because this is perceived to be clever or more efficient. But small and medium tests cannot be wrapped around this functionality if the build code and associated data steps are not modular. A balance needs to be struck between having fewer intermediate data steps and having lots of data steps that can be isolated and tested.

A good indicator that the build code is not sufficiently modular is that you have to go to significant effort in a test script to prepare datasets for the test. In extreme cases, parts of the build end up being rewritten in the test code to facilitate testing. Imagine how more difficult it would be to write a medium test around the field mapping if the example build's data flow looked like that of Figure 55. There is no easy way to pull apart each system's mapping or inspect the appended dataset before HR information is added to it.

14.4.3.2   Guerrilla Analytics Approach

At a minimum, identify critical marker datasets that need to be written into intermediate datasets from the build process. Implement build code with testing in mind.

14.4.3.3   Advantages

Small and medium tests can easily be wrapped around critical data steps and intermediate datasets to test important parts of the build data flow. Testing code is kept to a minimum and tests can execute quickly.

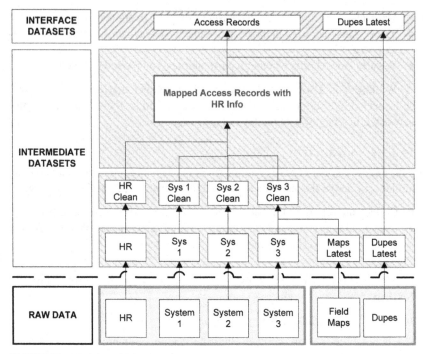

FIGURE 55 Modular build code makes testing easier

14.5 ORGANIZING BUILD TEST CODE

Tests datasets have to be stored somewhere. The test code also has to be stored somewhere. In build testing, only small tests map one-to-one with build code files and build datasets. More complicated medium and large tests may cover several code files and build datasets. This raises questions of how to clearly associate test code with both the build code and the build datasets under test. The following practice tips show how to best organize test code for this purpose.

14.5.1 Practice Tip 80: Use One Test Code File Per Test

14.5.1.1 Guerrilla Analytics Environment

The Guerrilla Analytics environment will require several build projects, each with their own build versions. This will result in many build code files and build datasets. Over time, a suite of tests will build up in the code base. This leads to confusion over which test code files perform which tests. The Guerrilla Analytics team do not want to waste time trying to coordinate and understand their own tests and code.

14.5.1.2   Guerrilla Analytics Approach

When discussing work product development and build development in previous chapters, it was recommended to have one code file per data output. This one-to-one mapping between code files and datasets helps to easily identify the code that created datasets in the DME, and encourages modular development that is easier to review, test, and report on. Testing is similar. It is best to have one test file per test.

14.5.1.3   Advantages

The advantages of one test file per test are as follows.

* **Debugging.** When a test fails, you can quickly locate the test file that reported the failure.
* **Maintenance of tests.** Test files are modular and easy to understand because they are small and do only one thing. A secondary benefit here is that if a single test script is becoming overly large and unwieldy, it is probably an indicator that the build is not sufficiently modular.

14.5.2   Practice Tip 81: Make Test Code Easily Identifiable with a Test Register

14.5.2.1   Guerrilla Analytics Environment

One of the most important advantages of writing a test is to help guide development. That is, a build developer should be able to write some build code and then execute the associated test code to gain confidence that his changes to the build have not broken the build. Testing is different to general analytics code where one code file creates one dataset. In testing, a particular code unit can be covered by multiple small and medium tests, each of which has their own test code file. This makes it difficult for a developer to know which tests cover their code, and quickly locate those test scripts to execute them.

14.5.2.2   Guerrilla Analytics Approach

The easiest way to solve this problem is to have a test register dataset that maps test UIDs to build code units and datasets. The creation and maintenance of this lookup dataset is owned by the test script writer. This means that when a contribution is made to the build code, the contributor should also be writing any necessary test scripts and registering them in the test register dataset.

Figure 56 shows what a test register dataset could look like for this chapter's illustrative build. Four tests have been registered in this example. Test 50 covers two datasets as it is a medium test. Three small tests cover dud character removal in the three system extract datasets.

Test registration should be done as part of the test's setup code so that it sits right beside the test script under version control. In practical terms this could be achieved in an RDBMS with UPDATE statements into the test register dataset.

TEST ID	DESCRIPTION	TYPE	DATASETS
50	Appended system access mapping	MEDIUM	APPENDED_SYSTEM_A CCESS
50	Appended system access mapping	MEDIUM	SYS_1_CLEAN
34	Dud character removal	SMALL	SYS_3_CLEAN
35	Dud character removal	SMALL	SYS_2_CLEAN
36	Dud character removal	SMALL	SYS_1_CLEAN

FIGURE 56   Test register dataset

14.5.2.3   Advantages

With a test register in place, the challenges of a fast-moving project with associated changes in the build are addressed. Specifically, build developers can easily identify the tests that cover their build code. This is achieved with a minimum of documentation where the only obligation is on test writers to register their test script.

14.5.3   Practice Tip 82: Make Test Code Part of the Build Code Base

14.5.3.1   Guerrilla Analytics Environment

Tests need to evolve with the build. As new features are added and some features are repaired or changed, so new tests need to be added or existing tests need to be changed. This means that test code only makes sense in the context of the version of the build code it is testing.

14.5.3.2   Guerrilla Analytics Approach

Test code should be under the same revision control system as the build code and build versions should contain the latest test code. Test code is as much a part of the code base as the build code.

14.5.3.3   Advantages

Taking this approach, a repaired bug in a particular build version can be verified to have been closed and covered with an associated test. A report can be run to list all tests and their descriptions from the test register along with their latest test results. This type of report can then accompany build delivery.

14.6   ORGANIZING TEST DATA

Test code uses and generates test data. Three types of data are associated with tests.

- **Test input datasets:** Some tests require a mocked up input dataset that contains data characteristics being tested. For example, if you were writing a small test around deduplication functionality, you would create a test dataset that deliberately contained duplicates and then pass this mocked up data to the code under test.

- **Intermediate datasets:** When a test executes, it may need to create some intermediate datasets of its own. This helps simplify and debug test code.
- **Test result datasets:** Ultimately, the result of the test and any details of a failed test need to be archived somewhere for future reference and for investigation.

The following tips show how best to organize these types of test datasets.

14.6.1   Practice Tip 83: Retain Intermediate Test Datasets

14.6.1.1   Guerrilla Analytics Environment

We already discussed how tests will often need to prepare supporting test datasets in a setup phase. These supporting datasets are essential to understanding why a test failed. If tests do not store these datasets then it can be time-consuming to investigate why a test failed.

14.6.1.2   Guerrilla Analytics Approach

A Guerrilla Analytics team should store intermediate datasets in an appropriate DME location when a test fails.

14.6.1.3   Advantages

- The team can quickly identify a failed test and locate its intermediate datasets.
- Time is not wasted having to rerun a test step by step to inspect what it does and understand why it failed.

14.6.2   Practice Tip 84: Store Test Results and Test Failure Details

14.6.2.1   Guerrilla Analytics Environment

Tests will be executed many times and every execution will produce a test result. Sometimes that result will be a fail and sometimes it will be a pass. If a log of test results is not maintained then it becomes difficult for the team to determine when a test began to fail and therefore determine the changes that might have caused this failure. If the data that caused the failure is not stored then it is difficult to investigate the cause of the failure.

14.6.2.2   Guerrilla Analytics Approach

Test results should be stored in a DME location. Again, in making results easy to find, it is best to store results in a namespace that contains the test UID. Every execution of a test writes its test results into its associated result dataset. Thus the result dataset is effectively a log of all executions of that particular test.

Different tests will fail in different ways. For example, a large test comparison of the user IDs in the raw data and the build interface might fail when one or more user IDs are lost in the build. A test failure would need to list these missing user IDs. When further detail on a test failure is useful, then this should be should be stored in a failure details dataset. While the results dataset has the same format across all tests, the details dataset can be allowed to differ depending on the specifics of the test that is failing.

14.6.2.3   Advantages

The Guerrilla Analytics team can quickly determine two things that greatly help the investigation of a failed test.

- **Time of failure.** By inspecting the results dataset, the team can see when a test began to fail.
- **Cause of failure.** By looking through the specific data records that caused a failure, the team can more easily determine why the test reported a fail and adjust their code or test accordingly.

14.6.3   Practice Tip 85: Establish Utility Data Structures in Setup

14.6.3.1   Guerrilla Analytics Environment

Some tests will rely on setup datasets before they can perform their test checks. For example, a large test checking that all user IDs are in a build interface dataset will have to first generate a list of all user IDs from the raw datasets feeding into the build. If every test creates its own setup datasets, space is wasted and tests take longer than necessary to execute.

14.6.3.2   Guerrilla Analytics Approach

Guerrilla Analytics takes the approach of identifying common utility datasets that serve several tests and building these datasets at the start of a test suite. Tests can then use these utility datasets instead of building them from scratch.

In the user ID example, a list of all raw user IDs is probably a useful dataset that could be availed of by other tests in the test suite.

Figure 57 shows a test suite code folder that contains setup scripts and the corresponding utility datasets for the illustrative test example. The need for two utility datasets has been identified. The User_IDs dataset is a list of all raw user IDs input to the build. The HR_IDs dataset is a list of all raw HR system IDs. There are several points to note about the organization of the code and datasets.

- There is now familiar one-to-one mapping between a utility dataset and the test script that creates the dataset.
- Setup scripts are stored at the top of the test script folder. They are the first scripts to execute because subsequent test scripts will use their output datasets.
- Subsequent test scripts then have their own folder that is named after their test UID.

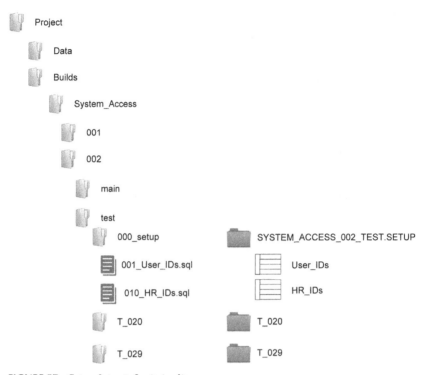

FIGURE 57   **Setup datasets for test suite**

14.6.3.3   Advantages

- Having utility datasets available avoids having to repeatedly generate them in the many subsequent tests that rely on them. This reduces test run time.
- Test scripts are simplified and this reduces the chance of bugs appearing in test scripts.

14.6.4   Practice Tip 86: Automate Build Test Execution and Reporting

14.6.4.1   Guerrilla Analytics Environment

As the test suite grows, it becomes increasingly cumbersome to manually execute all the test scripts and check for passes or fails. In a Guerrilla Analytics project, the build will change frequently and so tests should be executed and reported on. If test execution and reporting is a manual ad-hoc process, then it is time-consuming and expensive to do and hold up the release of new builds to the broader team. Furthermore, a key advantage of testing – to guide and accelerate development – is lost.

14.6.4.2   Guerrilla Analytics Approach

The obvious solution is to automate executing tests and checking results for failures. Test execution covers:

- Tearing down and rebuilding of the test suite setup datasets.
- Execution of each test script.
- Reporting of test scripts that have failed.

Automation includes not only the capture of test results, but also the first-level reporting of those results. As far as possible, tests should do the comparison of expected to actual, so an analyst need only get involved when a test starts to fail.

The build code will have a build code file that executes all the build code and produces fresh build datasets. This build file should also have the option to execute the build's test suite. In this way, testing is integral to the build and is run every time a new build is created.

14.6.4.3   Advantages

With test execution and reporting automated, several advantages are realized.

- Testing can be an integral part of the build process, improving quality, and identifying build defects early.
- The test suite can grow to include many test scripts without a significant operational cost for the team.

War Story 15: Better Late, Then Never

William was a test manager whose responsibility was to test a data build in a Guerrilla Analytics team. Unfortunately for William, the build did not have a very modular design. The build team struggled to implement significant changes to their code because a single feature change involved many changes throughout the build data flow. Because testing had not been tightly integrated into the build, William was always waiting for the build team to declare they had finished their work before William could begin his testing.

Testing was effectively put on hold for several days while the build was developed and executed. Testing always ended up lagging behind the build and pressure came on the build team to release results before they had been fully tested. When testing was eventually executed, scripts had to first unravel the tightly coupled build structures before testing them. In effective, much of the build code was being refactored in the test scripts. The whole project began to hinge on when the build was ready.

William decided to take a Guerrilla Analytics approach to testing. He met with the build manager, explaining where his test code required significant refactoring and how some minor changes to the build structure would benefit both teams. Build code would be more modular and testing would have to do less reverse engineering of the build data structures.

Once this build refactoring was complete, William then pushed for test code to be held within the main build code base. This meant that tests executed at the same time as the build code executed. There was no more waiting for the build to complete or worse still, results being issued before testing had completed. The build team benefited because they could publish a build accompanied by a verified set of passed tests.

14.7   WRAP UP

In this chapter, you have learned about testing data builds. In particular, this chapter has covered the following.

- A reminder of the structure of a data build with an illustrative example of building and deduplicating an analysis of system access permissions.
- The three categories of build tests.
  - Small tests wrap around a single code file or dataset.
  - Medium tests wrap around a data segment or several code files from the build.
  - Large tests wrap around the entire build and test its end-to-end processing.
- Test code development described tips for writing test code that is clear, traceable, and maintainable.
  - Test code should have a clear uniform layout for all tests.
  - Tests should store their results in a common results dataset structure.
  - Build code should be sufficiently modular to facilitate wrapping tests around priority segments of the build.
- Organizing test code described tips for storing test code so that it is easily identifiable.
  - There should be one test code file for each test.
  - Each test should have its own UID.
  - Each test should register itself in a central test register.
  - Test code should reside in the build codebase and be executed as part of the build.
- Organizing test data described tips for storing input datasets, intermediate datasets, and results datasets.
  - Input test datasets should be stored under their associated test UID.
  - Intermediate datasets from a test execution should be retained so that test failures can be investigated.
  - Test results should be stored in a common result dataset structure.
  - Test failure details should be stored separately.
- Executing tests covered operational tips for testing builds.
  - Tests should be executed often.
  - Where possible, common test datasets should be identified and created as utility datasets that other tests scripts can use.
  - Test execution and reporting should be automated so it is easy to run tests often and test results need only be inspected when there is a test failure.

Chapter 15

Testing Work Products

15.1 TYPES OF TESTABLE WORK PRODUCTS

If you think about all the possible work products that a team produces, it may seem like a daunting task to test all of these variations. There are presentations, written reports with embedded analytics, plots, visualization dashboards, data samples, enriched datasets, and many other outputs. However, all of these work products break down into two fundamentally different types of outputs that are tested in two different ways.

- **Ordinary work products:** These are a combination of program code and some output data. This output data could be used in many ways. It may be given to a customer or other team member to work on. It may also feed into a visualization to help the customer with some data insight. It may be one component of a larger report.
- **Statistical models:** These are models in the machine learning or statistical sense and statistical hypothesis tests. That is, they are a relationship between variables that the analytics team has derived or they are a statement about the acceptance or rejection of a hypothesis.

The next sections will describe how these two fundamental types of outputs are tested.

15.2 ORDINARY WORK PRODUCTS

Rather than being overwhelmed by the variety of ordinary work products, think more generally about how these work products are constructed. Some code is written to manipulate data. If a suitable build exists, this code may draw on the convenience datasets that this build provides. If no build exists, then the work product code will probably have to do more of its own data manipulation. Either way, a final set of result datasets is produced. These result datasets may be very small and simple if they are providing a single number for use in a report or some very high-level management information. Alternatively, the result dataset might be a significant data sample that the customer or wider team member wants to use in their own analyses. The result may be a base dataset on which a visualization or plot is constructed. Whatever the output, you have the usual structure of data manipulation code, result dataset and then some type of presentation layer. It is this code and result dataset that you need to test for defects.

In a manner similar to data testing, we can identify the following "5C" tests of ordinary work products.

- **Completeness:** Was the right subset of data used in the work product?
- **Correctness:** Is the work product code logically correct?
- **Consistency:** Is the work product consistent with previous versions? If not, how did previous versions of this work product differ from the current work product under test? If the work product is based on a build, does the work product data agree with the build data?
- **Coherence:** Does the work product have sufficient IDs to connect it back to its source data? If the work product has several related parts such as a plot and a table of data, are those parts in agreement with one another?
- **aCcountability:** Can you identify the exact versions of all data sources and build datasets used in the work product and can you clearly identify the work product generated by the program code?

The following sections will elaborate on each of these test types.

15.2.1   Testing Completeness

In Chapter 13 on testing data, a lot of time was spent covering the completeness of data delivered to the team. This focused on methods such as checksums to ensure that the data expected from the source was actually the data received and loaded into the Data Manipulation Environment (DME).

Completeness in a work product means that the correct population of data was used for the work product. For example, if you were asked to produce a visualization of sales data for the first quarter, have you clearly filtered by date to the first three months of the year? If you were asked for an analysis of a particular customer subset, have you clearly extracted that specific subset from the available data when producing the work product and were any customers missing?

Testing completeness of a work product therefore involves comparing the population in the work product dataset to the same population in the source raw or build dataset to ensure that the population has not being corrupted or truncated in the course of the work product's code. Sample tests would look like the following.

- **Comparison of the population in the result set to a known expected population.** Consider this example. A customer has asked the team for details on a specific set of registered website users. The specific users were provided by the customer to the team as a list of names. The work product involved sourcing the proper data identifiers for this list of names and then assembling the required data for those users. A work product test did a comparison of the input list from the customer and the names in the final result dataset. It showed that one registered user was missing. A conversation with the customer could then take place to see whether the provided name was incorrect or to source where the problematic user name came from.

- **Comparison of the population in the result dataset to the same population in the source datasets to check that data fields have not been dropped or corrupted.** This typically occurs when a work product has to enrich a build or raw dataset. In the course of this work, data can be dropped or corrupted. A good work product test will check that this has not happened.

15.2.2 Testing Correctness

Testing correctness of a work product is a much more nebulous endeavor. Unlike when you test data, you do not usually have a specification or business opinion on what the contents and distribution of the data should look like. The work product code is manipulating the data in new ways to reveal new insights, so how do you judge its correctness? For these types of test, you can appeal to all of the excellent work that has been done in traditional software testing.

When testing, you should check to see that data manipulations have been done in a modular way with clearly defined and commented data steps. You should review the program code to check its logic and approach. You should step into some of the intermediate datasets and do completeness tests. You should profile the result dataset to check for any data corruption and do an overall sense check of the results.

This type of testing is often neglected. Analysts tend to blindly trust their code, especially when it runs without errors. Bear in mind that data is full of potential issues and even a single broken field can have a dramatic effect on a data flow.

15.2.3 Testing Consistency

Work products can go through a number of iterations. The underlying build data may change because data is refreshed or because new data features are added to the build over the life of the work product. A customer may request changes to the work product or identify bugs in the data and analysis.

Testing consistency is about identifying and quantifying changes to the work product data that occur between delivered versions of the work product. This type of testing allows you to make statements or answer questions such as the following.

- The population of insurance claims has increased by 567 because our new build of data contained an additional 567 new claims after a data refresh.
- Adding trades from the previous month now increases the total population of trades in the dashboard to 1430, up from 1201.
- The duplicates you reviewed mean we were double counting sales for 20 sales managers and our total reported sales have now decreased by 310,000 USD.

As with consistency testing of data, consistency testing of work products involves comparisons with previous versions of the work product. This is made all the easier when all versions of work product datasets are stored in the DME or can be reproduced quickly from earlier versions of the work product code. (Section 9.10.)

Consistency tests are straightforward in principle but are often neglected in practice. Be ready to answer the customer's questions on why numbers have changed.

15.2.4   Testing Coherence

When we discussed coherence in data testing, it was all about whether the data could be joined together so that expected relationships in the data model were actually respected. Coherence of work products arises in two areas.

- **Multiple parts:** Very often, a single work product will be delivered in two or more parts. Imagine a data sample of website customer addresses and all their historical addresses. You might present this as one flat table where the website customer name repeats for every one of their addresses. However, your client wants to primarily focus on the latest address and only wants the historical dataset in case questions arise during their analysis. A good approach here is to deliver two datasets. The first dataset is the list of most recent addresses. This is where the client will do their work on customer address review. The second dataset is a historical list of addresses. This dataset is primarily for investigations and look up. If these datasets are coherent, every customer in the latest address dataset should have at least one address in the historical address dataset. The address that appears in the review set should be the latest address in the historical set.
- **Trace to source:** When producing a dataset for use in a report or visualization, it is tempting to include only the data fields that are of interest in the work product and removed supporting fields such as UIDs. This can lead to problems. When questions arise about the work product, there is no easy way to identify and connect back to the source of the work product data. This type of coherence involves including sufficient UID fields in the work product so that the source data can be identified and joined back to if necessary.

An example multiple parts test would do joins between the multiple parts, much like a join test in a data coherence test. This is illustrated in Figure 58. The

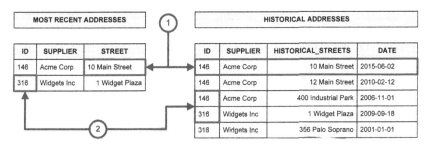

FIGURE 58   **Work product coherence test**

dataset on the left is the presentation dataset of most recent supplier addresses for two suppliers, Acme Corp and Widgets Inc. On the right is the full historical list of supplier addresses with the as-of date for each address. Acme Corp has had three addresses and Widgets Inc. has had two addresses. There are at least two coherence tests you should do on this data.

1. Is the most recent address for each supplier also the most recent address in the historical dataset?
2. Is every presented supplier in the most recent addresses also in the historical addresses dataset?

15.2.5 Testing aCcountability

The final type of work product test is that of "aCcountability." In work products, aCcountability is essentially about testing data provenance. As was covered previously, the following factors influence data provenance.

- Can all source datasets (from builds or raw data) be easily identified in the work product code?
- Can all result datasets be easily identified and reproduced from work product code?
- Can all outputs (spreadsheets, dashboards, graphics, etc.) be easily identified in the work product's outputs folder?
- Can multiple versions of the work product be easily identified and distinguished?
- Which team member contributed to each of these work products versions?

Testing for work product aCcountability is a matter of reviewing code and inspecting documentation. Ideally you should implement this through training and feedback augmented with the occasional audit of the team's work.

15.3 GENERAL TIPS ON TESTING ORDINARY WORK PRODUCTS

15.3.1 Practice Tip 87: Clearly Identify Work Product Test Code and Data

The team should already be structuring its work product code following Guerrilla Analytics principles. This means the analytics code will be in a folder with a work product UID and will be manipulating data in an area of the DME identified by that same UID.

- **Test code:** Keeping with similar conventions you have seen throughout this book, the test code files should have a similar name to the code files they test so that the files are understood to be related to one another.
- **Test data:** On the DME side, the test datasets reside under the same name space as the work product. This has two advantages. First, the associated test

datasets can be seen right beside the analytics datasets and perhaps delivered along with those analytics results. Second, if the analytics code follows the recommend Guerrilla Analytics practice of tearing down and rebuilding all datasets in its destination location then this will also force a rebuild of the test datasets.

15.3.2   Practice Tip 88: Sense Check Work Product Outputs

It is very difficult to specify test conditions for an ordinary work product. The odds are that this work product has never been created before. Therefore, it is difficult to know what to expect from the analytics code and accordingly what to set as expected in the test. Moreover, many common data mistakes can slip through a work product even if logical tests have passed. It is always advisable to do a quick senses check of outputs. Some common mistakes that arise in a dynamic and pressurized Guerrilla Analytics environment are listed below.

- **Poorly formatted values:** For example, large numbers may be printing in scientific notation or dates may be in datetime format with a redundant time component. This usually happens when exporting data out of DMEs.
- **Truncation at export:** Some analytics environments only print out a limited number of records by default. Does the final output contain all the data it should?
- **Missing data fields:** Are all intended fields included and are unnecessary fields removed?
- **Sensible:** Do the numbers make sense from your knowledge of the business problem?

Code reviews can pick up these mistakes but it is also advisable to train the Guerrilla Analytics team to take a few minutes to quickly sense check their work products.

15.4   TESTING STATISTICAL MODELS

At a high level, statistical models are a relationship between variables in the form of an equation. For example, variables such as customer's age, average current account bank balance, and average salary could be used to model the likelihood that they will default on a credit card balance. The input (or independent variables) of age, balance, and salary are combined as terms in an equation to calculate the probability of defaulting.

The related fields of statistical modeling and machine learning are vast and require trained experts to make judgments about choice of models, choice of variables, and interpretation of model outputs. A detailed discussion of testing is therefore beyond the scope of this book. However, since models and machine learning are often a critical component of analytics work and very much in vogue in "data science," it is worth mentioning some ideas around their testing.

There are two key ways to test a model.

- Model tests.
- Cross validate the model on new data.

The following sections explain these two approaches.

15.4.1 Model Tests

Many models can be tested in specific ways. For example, the quality of a regression model can be tested with statistical tools such as Cook's distance, Q–Q plots, P–P plots, and Box–Cox plots (Montgomery, 2012). Before generating such a model, the independent variables going into the model can be tested for correlations and suitable distributions. Each type of statistical model has its own quality tests and there is no escaping a requirement to be familiar with how to interpret these tests, if not the details of how these tests are derived.

What is equally important is that statistical tests and models are approached with a high degree of skepticism in terms of whether their assumptions are appropriate for the given data. Any model or statistical test which the team publishes should be supported by the necessary tests and data assessments.

15.4.2 Cross Validate Models

Even when statistical quality tests are passed, what ultimately matters is whether a model is a good representation of reality. The canonical way to quality check a model in terms of the quality of its predictions is to perform cross validation.

Cross validation involves partitioning the available data into a training dataset and a test dataset. The training dataset is used to build the model. The test dataset is used to assess how well the model performs on data it has not seen before. K-fold cross validation extends this concept. The available dataset is partitioned into K complementary subsets. The model is trained on K-1 subsets and tested on the remaining subset. This process is repeated for each of the K partitions. The performance on the model against each of the K-test partitions is then combined to give an overall model performance metric.

15.5 GENERAL TIPS ON TESTING MODELS

While model testing is a wide and varied field, there are several general tips that should be followed in a Guerrilla Analytics environment.

15.5.1 Practice Tip 89: Prefer Modeling Tools that Expose Model Data

While it is often helpful to have graphical tools and wizards for model building, these tools can restrict your ability to access the underlying raw data. If possible, use tools that expose that data. For example, a regression algorithm that allows you to access its residuals data lets you peek under the hood and assess the quality of your model. This gives you much more flexibility and power.

- You can further customize plots and store the output data back in the DME.
- Model outputs can be merged with other data for further analyses and testing.

15.5.2   Practice Tip 90: Store Model Versions for Comparison

When creating a statistical model, it is customary to try several different techniques and variables to determine which is most suited to the given data. For example, when clustering you may try both K-means and Hierarchical-clustering algorithms to see which is best suited to the problem. Although many might treat these early models as "throw away," they are important from the perspective of data provenance. Since the Guerrilla Analytics team must justify its choice of a particular model, the process of evaluating earlier models is important. Store all evaluated models for reference.

15.6   WRAP UP

In this chapter, you have learned about testing work products. In particular, this chapter covered:

- The two main types of work products.
- The five Cs of work product testing.
- The types of testing that can be done on ordinary work products.
- The types of testing that can be done on statistical models.

Part 4

Building Guerrilla Analytics Capability

This part of the book discusses building a Guerrilla Analytics capability. In particular, it will cover the people, process, and technology needed to create a Guerrilla Analytics team.

Chapter 16

People

16.1 THAT QUESTION AGAIN – WHAT IS DATA ANALYTICS?

Very early in Chapter 1, we discussed the meaning of the term "data analytics" and some of its variants such as business intelligence, business analytics, and data science. The debate about the remit of these fields is not within the scope of this book. What we *can* say is that the debate has been intense for several years and there is still a lack of consensus. This reflects the reality that "data" is a very broad area that has grown in recent years with the explosion of data availability. It is like asking what can be done with concrete when you do not have a definition of a civil engineer or architect.

If you think of oft-touted data science success stories, you probably think of Internet companies, social media companies, and digital companies. All of these organizations are growing immense customer bases through the innovative use of data and the creation of software and hardware to glean insights from that data. If you work in other industries, different "data analyst" roles may spring to mind. You may work with quantitative analysts in a financial services setting. You may think of actuaries who work with statistics in the insurance industry. I personally know geologists who deal with significant volumes of core sample data and run complex parameterized simulations across it. Companies have been mining data about customer behaviors for over a decade (Linden et al., 2003).

With these examples, you see a spectrum of activities. At one end of this spectrum, you find what can be considered data engineering activities. Data has to be put somewhere. Engineering activities involve the storage, management, and maintenance of data, and access to that data by the team. This may also include preparations applied to that data to facilitate these activities and support subsequent data analyses.

After engineering, you find data wrangling. As the name suggests, this is the common fight with the data that many analysts bemoan. Data must be cleaned. Derived variables are calculated. The data is reshaped to suit a particular analysis. Unstructured content is enriched with entities.

Once the data has been reshaped, there is sometimes a modeling phase. The reality is that on many Guerrilla Analytics projects, it is a sufficient win given project timelines to be able to summarize and report on the data at all – never mind building sophisticated models. However, when a model is required, it happens in this phase. A hypothesis is agreed and an appropriate model is selected, built, and evaluated. The model is then used to optimize a process and make predictions about the process.

Finally, the analytics results must be communicated to the customer. The format of this communication depends on the customer's requirements. It might be a conversation, a workshop, or a written report. Increasingly, it is a web application or dashboard where the customers can interact with the analytics to produce their own insights.

In the context of Guerrilla Analytics, a data analyst is anybody working with data to produce insight. If that data is an unstructured mass of website visits, then perhaps you use the current in vogue Big Data tools. If your data arrives with you in a fairly clean state and your job is to produce sophisticated models then you are more focused on the modeling process and reporting. If you are confronted with spreadsheets you probably spend a lot of time wrangling the data to get insight from it.

What makes you a Guerrilla Analyst is that you have to produce insight in dynamic circumstances while being quite highly constrained and facing frequent disruptions. This chapter focuses on the general skills of a Guerrilla Analyst rather than specific skills such as SQL, Hadoop, machine learning, or some of the other myriad technologies, languages, and techniques you may encounter.

16.2 GUERRILLA ANALYTICS SKILLS

Drew Conway's "Data Science Venn Diagram" (Conway, 2013) is an interesting perspective on the skills required in modern data analytics. The three expertise areas he identifies are as follows:

- **"Hacking" or programming:** This emphasizes the ability to access data and to think algorithmically. Data comes in a huge variety of forms and is stored in many ways. Team members need the skills to deal with this. They need to be able to get at this data and clean and manipulate it. This does not mean being an expert in computer science who can design compilers. Indeed it does not mean being an expert in database design and maintenance. It is a little bit of everything needed to get the job done. They need to recognize common database structures. They need to model data sensibly. Once data has been shaped into a good format, analytics is usually performed. This is where knowledge of algorithms and awareness of computer science topics such as complexity and data structures is advantageous. An appropriate data structure and an algorithm design can be all the difference between a feasible execution time and analyses that take hours to finish. The former is obviously the priority in Guerrilla Analytics.
- **Substantive expertise:** This is what is often termed "domain knowledge." The more your team knows about the business domain they are working in, the better placed they are to find, understand, and add value to the data they

must work with. A geologist estimating yields from a resource knows the order of magnitude of a sensible result. A marketing analyst should know the typical take-up rates of a particular type of campaign. Without this substantive expertise, the analyst is placing blind faith in their program code and their tools.

- **"Math and statistics" knowledge:** What Drew calls math and stats means some awareness of statistics as would be used in many machine learning and statistical analyses. If you want to get some insights from data beyond a ranking and a table of counts, you will need to apply a statistical analysis or machine-learning algorithm. Typical tried and trusted methods include regression, neural networks, Bayesian networks, decision trees, clustering, and association rule mining. To use these algorithms successfully, you need to understand the conditions under which they operate, the appropriate situations in which to use them, and the techniques for evaluating and tuning their performance.

There is currently much debate over whether these diverse skill sets can be found in a single individual. This is certainly less likely when you go further and include the additional skill sets your team will require on a variety of Guerrilla Analytics projects.

- **Communication:** Communicating with customers who are not data literate is critical. It is also important that team members can work constructively with one another.
- **Visualization:** Developing minimal, insightful, and beautiful visualizations to tell a story can often be the difference between analytics being understood and used by the customer or being discarded.
- **Software engineering**: Team members need an understanding of version control, build tools, documentation, specifications, and deployment. Without these techniques, the complexity of analyzing data can quickly turn into chaos. Second, if the team is ever to effectively consolidate its knowledge and increase its effectiveness, team members should appreciate how to build tools that can be reused. A sophisticated fuzzy match algorithm's value to the team is limited if it can only ever be used by its creator.
- **The data environment:** A lot of data resides in databases and most Guerrilla Analytics is done in a DME. While database tuning and management is a specialized skill, team members do need to understand how to set up database users, permissions, logs, and table spaces as well as how to connect to a database. Web applications are ubiquitous now. They are the front-end to many data sources and they are increasingly the presentation medium for analytics reporting. Team members need a working understanding of how web applications are structured, deployed, and developed.
- **Mindset:** Team members need to be able to prioritize work to add value incrementally. They obviously need a Guerrilla Analytics mindset where they can focus on data provenance despite project disruptions.

Your approach to building a team should be to find as many of these skills as possible in an individual team member while making sure that all skills are covered across your team. Let us now consider what each of these skill set areas involves in some more detail.

16.3 PROGRAMMING

16.3.1 Data Manipulation

It is simply impossible to do Guerrilla Analytics without advanced data manipulation skills. Data comes in a wide variety of forms and shapes and these are rarely the form and shape the analyst requires for their work. Data manipulation involves being able to quickly design short data flows that reshape data and calculate necessary derived data fields and datasets.

The Guerrilla Analytics environment puts a strong emphasis on this skill because very often there is no time to build data flows with sophisticated supporting tools. Some examples of this "data gymnastics" are as follows.

- Append together a variety of datasets that not only have some common fields but also differing fields.
- Identify the first and the last record within some partition of the data. For example, identify the first and the last system log record for a given user within a given day.
- Identify fuzzy duplicates across an arbitrary subset of fields in a dataset.

There are a large number of such patterns encountered in a Guerrilla Analytics project. These are covered in detail in the appendix "Data Gymnastics."

The Guerrilla Analyst must be able to dive into data, recognize these patterns, and quickly implement them with program code. This brings us to a related point.

To manipulate data with program code your team will need a data manipulation language. There is a variety of languages to choose from. SQL is necessary given its ubiquity in the relational database world. Other DMEs come with their own domain-specific language such as R (Crawley, 2007). As with anything, each language has its strengths and weaknesses. Assess these languages based on the types of data manipulation you need to do most often. Pick a minimum set of languages and get the team skilled up in their use rather than trying to cover all data manipulation scenarios.

16.3.2 Command-Line Scripting

You will encounter large data files and large numbers of data files. These files often cannot be opened with conventional text editors. Even if you could open them, you might need to do something a bit more sophisticated than read their contents. You might like to count the number of lines, sample some part of the file, sum a column of data, or append and sort multiple files. You might have to do this for a series of folders which all contain files of various dates and names. A command prompt and its associated scripting language are very useful in these scenarios where quick file manipulation is required.

At a minimum, your Guerrilla Analysts should be aware of command-line capabilities to do the following.

- **Iterate through files.** Iterate through a tree of folders to a given depth finding files with a given name pattern or other file property such as date stamp.
- **Append files.** Append one or more files together to produce a larger file.
- **Split files.** Conversely, split a file into a number of chunks based on line count, size, or some other rule.
- **Sort contents.** Sort a file by one of the columns in its content.
- **Find patterns.** Find a pattern within a file or count the occurrences of that pattern. For example, find all United States postcodes in a file.
- **Create samples.** Sample data extracted from between two given row numbers in a file. For example, extract rows 20,560 to row 20,600 from a file.
- **Find and replace.** Find and replace particular patterns within a file. For example, find the text "CUSTOMER: <FIRST NAME> <LAST NAME>" and replace with "CUSTOMER: XXX ZZZ" so that customer names are masked.
- **Compression.** Compress and decompress a file.
- **Character encoding.** Change the character encoding of a file.

These are some examples that you will encounter frequently. The more familiar and comfortable the team is with the command line, the better. It is a powerful, fast, and lightweight solution to data wrangling problems and is always available when more sophisticated tools may not be due to Guerrilla Analytics restrictions.

16.3.3   File Formats

There are several very common data file formats. Analysts need to understand what these formats look like and how to extract content from them. Comma-Separated Value (CSV) files are probably the most common format. XML and increasingly JSON are unavoidable. Programming languages such as Python (Lutz, 2009) provide functionality for iterating through and parsing these formats. Make sure that your team is able to work with these file formats and does not waste time writing file parsing code that already exists.

16.3.4   Data Visualization Language

Visualizing data is critical when exploring new data and when presenting data analytics to customers. Some languages have visualization libraries that allow plots of data to be produced from program code. Dashboard tools allow analysts to quickly prototype interactive data dashboards. Some combination of both approaches is required. Code-driven visualizations have all the usual advantages of version control, repeatability, and automation. Dashboard tools suit a more interactive approach to discovering relationships in data.

16.4 SUBSTANTIVE EXPERTISE

This is a vague and wide-ranging skill. It is best understood in terms of examples. How much better is a forensic data analyst if they have accounting experience, understand accounting rules, and know the main types of fraud? How much better is a data analyst in investment banking if they have worked in a trading environment? What about a data analyst who begins a customer analytics job having worked in marketing?

Few data analysts have a large amount of hands-on experience in a domain in addition to being skillful Guerrilla Analysts – there just is not enough time to be an expert in two or more fields. However, there is undoubtedly an advantage to the analyst who gains as much experience as possible in a domain to better understand the business drivers and challenges. Substantive expertise helps focus analyses quickly and avoids time being wasted in understanding irrelevant data patterns or pursuing useless analyses.

16.5 COMMUNICATION

It may seem obvious, but communication is a key skill for a Guerrilla Analyst. It is sometimes said that everything we do is about influencing others (Block, 2011). This is true for the Guerrilla Analyst as much as anybody else in a business environment. What use is an analysis if you cannot explain it and persuade a customer to use it? But communication is also important internally within a team. A Guerrilla Analytics environment cannot support lone rangers. There is too much going on in parallel and too much is changing for a go-it-alone attitude. A Guerrilla Analyst who communicates well also knows when to inform their team of issues, gives feedback constructively, and challenges team decisions with the right tone and language. It is important that the Guerrilla Analyst be able to communicate with the following audiences.

- **The customer.** You must be able to describe your analyses and their importance in simple business terms. A customer rarely cares about the sophisticated algorithms behind results. They only care about the bottom line and how your analyses support the decision they need to make. Know when to impress with knowledge of decision trees, data contortions, and data velocity stats, and know when to tailor communication at the right level.
- **Team members.** In a healthy Guerrilla Analytics team, there will be disagreements between team members and challenges to a particular approach that you are advocating. It is important to be able to understand where these challenges are coming from and present a reasoned non-emotional

argument for your position. Teams damage themselves irreparably because of arguments over technology and process. A good communicator can influence their technical peers, superiors and reports, and get their message across.

- **Management.** The higher up people go in management, the more removed they become from the details of Guerrilla Analytics. Over time they may forget how difficult it is to estimate analytics jobs before getting stuck into the data. This worsens as technology moves on. They forget how surprises are always lurking in every dataset. This causes problems when management expectations of delivery are not in tune with reality. A Guerrilla Analyst must be able to identify and communicate issues early and present incremental approaches to a problem. This makes management easier because managers have frequent visibility of progress and a "safety net" of delivery they can rely on even if the more advanced analyses and hypotheses do not come to fruition.

How do you improve communication skills in your team? The simple answer is practice. You must incentivize them to read voraciously, write in journals and blogs, and seek out opportunities to communicate analytics to a wide variety of audiences using a variety of media. While a peer review and feedback helps, there are also many self-publication channels that anybody can use such as blogs, twitter, and video websites.

16.6 "MATHS AND STATS"

This is another incredibly broad area that is impossible to cover in one book. There are simply hundreds of available statistical tests and modeling techniques. It would be arrogant to suggest that a data analyst could become expert in what is the full-time professional domain of statisticians and machine-learning experts. However, it is necessary and possible to be familiar with how these techniques are used and the right questions to ask of an expert when choosing an appropriate technique.

A Guerrilla Analyst involved in modeling should be familiar with the following fundamental concepts:

- **Independent variables.** These are the inputs to a statistical model.
- **Dependent variables.** These are the outputs from a model – the things that are predicted.
- **Transformations.** How to change and transform variables appropriately to make them suitable for an analysis.
- **Choice of variables.** How to assess whether variables should be included in a model.
- **Performance.** The concept of false positives and false negatives, and how to measure algorithm performance.
- **Testing.** Model validation as discussed in Chapter 15.

16.7 VISUALIZATION

Visualization is hugely important in communicating analytics results. Trends, changes, proportions, comparisons, connectivity—all are best communicated or supported with visualization. The ongoing increases in the volume and complexity of data only emphasize the importance of good visualization.

Excellent books by Nathan Yau (2013) and Edward Tufte (1990), and the ACM article "A Tour Through the Visualization Zoo" (Heer et al., 2010) are inspirational introductions to visualization.

For a Guerrilla Analyst, the key is to be able to recognize what they are trying to communicate and choose the appropriate visualization technique quickly. Here is a summary of typical visualizations that the team should be familiar with.

- **Changes over time:** Here you want to show how one or more quantities change over some time period. Bar charts and line charts (perhaps with multiple series) are a good option.
- **Static proportions:** In many cases you want to show the breakdown of a population. If the population is static, a pie chart or a tree map is a good option. A bar chart is also useful if various categories are being compared.
- **Changing proportions:** When data proportions change over time, an area chart or a stacked bar chart with time on the horizontal axis are good options.
- **Correlation:** This is when you want to demonstrate relationships between variables. For example, when variable A increases then variable B is seen to decrease. The scatter plot is the classic way to demonstrate correlations.
- **Distribution:** Sometimes you want to know how a population breaks down into buckets. This is a distribution and is best represented by a histogram.
- **Comparisons:** In these cases you want to compare a variable in terms of its distribution and key statistics such as median, mean, and range. A box plot offers a concise but information-dense way of doing this.
- **Outliers:** Here you are looking at particular variable values that are significantly different from the rest of the population. Again the box plot is very useful here. If outliers as a combination of variables are of interest, then a scatter plot quickly demonstrates interesting cases.
- **Geography:** If locations are of interest then the obvious solution is a map. You can color regions, or place bar and pie charts at locations to bring out variables at that particular location.
- **Connectivity:** Connectivity often arises when you look at networks and relationships. For example, you might consider email or phone call traffic, or connections between web pages. In these cases a network diagram is best.
- **Hierarchy:** The canonical way to represent a hierarchy is with a tree diagram.
- **Change in rank:** In some cases you would like to know how the rankings of items have changed between two points in time. This is where a slope chart comes into play.

- **Sequential additions and subtractions:** In some scenarios you would like to understand the cumulative effect of sequentially introduced additions and subtractions. This is where a waterfall chart is very useful (Rasie, 1999).

16.8   SOFTWARE ENGINEERING

A Guerrilla Analytics team needs to be able to do more than code against data. They are also creating sophisticated data and service builds. This type of coding is closer to traditional programming, but there is a surprising lack of knowledge of software engineering amongst data analysts. Software engineers have been thinking hard about problems of workflow management, version control, testing, coding conventions, configuration, and many other project operational challenges that data analysts ignore or struggle with. The following sections summarize the key software engineering skills that your Guerrilla Analytics team needs to know.

16.8.1   Source Code Control

Source code version control is probably the most important and fundamental aspect of software engineering. Guerrilla Analysts are not building million line code bases with support for multiple active releases. Guerrilla Analysts are however dealing with another type of complexity – that of changing data and requirements, as well as outputs that span several languages and formats. Version control is critical across the Guerrilla Analytics workflow in the maintenance of data provenance. A Guerrilla Analyst would benefit from understanding:

- **Concept of workspaces and code repositories:** The basic set up common across all source code control, which is that of a repository and workspaces. The repository centralizes and manages all the team's code. Individual workspaces are where a team member works on their copy of the code.
- **Repository/depot:** The repository is where files and their version history are stored. It may be on a separate server or can be local to the project files.
- **Checkout:** How to take a copy of the latest code or a specific version of the code from a repository into a local workspace.
- **Commit:** How to put code changes made in the local workspace back into the repository.
- **Update/sync:** How to pull the latest code file version from the repository into a local workspace.
- **Conflict:** How to recognize conflicts when more than one user has modified a file in their respective workspaces and how to resolve those conflicts by stepping through a conflict report.
- **Trunk/mainline/baseline:** The main code development.
- **Branch/fork:** Branching or forking involves taking a copy of the main/trunk code at a point in time. That branch of code can then develop independently. Branching is useful when you want to create a release for a customer.

- **Integration:** This is the process of taking changes made in a branch and merging them back into the mainline/trunk.
- **Tag/label:** This is a snapshot across all versions of files at a point in time. A tag/label can be equivalent to a version in the sense of a software product. Tags are generally named in some descriptive way and perhaps following a convention.

There are many tools for handling source code control (Collins-Sussman et al., 2008; Loeliger and McCullough, 2012). Choose one tool and get the team trained in its use.

16.8.2   Deployment Environments

The concept of local, test, and production environments is fundamental to software engineering.

- The local environment is where the developer tests their own changes to the data and code.
- The test environment is where all local changes from several developers are brought together and tested.
- The production environment is where tested code is rolled out for the customer.

Similar principles can be usefully applied in Guerrilla Analytics, especially when consolidating knowledge in builds. Your team needs to have this basic discipline and awareness when producing code that is deployed to customers.

16.8.3   Testing

Testing is another well-established area of software engineering. Some methodologies even advise writing tests before actually writing application code. Testing Guerrilla Analytics work has its own peculiarities – so much so that several chapters of this book are devoted to testing.

16.9   MINDSET

Finally, a Guerrilla Analyst needs to have the right mindset. Fast moving, poorly understood data with changing requirements can be an intimidating and frustrating environment to work in. Database tuning, algorithms, software releases, pattern matching – it can feel like you are a jack of all trades and master of none. The most successful Guerrilla Analysts will have the following mindset.

- **Curiosity:** They must relish tearing data apart, and twisting it inside out to find insights. Many of their lines of attack will lead to nothing but the Guerrilla Analyst must enjoy that exploratory process rather than expect a specification of what they need to do.

- **Passion:** They must care about presenting results in a beautiful and insightful way so that they influence customers. Fancy algorithms and data gymnastics are irrelevant to telling a data story. The Guerrilla Analyst must want to explain their analyses and improve them.
- **Discipline:** Maintaining data provenance requires discipline. An analyst needs to keep versioning, testing, conventions, and quality code in mind despite a sometimes chaotic project environment. Hacking around datasets carelessly without regard for the data provenance implications creates technical debt.
- **Patience:** Data is like a box of chocolates – you never know what you're going to get (Zemeckis, 1994). Some might naively think it is just a matter of "add another column." The reality is that there are always surprises lurking. A Guerrilla Analyst needs to be able to deal with the unexpected setbacks and persevere with wrangling insight out of the data they have been dealt.

16.10 WRAP UP

In this chapter, you have learned about the skill sets needed in Guerrilla Analytics. In particular, you should now understand the following.

- Data analytics is a wide ranging diverse set of activities. What defines a Guerrilla Analyst is that they have to produce insight in dynamic circumstances while being quite highly constrained.
- It is unlikely that any individual would have all the required skills of a guerrilla data analyst; however, you should ensure your team overall has as many of these skills as possible.
- The main skill areas for a Guerrilla Analyst are:
  - **Data wrangling:** The ability to quickly manipulate data according to frequently encountered patterns.
  - **Programming:** The ability to automate routine tasks, write and understand algorithms, understand the many technical environments and systems they will encounter.
  - **Substantive expertise:** Knowing and understanding the problem domain from the business perspective.
  - **Communication:** The ability to communicate results and issues within the team and with the customer.
  - **Maths and stats:** Some knowledge of statistical models and machine learning, how to choose appropriate approaches and how to evaluate them.
  - **Visualization:** The ability to choose and implement the right data visualization to communicate about data.
  - **Software engineering:** Knowledge of version control, deployment, and testing as appropriate for data analytics work.
  - **Mindset:** The right combination of curiosity, patience, discipline, and passion to deal with analytics setbacks and extract insights from complex data.

Chapter 17

Process

17.1 WHAT IS WORKFLOW MANAGEMENT?

Many of the things you do can be considered as workflows. Think about the creation of a work product such as this book. Writing the book involves a sequence of activities. I write each chapter in turn (not necessarily in reading order) then review and modify those chapters as new ideas occur to me. When the book's text is complete, it is copy edited. This can involve iterations of review and discussion with the copy editor. Eventually the book is printed so it can be put on sale. The work product I am producing goes through various states such as "in planning," "being written," "under review," "published," and "on sale." The work product can also jump back into previous states. For example, reviewers' comments could put the book back into a state of "being written" as their comments are incorporated into the book.

A workflow then is a set of defined activities on a work product that take place in a prescribed order. Each activity moves the work product into different allowed states such as the "being written" state in our book writing example.

A workflow management *system* is a process or a software tool for monitoring activities and states of work products and controlling the allowed transitions between those states.

17.2 WORKFLOWS IN ANALYTICS

The roadmap through much of this book is based on the Guerrilla Analytics workflow of Figure 59. This is the sequence of activities that is applied to data from extraction through to delivery as team work products and reports. As you are well aware by now, there are various activities that the analytics team member engages in. We have seen activities such as loading data, coding, testing, and presenting results. We could map out all the nuances and checks of data loading and data testing. We could specify the steps to take when choosing and validating a model. Any of these activities could be described in a workflow and therefore could be managed with a workflow management system. To specify every possible analytics activity with a workflow would be overwhelmingly complex and would hamper the agility required for Guerrilla Analytics. In keeping with the principle of light-weight processes, this chapter focuses on

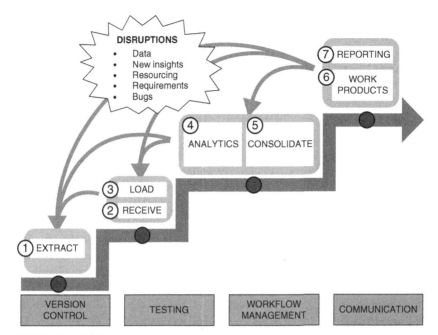

FIGURE 59   **The Guerrilla Analytics workflow**

the key activities that benefit from a minimal workflow management. As illustrated in the Guerrilla Analytics workflow, workflow management is one of the supporting functions of all of these activities.

17.2.1   Types of Workflow

There are three basic types of workflow management needed in Guerrilla Analytics projects.

- **Data receipt and load:** This is effectively the management of data logging and data tracking. Data gets a special workflow of its own because of its importance. Data loss has very serious repercussions for the team and the customer. As mentioned on many occasions, losing data provenance is the root cause of team inefficiency. The team needs to know where data came from, when it arrived with the team, where it is stored on the file system, and where it was loaded to in the Data Manipulation Environment (DME). Workflow management can help with this.
- **Producing work products:** These are all the ad-hoc analytics activities engaged in by the team. Specifically they are the activities at data extraction, coding, testing, and reporting. As mentioned before, you do not want to delve into the detail of each activity but you do need to know which activities are open, in review, and delivered as well as who is working on what.

- **Programming a build:** These are the build development and testing activities engaged in by the team. The workflow management of build activities is closest to workflow management in a traditional software engineering project (Doar, 2011). The build will be architected into components and these will be coded by team members. Bugs will be reported against versions of a build and these bugs have to be repaired. Releases of builds and versions of new builds need to be coordinated. Workflow management excels here.

The three workflow types described above have been sufficient to coordinate all my teams' activities in very complex and fast-paced projects.

17.2.2   Common Workflow States and Transitions

Although the various analytics workflows differ in the information they need to track, they can all be described by the same high-level activities and states illustrated in Figure 60. We will first look at this common structure before describing how the activities differ in each workflow type.

The workflow begins when a new work product arrives with the team. In data logging, this is a new delivery of data. For producing work products, it is a new piece of work the team has been asked to do. For build activities it will be some feature that needs to be implemented or a bug that needs to be fixed in the build.

The team member who picks up this activity from the customer describes it with appropriate detail and places the work product into a state of Open. The work is now on the team's radar.

Once Open, the work product remains in this Open state until one of two things happen. First, being a very dynamic project, it is quite possible that

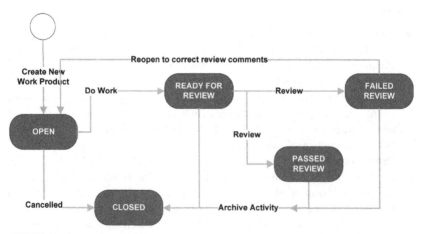

FIGURE 60   A simple workflow

somebody will decide the work product is no longer needed and so the workflow can be closed down. Alternatively, a team member can begin the activity needed to complete the work product. This could be coding, writing, testing, or any of the myriad of team activities. When this is completed, the team member marks the work product as "Ready for Review." Somebody now needs to pick up this work product and review it for correctness.

The review process places the work product into one of two states. Either the work product passes review or it fails review. A failed review leaves the work product in a state of Failed Review. The original team member can then pick up this work product to make changes to it. This pushes the work product back into the original state of Open. The process begins again. If the work product passes review it can go on to be delivered to the customer (internal or external).

What we have here is a minimal set of states and transitions that describe any team activity and review.

17.2.3   Common Information

The analytics workflows are actually very similar and have a lot of descriptive information in common. This descriptive information is needed when the work product is created, when it is worked on, and when it is reviewed. Some typically useful information to track includes the following.

- **Creating the work product:** This is the initial registration of the work product in the workflow tracking system.
  - The customer who requested this work product. This facilitates rapid interaction with the customer and allows themes to emerge.
  - The project work stream that will use the work product.
  - When the work product was requested.
  - The UID of the work product.
  - Which team member is assigned to complete the work product.
- **Completing the work product:** This is the activity of doing the actual work on the work product. Keeping with the Guerrilla Analytics principles, interruptions to doing actual work should be minimized. That said, it is useful to track the following information while completing a work product.
  - Any helpful comments on lessons learned, exceptions, and other context that would help somebody else understand the work product. For example, in a modeling activity, a team member should note their observations about the data and their rationale for choosing a particular model. This is helpful if the original executing team member is no longer on the team or is not available.
  - Any conversations with the customer that helped shape or change the work product as originally described. This is useful if particular design decisions and interpretations of outputs are questioned in the future.
- **Review of the work product:** This is the activity of reviewing the completed work product. Here it is important to capture.

- Who reviewed the work product. This person is different from the work product executor.
- When the reviewer did their review.
- Any comments and feedback on the work product. It is important to capture this information so the evolution of the work product can be understood and also so that junior team members have a record they can refer back to and learn from.

The information above greatly helps in tracking and understanding a work product as well as in any handover of work to other team members.

Given that there are differences between the three types of analytics workflow (data tracking, work products, and build activities), so there are some differences in the information that should be captured about those workflows.

17.2.4   Specific Information for Data Receipt and Load

With Data Receipt and Load, you should track as much of the following key information as possible.

- **Data description:** A short description of the data and any issues reported at delivery time. Some examples include the source system the data came from, the purpose of the data and any known issues or limitations of the data reported by the provider.
- **Delivery details:**
  - Who delivered the data to the team and who in the team received the data? This helps if there are follow-up questions about the data.
  - When did this happen?
  - Any associated communications around the data delivery.
- **Data storage and Load:**
  - Where was the data stored on the file system?
  - Where was the data loaded to in the DME? When loading data files into the DME, you can enforce that the data UID is first in the dataset name. This ensures all raw data list sequentially in the DME and aids in referencing back to the workflow management system.
  - Any issues encountered during data load.
- **Related work:** A link to the work product UID where checksums and other related data tests were performed.

17.2.5   Specific Information for Builds

Build workflows are closest to traditional software development efforts. As such they benefit from incorporating information such as:

- **Bug tracking:** A Bug ID from a bug tracking system when a work product involves fixing a bug.

- **Version control:** A version name and number of the build against which a work product is being applied.
- **Related development:** A link to any associated test scripts and code files.
- **Change control:** Details of the changes requested and features implemented in a particular build version. This aligns expectations as to when new and updated build datasets will be available.

Again, this tracking information is far from the detail offered and used with traditional software engineering projects. Remember, you are not in a traditional software engineering project. You are producing a data build, not a data warehouse and you need to do that in a Guerrilla Analytics environment. What I have listed here is the bare minimum you need to track to get the maximum improvement in your team's resilience to disruptions.

17.3   LEVELS OF REVIEW

A key team activity is to review one another's work. The high level example of workflow from Figure 60 shows only one level of review. In reality there is often a need for two levels of review in analytics projects. This is especially the case for very high profile work products such as reports.

Peer review is where team members review one another's work. Peer review is typically quite technical. It helps identify errors in analytics code or errors in an analytics approach. It also helps more junior team members benefit from the experience and coaching of more experienced team members.

Supervisor review is where an activity is given a second check usually at a higher and less technical level than a peer review. Supervisor reviews focus on management concerns. That is, whether the work product meets customer requirements, whether it complies with the team's processes, and whether data provenance is preserved.

The high-level workflow described by Figure 60 has only one level of review for simplicity. Adding supervisor review would be straightforward. The amount of required review will depend on the importance of the work product.

War Story 16: Team Spirit

Dave was brought into a fairly broken and distressed team on a very high-pressure project. Team members were disconnected from the customer and morale was very low. Being a Guerrilla Analyst, Dave's initial objective was to get team processes in order so he could achieve data provenance and better coordinate the team.

He started by introducing the practice tips and processes you have been reading about throughout this book. However, from the start there was resistance from some team members. As a new manager of the team there was suspicion of his "new rules." To the team they probably seemed whimsical and unnecessary. "Put all my data here and name it this way? Who is this guy?!." Of course they were not in the project steering meetings where Dave was getting an earful about the lack of coordination and quality in the team and how he had better get to grips with his new role and fix it fast.

Dave began by reviewing work products himself so he could get a handle on the project, the data, and whether the team was doing things in a uniform way as required. In the early days, there was lots of feedback and work products went through several iterations until they met Dave's bar of data provenance. This of course wasn't sustainable with 10 direct reports – he was going to need to delegate these reviews. Also, the team was going to need to understand why they had these rules and processes and follow them because it was the right thing to do.

Dave identified the senior analysts in the team and took them aside individually. He explained how they were role models for the junior team members and how their expertise was important to the success of the project. All expressed a desire to grow and agreed that coaching others and imparting their wisdom was an important part of that growth. Dave then assigned them as first-level reviewers of work products. Anybody creating a work product had to consult with senior team members to find a suitable reviewer who was free. The result was apparent within days. Suddenly, when confronted with a mess of code in many locations, disappearing data, undocumented work products, etc., team members began to understand the importance of the simple rules, conventions, and processes. Reviewers understood how frustrating it was when every one of their reviews began with a long walk-through of a work product and all its unique and ad-hoc nuances. Equally, reviewees would be proud to pass a review from a senior they admired and always strived to get their work product through on the first attempt. Team spirit and data provenance improved and the team was freed up to start adding real value to the project instead of chasing their own tails.

17.4 LINKING WORK PRODUCTS

You have seen how many of the team's work products are associated with one another or follow on from one another in some way. For example, a work product involving checksums of data is obviously associated with the work product that involved logging and loading that data into the DME. Any general work product may be a follow-on or tangent from a previous work product. It is important to be able to capture these linkages as it again helps track and understand the history of a work product as well as identifying customers and team members who were previously associated with a related work product. Since all work products have a UID, linking is simply a matter of listing a work product's linked UIDs and the reason for their linkage. Here are some examples.

- This data test is linked to the follow data import UID.
- This build feature is a fix of the bug with the UID 516 and updates the feature implemented under UID 389.
- This work product is UID 658 and is a report that uses a customer list loaded under UID 380.

17.5   CLASSIFYING WORK PRODUCTS

There are various ways that work products can be classified depending on project needs. I have found the following classifications helpful.

- Be able to distinguish work products by whether they are for internal or external delivery. Customer work products are always more sensitive than ones delivered only to the analytics team.
- Be able to identify work products that have gone into reporting and the particular report they were used in. This is because these work products are particularly sensitive. Reporting and the challenges of data provenance are discussed in detail in a chapter Chapter 10.
- On larger projects, it may be helpful to classify work products by their project work stream.

17.6   GRANULARITY

Probably the biggest decision you will face when putting workflow management into practice is the level of granularity at which you describe the three workflow types. Granularity refers to the number of discrete states and activities that the workflow tracks. The simple analytics workflows put forward in this chapter have the minimal number of states I have found necessary in analytics projects. Those projects have ranged from 3 to 12 team members with local and off-shore resources. These workflows balance the time it takes for the team to update the workflow management system with the desire to coordinate and report on team activities in detail.

Some workflow management software will divide a work product into finer grain states such as "Opened," "Reopened," "In progress," "On hold," "In Review," "Ready for Delivery," etc. with the aim of tracking hours spent in each activity. Think carefully before doing anything more granular than the workflows described in this chapter as maintenance of the work product states in the workflow management software is an administrative overhead on the team. Heavy processes in a Guerrilla Analytics environment are doomed to fail.

17.7   WHEN TO USE WORKFLOW MANAGEMENT

The following considerations should influence your decision to use workflow management in your team and the type of workflow management to implement.

- **Team size:** Once a team has more than about three members, it quickly becomes difficult to have a view of what the team is doing. Which work products are being worked on? Who is doing the work? Is everything being reviewed? Has every customer request been picked up by somebody? What's the next thing I need to do? If a team is going to be of even a moderate size, consider using some basic workflow management – even if that is a simple spreadsheet shared by the team.

- **Project dynamism:** If the project is very dynamic with many work products ongoing then requests for work can get overlooked. A workflow management solution can help capture everything that the team must do, even if they are too overloaded to begin that work immediately.
- **Team experience:** If the team has relatively inexperienced members, their work should be reviewed more thoroughly than other team members. Tracking these reviews and capturing feedback for the benefit of inexperienced team members is best done in a workflow management process.
- **Life of project:** If a project is going to last more than 6 to 8 weeks then two factors come into play. It is more likely that the team composition will change both on the analytics and customer side. This means that the history of past work products could be lost. Twelve weeks later, how many of the team will remember why the build does not have a particular feature that seems obvious and necessary? A workflow management system captures the conversations and project folklore so that the context of past decisions and work products can be retrieved. Second, handovers between team members are greatly facilitated if the leaving team members can simply look up all the work products they produced.
- **Importance of traceability:** In some types of project, it is imperative that every piece of work and the team members associated with it can be tracked. Any work that contributes to legal cases, for example, must be completely traceable. In these types of project, workflow management is very beneficial.
- **Geographically dispersed teams:** Geographically dispersed teams are common in today's globalized world. Off-shoring, near shoring, and customers with operations in a variety of locations can all cause teams to be physically dispersed. A workflow management tool helps these teams coordinate. It works almost like a notice board where teams can communicate and coordinate their tasks with one another even though they might have little overlap in their working hours.

Clearly these considerations will influence the sophistication of workflow management you put in place. Guerrilla Analytics projects have used everything from simple spreadsheets to full-blown web-based applications as project needs dictate.

17.8 WRAP UP

This chapter has discussed workflow management for Guerrilla Analytics. Having read this chapter, you should now understand.

- What is workflow management?
- What are the types of workflow management needed in Guerrilla Analytics?
- A common high-level workflow that describes all Guerrilla Analytics activities.

- The common information that should be tracked in workflow management for Guerrilla Analytics.
- Tracking information that is particular to each of the workflow types.
- Work product review and how this can be implemented with one or more levels of review.
- The concept of linking work products and why this is often useful.
- Some common classifications of work products.
- The factors that influence a decision to use workflow management in a Guerrilla Analytics project.

Chapter 18

Technology

18.1 ANALYTICS CAPABILITIES

There are some technologies that are absolutely essential to a successful Guerrilla Analytics team and in addition some secondary technologies that are highly desirable, if time, resources, and circumstances permit. The essential technologies are as follows.

- **Data Manipulation Environment (DME):** This book has referenced a DME throughout. The DME is some place to store and manipulate data. This may be a domain-specific DME such as the R environment (Crawley, 2007) or may be a more generic relational or NoSQL database. The choice between relational and NoSQL will depend on the type of data analyzed. Sadalage and Fowler (2012) give a good overview of NoSQL technologies.
- **Source code control:** Source code control provides the ability to track the version history of program code, roll back to previous versions of work, and highlight changes made to code between versions. Specific software is not strictly necessary for simple version control, and appropriate Guerrilla Analytics approaches to simple version control have been discussed in earlier chapters. That said, source control tools such as Git (Loeliger and McCullough, 2012) make the management of versions of code much easier.
- **A command line:** A command line (sometimes interchangeably called a shell or terminal) is a window where a user can type commands to interact directly with files stored on the underlying operating system. Because the command line is programmable and lightweight, it can be used to explore and interact with large data files on the file system. This is useful for the "quick and dirty" data profiling and manipulation without the overhead of loading all the data into a heavy weight DME. This helps the Guerrilla Analyst under time constraints. Command lines are also useful in the automation and scheduling of other analytics operations, as is typical when a combination of tools and techniques are brought to bear on a problem.
- **A high-level scripting language:** This is a programming language that is abstracted away from the details of the particular computer and operating system. This makes programs quick to develop and easy to understand.

These languages are great for stitching together analytics stages and activities. Typical popular languages include Python (Lutz, 2009), Perl (Christiansen et al., 2000), and PHP (Tatroe and Lerdorf, 2002).

- **Visualization/presentation:** The team needs to have some methods for visualizing data and presenting results back to the customer. Visualization can take a variety of forms from simple charts within spreadsheets through to web applications hosting sophisticated interactive dashboards.
- **A build tool:** A build tool is a tool for automating the configuration of an environment and the execution of program code in that environment, as well as automating various repetitive tasks the team needs to perform. A build tool could automate tasks such as running all analytics build code, archiving data, and creating the setup on the file system and DME for a new work product.
- **Access to the Internet:** If a team is working with data that is online such as social media data, data on web pages, or open datasets, then some form of Internet access is required. Data security concerns often limit this access in analytics projects but there are ways to provide Internet access for the team while mitigating these concerns.
- **Encryption:** Data security is often important in projects. In very fast-paced Guerrilla Analytics projects, good quality encryption software should be available to the team to mitigate risk of data loss during transfer of data to the team and during delivery of results back to the customer.
- **Code libraries for data wrangling:** Guerrilla Analytics involves an incredibly wide range of data manipulation activities on diverse datasets. There are plenty of tools to help with the most common problems. There may be some tools that evolve from within the team because of recurring project needs. Whether you buy your data wrangling functionality or write it in-house, make sure it is easily available to all teams with clearly labeled versions for data provenance.
- **Code libraries for machine learning and statistics:** If your Guerrilla Analytics team intends to do even the most basic descriptive statistics, then some type of code libraries for statistics and machine learning will be required. Nobody should be wasting time writing their own histogram plotting function, and few people are qualified to write their own neural network library. Source these libraries from third parties and make them available to the team.

In addition to these core technologies, life is made a lot easier and even more efficient for a Guerrilla Analytics team, if they have the following secondary technologies at their disposal.

- **A workflow management tool**: There is a lot going on in a busy Guerrilla Analytics project full of disruptions. Workflow management helps track team activities in the Guerrilla Analytics workflow, bugs, and work product reviews.

- **Automated code documentation tools:** Documentation is time-consuming but very necessary. These tools allow the team to automatically generate and publish presentation quality documentation directly from the team code base.
- **Virtual machine capabilities:** Virtual machines allow rapid deployment of standard analytical tools to new projects, prototyping, and testing in a safe sandboxed environment. When an analytics stack is agreed, this can be maintained as a virtual machine image that can be quickly booted up for new projects, saving the team's precious time in standing up their analytics environment.

The following sections now look at each of these technologies in more detail.

18.2   DATA MANIPULATION ENVIRONMENT

As discussed throughout this book, a DME is an absolute necessity for a Guerrilla Analytics team. A DME is simply "some place" where data can be stored, transformed, profiled, and manipulated with program code.

Two typical approaches to a DME environment exist. There is what is referred to as domain-specific tools. These are both dedicated data storage and data manipulation language all packaged together. Examples of this are the R environment (Crawley, 2007) and the Pandas environment (McKinney, 2012). Alternatively, there are generic databases that can be used and enhanced for analytics. Any relational or NoSQL database can serve this purpose. Analysts then interact with the database using some other external programming language or data manipulation languages such as SQL, SPARQL, and XQuery.

18.3   SOURCE CODE CONTROL

At its simplest, source code control is technology that manages and tracks changes to program code, configurations, and documentation. In any Guerrilla Analytics project, the code, documentation, and configuration are changed many times and these changes will be made by more than one analyst. Source code control software keeps track of these changes in multiple versions of program code. It tracks every change that team members make to code, and can roll back to earlier versions of code. More advanced use allows a team member to take an experimental copy of code and try some development "in parallel" to the team before merging their changes back into the team's code. This is critical for the Guerrilla Analyst who is dealing with changing requirements. Specific versions of files can be "tagged" and released as versions to the customer. If there are bugs or questions about older work products delivered to the customer, the version control system lets you roll back and inspect the history of changes to a particular version of a work product.

The availability of version control software makes Guerrilla Analytics so much easier. Work products can be tagged so that older versions can be recovered and rerun. Team members working on the same code base can coordinate better with one another. Individual changes to code can be tracked and traced back to a team member.

18.3.1   Level of Training and Expertise

Source code control is a significant subfield of software engineering. Things can get quite complex on large software projects. A team may have several released and maintained versions of their code base with associated bugs and fixes in each version. Team members will be producing code for interfaces, testing, configuration, as well as core functionality. This is more than is needed in Guerrilla Analytics, so a judgment call must be made on the source code control features that your team will use and the associated training required.

18.4   ACCESS TO THE COMMAND LINE

As mentioned earlier in this chapter, a command line (sometimes interchangeably called a shell or terminal) is a window where a user can type commands to interact directly with files and the underlying operating system. Because command lines are programmable, very lightweight, and efficient, and have been around for a very long time, they typically have a wide range of useful commands available. These commands expose functionality that would be very cumbersome or simply not possible in a graphical windowed environment.

Consider this problem. You receive hundreds of large text files containing phone call data. This data describes a "from" dialing number and a "to" dialed number. These files are scattered in an arbitrary folder tree, so some are one folder deep while others are up to five folders deep. There is no regular pattern to this folder structure. Now, suppose you are asked to quickly summarize all phone numbers in all data files, and determine if any international calls were made. How would you go about this? Here are some of the approaches I've seen analysts undertake.

- Begin trying to open the files in a text editor and search for phone numbers with the editor's "find" command. This is time-consuming, error prone, and many of the files will not open in a text editor because they are too large.
- Begin loading the text files into a DME. This is a bit better since the analyst at least realizes they are dealing with a data problem. But it's overkill. We're really just facing a simple search problem here and do not need the data manipulations that a DME provides.
- Begin writing a script in a language like Python (Lutz, 2009) so you can walk through all the files in the folder tree and use a regular expression to identify phone numbers.

The third approach is much better! This is a Guerrilla Analytics approach because it is quick and simple. But do we really need to fire up a script in a high-level programming language (assuming an interpreter is available for that language in the constrained Guerrilla Analytics environment)?

There is a better solution. The command line has a rich variety of tools available for iterating through files, editing them, finding patterns, and chaining these commands together. Here are some of the things you can do.

- **Edit large text files:** Find and replace arbitrary text in very large files. Example tools for this are *sed* and *awk* (Dougherty and Robbins, 1997).
- **Find patterns:** Find and filter on text patterns using regular expressions. An example tool is *grep* (Bambenek and Klus, 2009).
- **Examine the beginning or the end of a file:** Return a specified number of lines from the start or the end of a file. Example tools are *head* and *tail*.
- **Count the number of words and lines in a file.** An example tool is *wc*.
- **Sort data files.** An example tool is the aptly named *sort*.
- **Find duplicate rows in a file.** The tool *uniq* comes in very useful.
- **Append files:** Join one or more files together end to end. An example tool is *cat*.
- **Strip a column of data out of a file.** An example tool is *cut*.
- **Join files horizontally:** This is the horizontal equivalent of vertically appending files. An example command is *paste*.
- **Download web pages:** The "wget" command allows you to download web pages and follow hyperlinks.
- **Schedule tasks:** "cron" allows you to schedule when some other program runs. This is helpful when some time-consuming or intensive processes need to be set up to run over night.
- **List files and directories:** Commands such as "ls" and "find" allow us to return all files that match names patterns in some or all of a folder tree.
- **Chain together commands.** With "pipes" you can have one command run and then "pipe" its output into the input of another command.

The phone number problem could be solved at the command line with a strategy like the following.

- Iterate through all data files in the folder tree using a directory listing command.
- Search each file for text patterns that look like a phone number using "grep" and redirect these in a single output file that lists the data file name and phone number text using "sed."
- When finished, count the number of *international* phone numbers in the output file using another "grep."

Availability of a command line is simply essential for many Guerrilla Analytics tasks.

18.5   HIGH-LEVEL SCRIPTING LANGUAGE

Command-line scripts are quick and dirty. While they can be fully functional programs in their own right, sometimes you want the extra features and ease of use of a high-level scripting language. This is a programming language that is abstracted away from the details of the computer and operating system. It makes programs quick to develop and easy to understand. These languages are great for stitching together analytics activities. For example, you may want logging, debugging, and the use of third-party libraries for tasks such as parsing XML files and converting PDF files into text.

18.5.1   Which Language to Use?

There are plenty of scripting languages to choose from: Perl (Christiansen et al., 2000), PHP (Tatroe and Lerdorf, 2002), and Python (Lutz, 2009) are some examples. The choice of language should consider the following factors.

- **DME connectivity:** The language should be able to connect to the DMEs your team uses, pull data out of them, or write data into them.
- **Parse file formats:** The language should be able to interact with a range of file formats such as HTML, XML, PDF, email archives, CSV, and office applications. Data often comes in these formats and you want to avail of all the hard work that has been done to usefully expose these data formats with scripting language libraries.
- **Software engineering features:** Many high-level scripts become full-fledged project tools in their own right. It then becomes important that they have associated language features such as logging, testing harnesses, and error trapping for example.

18.6   VISUALIZATION

There is not much point in doing analytics work if you cannot then present your findings. While a simple dataset is sometimes a sufficient medium for communicating a result, in many cases something more sophisticated is required.

At a basic level, a team should have spreadsheet software available. This allows a team to use a spreadsheet's plotting capabilities to visualize data from the DME. Ideally the spreadsheet can connect to the DME to pull datasets out of it.

One of the problems with spreadsheets is that without some significant effort from the analyst, they allow the underlying data to be modified and potentially broken or corrupted. This is a problem for the Guerrilla Analytics who wishes to maintain data provenance. However, some customers want to be able to interact with their data and cut it in various ways to understand it. In these scenarios, it is beneficial to have a dashboarding tool available to rapid prototype visualizations that customers can interact with. Some tools allow dashboards to be packaged up with their data and delivered to a user who does not have access to the DME. This is helpful because it effectively gives your user the visualization flexibility of a spreadsheet, but shields the user from the complexity of the underlying data.

Spreadsheets and dashboards are limited in size to the amount of data that the end user's machine can process. The most flexible and scalable approach to visualization is to host visualizations in web applications. A server does the heavy lifting and preparation of data in response to the user's interactions, and presents the results in lightweight web pages that the user can consume with nothing more than a modern web browser.

18.7   BUILD TOOL

You have seen how Guerrilla Analytics work products frequently require executing several program code files, perhaps in a variety of programming languages. Some of these code files may be command-line scripts. Some may be written in scripting languages. Some may be query files that manipulate data in a DME. In addition to executing code in some defined order, the team will often want to move things around on a file system, perhaps tear down databases, and rebuild them. Perhaps applications need to be deployed on a web server. You probably want to generate your documentation using the tools we described earlier in this chapter to save precious time. There are two problems here. Mundane and repetitive tasks such as moving files around are error prone and do not add direct value. Second, the inevitable variety of tools the team brings to bear on a problem each have their own options, switches, and configurations. Figure 61 shows an example of the command-line options available to the Microsoft SQL Server sqlcmd utility. A Guerrilla Analytics team is too busy to have to remember and retype this information every time they execute some code.

Build tools are used for automating all of these varied types of repetitive and error prone tasks that an analyst needs to do, and abstracting away complex commands that are tiresome to repeatedly type out.

18.8   ACCESS TO THE INTERNET

Access to the Internet may seem like an obvious necessity. However, many analytics environments deny access to the Internet because of perceptions around security of data. Given the current emphasis on unstructured data from social media and the increasing availability of open datasets, it is becoming increasingly important that data analysts can access websites with appropriate web scraping tools. Additionally, most software documentation is hosted online for search by users.

You need to find a setup that allows your team to access the Internet in a secure way with minimal disruption to their normal work flow.

18.9   ENCRYPTION

Data will need to leave the Guerrilla Analytics team, as work products and data will need to be transferred to the team (physically or electronically) when provided by a customer. Losing this data to a third party can have extremely serious consequences for the customer and for the analytics team. To protect data, high-quality encryption software should be available to every team member.

```
sqlcmd
    -a packet_size
    -A (dedicated administrator connection)
    -b (terminate batch job if there is an error)
    -c batch_terminator
    -C (trust the server certificate)
    -d db_name
    -e (echo input)
    -E (use trusted connection)
    -f codepage | i:codepage[,o:codepage] |
o:codepage[,i:codepage]
    -h rows_per_header
    -H workstation_name
    -i input_file
    -I (enable quoted identifiers)
    -k[1 | 2] (remove or replace control characters)
    -K application_intent
    -l login_timeout
    -L[c] (list servers, optional clean output)
    -m error_level
    -M multisubnet_failover
    -N (encrypt connection)
    -o output_file
    -p[1] (print statistics, optional colon format)
    -P password
    -q "cmdline query"
    -Q "cmdline query" (and exit)
    -r[0 | 1] (msgs to stderr)
    -R (use client regional settings)
    -s col_separator
    -S [protocol:]server[\instance_name][,port]
    -t query_timeout
    -u (unicode output file)
    -U login_id
    -v var = "value"
    -V error_severity_level
    -w column_width
    -W (remove trailing spaces)
    -x (disable variable substitution)
    -X[1] (disable commands, startup script,
environment variables and optional exit)
    -y variable_length_type_display_width
    -Y fixed_length_type_display_width
    -z new_password
    -Z new_password (and exit)
```

FIGURE 61   Example arguments for a command-line tool

Agree to an appropriate encryption method and an encryption software, and make this easily available to the team. Remember, a team in a dynamic Guerrilla Analytics project will need to quickly package up work products and deliver them. Encrypting these work products should be one click away so that encryption is not a disruption to work and efficiency.

If data is being transported around on portable media, there is a danger that the media and the data contained on it could get lost. Make sure the team has a process for:

- Encrypting media.
- Wiping data from media as soon as the data has been stored in a secure environment.
- Controlling storage of unused media so that you know which media are in the field and who is responsible for them.

18.10 CODE LIBRARIES FOR DATA WRANGLING

There are many data formats out there. Every web page is different. Much data is still provided in spreadsheets or PDF documents with an endless variety of formatting and layouts. It is important that the team's scripting language and DME are supported by the right libraries to handle these formats.

When evaluating a scripting language and DME for a team, consider these typical functionalities.

- Ability to convert PDF files into structured text.
- Ability to programmatically navigate HTML, XML, JSON, PDFs, office documents, and other common file formats.
- Ability to handle image formats, resizing, and converting them between different formats.
- Availability of other supporting software engineering functionality such as logging services and testing harnesses.
- Overlap with other technology needs such as visualization and machine learning.

18.11 MACHINE LEARNING AND STATISTICS LIBRARIES

Very often, getting the data into shape and doing some descriptive statistics and visualization are enough to complete a Guerrilla Analytics job. However, you may sometimes need to go further and do statistical modeling such as regression, decision trees, and clustering. You may also need to do machine learning such as association rule mining, neural networks, or Bayesian networks. These types of algorithms are difficult to write correctly and to scale. Plenty of others have done this work before anyway.

The team should have some machine learning and statistics libraries available so they can do this more advanced data science. Perhaps this capability is in a dedicated domain language such as the R environment (Crawley, 2007) or you may opt for some combination of libraries in a general programming language such as the Pandas environment has done with the Python language (McKinney, 2012).

18.12 CENTRALIZED AND CONTROLLED FILE SYSTEM

It is essential to have a centralized file server location where all projects are stored. This facilitates archiving older projects and rolling onto new projects. The process of starting up new project folders in this location should be controlled so that the project folder area does not become a chaotic mess.

We saw in an earlier chapter how all data gets stored in one folder location without trying to create complex folder structures. These confuse users and make it difficult to find data. The same principle applies with project folders. Give every project an ID and label, and name its folder with that ID and label. This saves the Guerrilla Analytics team precious time when leveraging existing knowledge and assets from previous projects.

18.13 ADDITIONAL TECHNOLOGY CAPABILITIES

Although the key capabilities might seem extensive, it is quite possible to achieve them with 5–10 pieces of software and access to a command line. Even the most dynamic environments can usually provide these key capabilities. There are some further secondary capabilities that are very helpful but that usually require installation of more niche software. These capabilities are described in this section. If your customer's analytics environment is flexible or you are working from your team's home environment, then get these tools in place.

18.13.1 Workflow Management

Workflow management is about controlling and tracking the team's activities, and the order in which those activities happen. Workflow management was discussed in the chapter on process.

Workflows can quickly become complex, and tracking them for many team members simultaneously is beyond the capability of a spreadsheet. Workflow management tools take care of this. You can specify the types of activities the team engages in, the states those activities can be in, and the transitions between each of those states. While there are no dedicated Guerrilla Analytics workflow trackers, you can choose one of the existing highly customizable software engineering tools and customize it for your team's analytics workflows (Doar, 2011).

18.13.2 Automated Code Documentation

Most work products require some type of code documentation. Think how hard it can be to understand your own code when you return to it after several months. Now imagine what that is like for a customer or another team that is inheriting your work. Guerrilla Analytics focuses on minimizing time wasted in understanding work products during handovers and reviews. Having well-documented code helps with this.

There are two basic aspects to code documentation. The first is some overall documentation that describes any configuration and operation of the code or application, sources of data, business rules, and outputs. The second aspect is documentation of the actual program code files to explain particularly complex pieces of program code, and give an overview of what a code file does.

18.13.2.1   Overall Documentation

This documentation is separate from the technical analytics work, but must be written and maintained in sync with the analytics work. For example, your final report will document data sources, business rules, and key assumptions in your analysis. So while the majority of this documentation is "business level," it must also relate to the latest state and outputs of the technical analytics work. Maintaining this type of documentation is made much easier if the documentation is written in a file format that can be usefully put in source code control alongside the analytics code and outputs. By "usefully" I mean that it is in some type of plain text format that can be compared between versions as opposed to binary document formats.

The obvious solution here is to write documentation in plain text. But plain text is not very pretty and we might be giving documentation to a customer or stakeholder. A great candidate for professional looking documentation that can be maintained in source code control is Markdown (Gruber, 2004). Markdown allows one to create documentation in a format that is easily readable (plain text), and then convert that documentation to a multitude of formats such as HTML and Microsoft Word. This has two advantages. First, the team can maintain documentation in source code control, close to their analytics work with minimal disruption. Second, you can build the documentation into a presentation output format when required, by applying whatever style is most appropriate. Need all headings to be dark blue? Simply change one line of the configuration file. Need all paragraphs to have 1.5-line spacing? Simply change another line of the configuration file.

18.13.2.2   Code Documentation

It is one thing to have overall documentation of the project. This is useful for managers and customers who want to understand the project at a business level. However, the data analysts also need documentation at their level – down in the code files they write and the analytics they produce. When documenting code, some teams make the mistake of keeping separate documentation that sits alongside the code files. This just does not work in practice. It breaks that fundamental Guerrilla Analytics principle of keeping analysts close to their work.

If the team have to step out of code into some separate parallel documentation, you will find that they forget to document or do not bother. Documentation then goes out of date and is effectively useless.

Code should be documented using code comments that sit right beside the program code that the comments describe. This is still a little problematic. It is very difficult to get an overview of the code base so that you can find a particular functionality or know where to get stuck in to understanding the code. This is where automatic code documentation tools such as Javadoc and Doxygen (van Heesch, 1997) excel. These tools read code comments that are tagged in a particular way, extract those comments, and automatically generate documentation in a variety of output formats. As well as producing high-quality code documentation the use of these tools encourages uniformity in code commenting styles – a further time saver for the Guerrilla Analyst.

18.14   WRAP UP

This chapter described the technology needed to enable a Guerrilla Analytics team. The chapter was not prescriptive about particular technologies as these improve and evolve all the time. Instead, this chapter focused on what a Guerrilla Analytics team needs to be able to do with data and the associated technology choices to enable this. After reading this chapter, you should now understand the following.

- **Core capabilities:** There are some essential technological capabilities to make available to the Guerrilla Analytics team. Without these, a team will struggle to be effective in a dynamic project with frequent disruptions. The core capabilities covered the following:
  - **DME:** Provide a DME. You may need to consider domain-specific options or generic databases. You will also need to consider the type of data modeling such as relational and NoSQL.
  - **Source code version control:** The team needs to be able to track revisions to their code, tag versions of their code, and roll back to previous versions of the code. There are many technologies to choose from, but only a subset of functionality is required for the vast majority of data analytics projects.
  - **Access to a command line**: The command line allows powerful automation of data analytics tasks that could not be achieved in a point-and-click windowed environment, and is also useful for quick and dirty analyses without a heavyweight DME. There are a small number of commands the team should be aware of for data analytics. Choose one type of command line that has these minimum capabilities.
  - **High-level scripting language:** Make a scripting language available for quickly writing short programs that are more sophisticated than a command line script and for gluing together various analytics components.

- **Visualization:** Make sure there is a method for presenting data visually. There are several options that vary in sophistication. Simple charts within spreadsheets are widely available and well-understood. Dashboards are more sophisticated but also more expensive, and require specialist skills. Web applications are the most flexible and scalable but require some complex technology decisions, as well as a significant upskilling of an analytics team.
- **Encryption:** Make sure the team has software encryption readily available to them and ensure they know how to use it consistently as a team. Put in place a process for controlling external media and wiping its contents as soon as data has been delivered.
- **Common code libraries:** Establish common code libraries for data wrangling and for machine learning. Make these libraries available in a central location with clearly documented versions.
- **File system:** Have a central file server where all projects are located and where all data is stored.
- **Additional capabilities:** There are also some additional secondary capabilities that are very beneficial but perhaps a little more difficult to introduce into the usual Guerrilla Analytics environment. The additional capabilities that are good to have are as follows.
  - **Workflow management software:** This helps coordinate what the team is doing, work products that have been delivered, and data that has been received.
  - **Automated code documentation:** This saves time producing reports and descriptions of analyses and code.

Chapter 19

Closing Remarks

19.1   WHAT WAS THIS BOOK ABOUT?

Certain types of analytics projects are particularly difficult because they are very dynamic and yet the team is highly constrained. They are dynamic because data and requirements are changing often. They are constrained by tight time-lines, limited tooling, and the expectation of testable, traceable analytics out-puts. These projects are Guerrilla Analytics projects and their typical workflow is illustrated in Figure 62.

It turns out that much of the confusion, inefficiency, chaos, and frustration of these analytics projects is due to a lack of data provenance. The Guerrilla Analytics principles are a set of guidelines for maintaining data provenance despite the many disruptions of a Guerrilla Analytics project. The principles are as follows.

- **Principle 1:** Space is cheap, confusion is expensive.
- **Principle 2:** Prefer simple, visual project structures over heavily document-ed and project-specific rules.
- **Principle 3:** Prefer automation with program code over manual graphical methods.
- **Principle 4:** Maintain a link between data on the file system, data in the analytics environment, and data in work products.
- **Principle 5:** Version control changes to data and program code.
- **Principle 6:** Consolidate team knowledge in version-controlled analytics builds.
- **Principle 7:** Prefer analytics code that runs from start to finish.

You may have picked up this book for several reasons. Perhaps you were struggling with the complexity of your analytics projects. Or, you had become demoralized by analytics chaos and were looking for a better way to produce insights from data. Perhaps you wanted a straight-forward perspective on how to approach analytics work with real-world data on real-world projects.

Whatever the reason, hopefully you have found this book to be a useful reference as you work in and manage teams in any stage of the Guerrilla Ana-lytics workflow. The seven Guerrilla Analytics principles above lead to almost 100 practice tips that span the entire Guerrilla Analytics workflow. These can be used as and when needed – different tips will come in handy on different

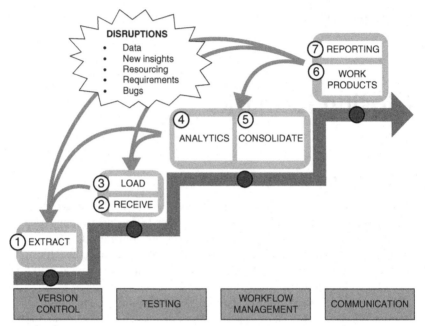

FIGURE 62   **The Guerrilla Analytics workflow**

projects – and all have been designed to help make your projects run more efficiently and provide you with better results.

For those with a strategic remit, the book also covered the people, process, and technology needed to build a Guerrilla Analytics capability. There is a comprehensive list of skill sets that you should cover in your team if you want to get the most out of your Guerrilla Analytics projects. We also discussed the workflow management needed to manage teams and the technology that you should provide to make the most of their skills.

19.2   NEXT STEPS FOR GUERRILLA ANALYTICS

This book has covered much of what I have learned and implemented over the past 10 years in analytics research, pre-sales, and professional services. In that time, there has been a phenomenal growth in the data volumes and data variety produced around the globe as well as amazing innovations in the technology to do new (and old) kinds of data analytics. Despite or perhaps because of these changes, it still remains complex and difficult to do data analytics. If anything, the number of moving parts on an analytics project has increased. There are more types of data manipulation environment, programming languages, visualizations, web frameworks, etc. than ever before. As long as this is the case, and as long as poorly understood data exists then the Guerrilla Analytics principles will always be required. Here are my thoughts on some of the priorities for Guerrilla Analytics in the coming years.

19.2.1   Better Education in Software Engineering

If there were one course of study that would produce a better Guerrilla Analyst who is ready to work on real-world data, it would probably be software engineering. Many Guerrilla Analytics challenges have already been encountered in a different guise in software engineering. Version control, migration of data, data quality, testing, workflow tracking are well understood and supported by the tools and training of software engineering. Analytics has not yet reached that level of maturity. The approaches in this book are the bare minimum you should do to better control disruptions in the typical analytics project. Much more thinking, training, and tooling needs to be devoted to the equivalent of software engineering for Guerrilla Analytics and analytics in general.

19.2.2   Better Analytics Workflows

Many of the challenges in Guerrilla Analytics are due to the wide variety of activities and tools required to extract insight from ever-changing data. A significant proportion of this book was devoted to overcoming those challenges with existing technology adapted for Guerrilla Analytics and simple conventions to preserve data provenance. This is good but not enough. The analytics workflow needs to be better understood and supported with tools that embrace its dynamism and disruptions. There is a need for better ways to trace data provenance that do not get in the way of doing analytics.

19.2.3   Better Analytics Testing

Data is fundamental to everything that is done in data analytics. In spite of this, the ability to test data and analytics work with powerful tools and well-grounded thinking is almost nonexistent. What is needed is the equivalent of software test frameworks for the five Cs of Completeness, Correctness, Coherence, Consistency, and aCcountability. Yes, these are supported in the fields of data quality and master data management but they do not quite work in the reality of a Guerrilla Analytics project.

19.2.4   What About Big Data?

I have deliberately avoided mentioning Big Data throughout this book. I made this decision because the definition remains muddled and influenced by both technology vendors and by sales pitches. Perhaps that will change in the near future. Nonetheless, there has certainly been a change in the technologies that permit analytics on large volumes and varieties of data. That will not disappear. This begs the question of whether and how Guerrilla Analytics should change to support Big Data. What I suspect will happen is that the convergence of software engineering and analytics will accelerate as more analytics is done on large powerful software platforms, rather than with a mixed bag of tools borrowed from other fields. The principles of Guerrilla Analytics can certainly help with this, as this scale of data also needs to be explored, analyses need to be version controlled and data provenance will remain of primary importance.

19.3 KEEP IN TOUCH

That brings this book to an end. The principles, practice tips, and war stories described in this book are abstracted from many real-world analytics projects. The hope is that my experiences can help you with your analytics projects in consulting, industry, research, or elsewhere. It has certainly helped me clarify and consolidate my own thinking and experiences over the years. I am always happy to answer questions, provide further detail, and receive feedback about this book.

Also, I am always looking for opportunities to help organizations understand their data and find value in it. This may be through both tactical consulting work and the strategic development of Guerrilla Analytics teams and technology. I welcome any opportunities to share ideas and seek out ways to work together.

You can find the latest news on Guerrilla Analytics at my personal website that I set up for this book - www.guerrilla-analytics.net. Please contact me on Twitter @enda_ridge or via email at guerrillaanalytics@gmail.com.

ACKNOWLEDGMENTS

This book would not have happened without my friend and colleague Edward Curry. The early thoughts on formalizing what became Guerrilla Analytics were shaped through many conversations and several conference presentations with Ed. My heartfelt thanks go to Ed for his early encouragement.

Guerrilla Analytics gathers together all my lessons learned in doing data analytics over many years. My industry and research work was not done in isolation. I thank all my colleagues present and past that supported, challenged, and encouraged me and those who were the guinea pigs and contributors to some of what eventually became the principles of Guerrilla Analytics.

I am very grateful to Andrea Dierna, Acquisitions Editor at Elsevier for guiding me through the book proposal, Kaitlin Herbert and Steve Elliot for their project management support throughout, the copyeditors Priya and Ritu, and other Elsevier staff who made this possible.

I wish to thank my parents and family for their support (and home-cooked meals during some of my most productive writing sessions at home in Galway). Finally, a thank you to Sarah, my patient and supportive sounding board whose proof reading provided a different non-data perspective to help round out the book.

Go raibh míle maith agaibh go léir.

Appendix

Data Gymnastics

DATA GYMNASTICS PATTERNS

It is of not much help to say "be good at hacking" or "learn {insert data language of your preference/bias}." I know that whenever I begin to learn a new language, I find it frustrating. I know what I want to do with the data but I lack the vocabulary and the expressiveness in my new language to actually execute what I want to do. The peculiarities of Guerrilla Analytics make it difficult to find advice on what to learn in traditional books on data manipulation.

What follows are the most common patterns your team will encounter time and again in Guerrilla Analytics work. A top performing team will have one or more people who can quickly recognize and execute these patterns in the team's Data Manipulation Environment (DME) of choice.

Pattern 1: Dataset Collections

Data often needs to be sifted through and broken out into different buckets. You may need to track versions of data and versions of analyses. You may need to identify subsets of data.

This pattern means having a method to place certain datasets matching a pattern into a collection so they can be considered together. Some examples include the following.

- Creating views over a subset of relational tables and schemas that match a pattern.
- Moving tables and views between database schemas.
- In a document database (Sadalage and Fowler, 2012), this could mean creating collections and placing documents into these collections depending on certain document properties.
- In a graph database (Sadalage and Fowler, 2012), this may mean labeling nodes and edges so they can be grouped together.

Whatever the DME, the analyst must have a method to form data collections.

DISPARATE DATASETS			
ID	**TRADE_DT**	**VALUE**	**STATUS**
3477	2014-03-16	150,000.00	SETTLE
4598	2014-03-17	45,000.00	SETTLE
4599	2014-03-17	10,015.00	AMEND
5134	2014-03-20	-2500.00	AMEND

ID	**DATE**	**VALUE**	**STATUS**
5670	2014-03-14	99,140	S
7101	2014-03-15	35,500	CCA
7200	2014-03-17	80,000	S

APPENDED DATASETS				
ID	**TRADE_DT**	**DATE**	**VALUE**	**STATUS**
3477	2014-03-16		150,000.00	SETTLE
4598	2014-03-17		45,000.00	SETTLE
4599	2014-03-17		10,015.00	AMEND
5134	2014-03-20		-2500.00	AMEND

ID	**TRADE_DT**	**DATE**	**VALUE**	**STATUS**
5670		2014-03-14	99,140	S
7101		2014-03-15	35,500	CCA
7200		2014-03-17	80,000	S

FIGURE 63   Appending data with common fields

Pattern 2: Append Data Using Common Fields

Data is often broken up into many datasets. For example, log data is often written into daily files. To analyze a year of logs you would have to put all these files together end to end. Occasionally, data needs to be broken into chunks to help it load successfully into the DME and then appended together once safely in the DME.

You need to be able to stick datasets together end to end. What makes this a little more challenging is that the various dataset you are appending may not all have the same fields. Lining up these fields manually in code quickly becomes very cumbersome and error prone. Figure 63 shows a simplified relational database example. On the left are two datasets from two different financial trade systems. You need to append these together so that all common fields line up and the remaining fields are kept in the final appended dataset. One of the datasets has a field called TRADE_DT while in the other it is called DATE. The other fields are common to both datasets although the STATUS field seems to have a different range of values. On the right is the desired result. This result dataset has all the fields of both datasets. Where fields are common (ID, STATUS, and VALUE), they have been lined up. Where fields are different, they have been blanked out in the dataset they do not exist in. There is more work to do of course. TRADE_DT and DATE should now be combined and the coding of STATUS should be unified, for example. However, having the ability to quickly append datasets and not lose information has removed what is normally a cumbersome and error-prone process.

Pattern 3: Map Fields to New Field Names

As discussed already, data can arrive chunked into a number of separate datasets that must be appended together. In addition, these individual datasets may have different names for common fields. For example, a customer identifier field in one dataset may be called "ID" but may be called "CUST_ID" in another

DAY_ID	CUSTOMER	PCH	VAL
3477	2014-03-16	150,000.00	SETTLE
4598	2014-03-17	45,000.00	SETTLE
4599	2014-03-17	10,015.00	AMEND
5134	2014-03-20	-2500.00	AMEND

ORIGINAL DATASET

SOURCE_DATASET	FROM	TO
PURCHASES	DAY_ID	ID
PURCHASES	PCH	PURCHASE
PURCHASES	VAL	VALUE

MAPPING DEFINITION DATASET

ID	CUSTOMER	PURCHASE	VALUE
3477	2014-03-16	150,000.00	SETTLE
4598	2014-03-17	45,000.00	SETTLE
4599	2014-03-17	10,015.00	AMEND
5134	2014-03-20	-2500.00	AMEND

MAPPED DATASET

FIGURE 64 Map fields to new field names

dataset. This quickly becomes difficult when you are faced with a large number of datasets and a large number of differing field names.

Figure 64 illustrates what this looks like. The mapping dataset defines a list of original field names and their target new names in the "FROM" and "TO" fields, respectively. The original dataset is passed through this mapping dataset to give the output at the bottom of the figure. Any fields mentioned in the mapping dataset have now been renamed. Other fields such as "CUSTOMER" have been ignored. The mapping dataset is a convenient reference dataset that can be version controlled and signed off by the customer.

Pattern 4: Identify Duplicates Without Removing Data

Time and again you will encounter duplicates in data. You know from earlier chapters that it is preferable to flag duplicates rather than delete them outright as this preserves data provenance.

ORIGINAL DATA			
ID	NAME	CITY	COUNTRY
4551	Joe Smith	Dublin	Ireland
4978	Jane Darcy	Lincoln	U.K.
5100	Jane Darcy	Lincoln	United Kingdom
6788	Joseph Smith	Dublin	Ireland
8000	Albert Stein	Glasgow	UK

DATA FLAGGED FOR DUPLICATES					
ID	NAME	CITY	COUNTRY	GROUP	MEMBER
4551	Joe Smith	Dublin	Ireland	50	1
4978	Jane Darcy	Lincoln	U.K.	23	1
5100	Jane Darcy	Lincoln	United Kingdom	23	2
6788	Joseph Smith	Dublin	Ireland	50	2
8000	Albert Stein	Glasgow	UK	51	1

FIGURE 65   Identify duplicates without removing data

This pattern involves being able to identify and flag all duplicates in a dataset using some or all data fields. Figure 65 shows an illustration of what this looks like. The dataset on the left contains five records. Two of these are duplicates. A common approach is to compare records across columns and removed any duplicates detected. The Guerrilla Analytics approach instead flags duplicate groups as shown in the dataset on the right. The "GROUP" field is an identifier for duplicate groups found in the data. Records that are deemed to be duplicates of one another are given the same group identifier. Records within a group are numbered. With this approach,

- Duplicates are visible in the data and can be inspected.
- Deduplicating the dataset is a simple matter of selecting the first member from each duplicate group.
- Duplicate group sizes can be calculated to prioritize the areas of the data that have the largest duplicate issues.

Pattern 5: Uniquely Identify a Row of Data With a Hash

Because you are often extracting data from a multitude of disparate sources, these sources will either have completely incompatible ID fields or will have no ID at all such as in the case of web pages and spreadsheets.

A key skill is the ability to deterministically ID a row of data. The best way to do this is with a hash code. However, it is not simply a matter of applying a hash function (if one is available in the DME). How are blanks and NULLs handled? How should the data be parsed so that every row's calculated hash code is unique? Team members need to have access to and understand how to consistently use a hash function for row identification.

Pattern 6: Summarize Data

It is critical for reporting, data exploration, and data testing that an analyst can summarize data quickly. Some useful summaries that an analyst should be able to produce are:

- Date and value ranges.
- Counts of labels, both overall and unique.

- Sum, average, median, and other descriptive statistics.
- Placing data records into quartiles, deciles, etc.
- Ordering data by time or some other ordering field and then selecting the *N*th item from that ordered list.
- Listing the field types and field names in all datasets.

Pattern 7: Pivot and Unpivot Data

A natural relational structure or document structure is very often not how data gets reported. People prefer data organized in pivoted tables. Conversely, data often arrives with a team in this presentation format and needs to be unpivoted before it can be used. This is typical with survey data, for example. Analysts need to be able to move data back and forth between these two formats quickly in program code.

Pattern 8: Roll Up Data

Data can be provided such that a key field has values split across many rows.

Figure 66 shows a typical dataset representing a simplified transaction log. The transaction log has been sorted by user and by event so that all events for a given user appear in event order beside that user. The user "Andrea Lazar" has three events and Albert Stein has two. Now, in many applications and for some presentation purposes you should like to produce the dataset shown in the right of the figure. All events associated with each user have been "rolled up" onto a single row separated by a "/"delimiter. It is now a simple step to produce one row of data per unique user.

Pattern 9: Unroll Data

Unrolling data is the exact opposite of "rolling up data." In this case, data is provided rolled up in some type of delimited format such as the "/"delimiter of the previous example (see Figure 66). The objective is to break this out into a new row for every item in the delimited list.

ORIGINAL DATA		
EVENT	USER	TYPE
1004	Andrea Lazar	Login
1010	Andrea Lazar	E-mail
1020	Andrea Lazar	E-mail
1003	Albert Stein	Login
109	Albert Stein	Logout

DATA ROLLED UP			
EVENT	USER	TYPE	TYPE_ROLLED_UP
1004	Andrea Lazar	Login	Login / E-mail / E-mail
1010	Andrea Lazar	E-mail	Login / E-mail / E-mail
1020	Andrea Lazar	E-mail	Login / E-mail / E-mail
1003	Albert Stein	Login	Login / Logout
109	Albert Stein	Logout	Login / Logout

FIGURE 66   Roll up data

Pattern 10: Fuzzy Matched Data

When bringing together disparate data sources, it can happen that they will not have a common join key that can be used. In these cases you must resort to fuzzy matching the datasets against one another. Fuzzy matching is simply a way of comparing two pieces of text and measuring how similar they are. For example, "bread" and "breed" are very similar because they differ only by one letter in the same location. "Bread" and "butter" however are less similar.

Figure 67 illustrates two datasets that are fuzzy matched into a new result. At the top of the figure are two source datasets that must be joined together. They have come from different systems and so do not share any common key that would permit the usual joining together of datasets. On the left is a list of actor names and their country of residence. On the right is a list of typed actor names (with typos) and the year of the actor's last film. After fuzzy matching the two datasets on actor name, you see the result at the bottom of the figure. Schwartzeneggar has not been matched to anything. Gleeson and Downey have been matched to two candidates in decreasing order of similarity.

The technical and mathematical details of fuzzy matching are beyond the scope of this book. However, the analyst needs to be familiar with the use of fuzzy matching algorithms, how they can be tuned, and how to interpret their outputs.

DISPARATE DATASETS

NAME	COUNTRY
SCHWARTZENEGGAR	USA
DOWNEY	USA
GLEESON	IRELAND

ID	ACTOR	LAST_FILM
5670	GLEASON	2013
5970	EASON	2001
10943	DOWNS	1997
7200	DOWNEY	2013

NAME	COUNTRY	ID	ACTOR	LAST_FILM
SCHWARTZENEGGAR	USA			
GLEESON	IRELAND	5670	GLEASON	2013
		5970	EASON	2001
DOWNEY	USA	7200	DOWNEY	2013
		10943	DOWNS	1997

FIGURE 67 Fuzzy-matched datasets

Pattern 11: Fuzzy Group Data

Fuzzy grouping is closely related to fuzzy matching. Fuzzy grouping occurs when you want to find similar groups of data records or documents within the same dataset. This may be because you are looking for duplicates or because you are interested in similar groups. Fuzzy grouping is effectively a fuzzy match where the dataset is fuzzy joined on itself to determine how similar a dataset's records are to one another.

Pattern 12: Pattern Match With Regular Expressions

When searching data, parsing it and doing certain types of matching, it is useful to be able to identify patterns. This is where *regular expressions* come into play. Regular expressions (Goyvaerts and Levithan, 2009; Friedl, 1997) are like a language that allows you to succinctly express text-matching conditions. For example, imagine trying to match all email addresses in some data. If you attempted a procedural approach to this problem it would require a significant amount of program code. You would have to iterate through each piece of text looking for a single "@" symbol followed by several letters, a "." symbol and then some more letters. Having found that, you would then need to go back and capture the entire string of text containing this pattern.

Regular expressions instead allow you to succinctly express a pattern matching string that can catch all variants of email addresses using a rule such as "must contain the @ character followed by some amount of characters including at least one "." after the "@" symbol." Other examples of where regular expressions are very useful are:

- Find valid postcode and zip code patterns.
- Determine if a transaction code matches an expected pattern.
- Parse a web log into each of its fields such as timestamp and return code.
- Parse a name field into first name, optional middle name, and last name separated by a comma or one or more spaces.
- Join together two data records where they both contain the string "Name:"

Pattern 13: Select the Previous or Subsequent *N* Records

Time series data is everywhere. Financial transactions, machine logs, website navigation and click through, and shopping checkouts are all time series data. Over time, some set of activities occurs and you would like to better understand patterns and trends in those activities. In these problems, it is necessary to "look back" into the data or "look ahead" into the data. That is, you would like to ask questions such as "show me five records previous" for this user or "show me the next record after the current one" or indeed "show me everything that happens between the current record and the next 10 records."

Pattern 14: Compare Data

Data arrives with the team in many versions and work product iterations. Analysts often struggle to determine if there are differences between datasets and where exactly those differences are located.

An analyst should know how to quickly "diff" two datasets by certain fields and by an entire row.

Pattern 15: Convert All Blanks to Null and Nulls to Blanks

If there is one area that causes more data analytics bugs than any other, it is probably the presence of NULLs and blanks in data. Whether you use one or the other depends very much on circumstances. Regardless, you will need a way to go through data fields and switch all NULLs to blanks and vice versa.

Pattern 16: Checksum Data

The chapter on data testing emphasized the importance of checksums. An analyst needs to understand and be able to quickly calculate checksums on both text files and DME datasets for a variety of data types.

WRAP UP

This appendix has described some of the most common data manipulation patterns encountered in Guerrilla Analytics projects. A high-performing team will be able to recognize these patterns and implement them in program code.

References

Bambenek, J., Klus, A., 2009. grep Pocket Reference. O' Reilly Media.

Beck, K., 1999. Extreme Programming Explained: Embrace Change. Addison Wesley.

Beck, K., 2002. Test-Driven Development. Addison Wesley.

Block, P., 2011. Flawless Consulting: A Guide to Getting Your Expertise Used. John Wiley & Sons.

Chapman, P., et al., 2000. CRISP-DM 1.0: Step-by-Step Data Mining Guide. IBM.

Christiansen, T., Schwartz, R.L., Wall, L., 2000. Programming Perl. O' Reilly Media.

Collier, K.W., 2011. Agile Analytics: A Value-Driven Approach to Business Intelligence and Data Warehousing. Addison-Wesley Professional.

Collins-Sussman, B., Fitzpatrick, B.W., Pilato, C.M., 2008. Version Control with Subversion, Second ed. O' Reilly Media.

Conway, D., 2013. The Data Science Venn Diagram. Available at: http://drewconway.com/zia/2013/3/26/the-data-science-venn-diagram [Accessed November 24, 2013].

Crawley, M.J., 2007. The R Book. Wiley-Blackwell.

Davenport, T.H., 2006. Competing on analytics. Harv. Bus. Rev. 84 (1), 98–107, 134. Available at: http://www.ncbi.nlm.nih.gov/pubmed/20929194.

Doar, M.B., 2011. Practical JIRA Administration. O'Reilly Media.

Dougherty, D., Robbins, A., 1997. sed & awk, Second ed. O' Reilly Media.

Duvall, P.M., Matyas, S., Glover, A., 2007. Continuous Integration: Improving Software Quality and Reducing Risk. Addison Wesley.

Franks, B., 2012. Taming the Big Data Tidal Wave: Finding Opportunities in Huge Data Streams With Advanced Analytics. John Wiley & Sons.

Friedl, J.E.F., 1997. Mastering Regular Expressions. O' Reilly.

Gamma, E., et al.,1994. Design Patterns: Elements of Reusable Object-Oriented Software. Addison-Wesley Professional.

Goyvaerts, J., Levithan, S., 2009. Regular Expressions Cookbook. O' Reilly Media.

Gruber, J., 2004. http://daringfireball.net/projects/markdown/.

Heer, J., Bostock, M., Ogievetsky, V., 2010. A Tour Through the Visualization Zoo. Queue 8 (5), 20, Available at: http://dl.acm.org/ft_gateway.cfm?id=1805128&type=html [Accessed December 14, 2013].

Humble J., Farley D., 2011. Continuous Delivery: Reliable Software Releases through Build, Test, and Deployment Automation.

Jensen, K., 2012. CRISP-DM Process Diagram. Wikipedia2a, p. 1. Available at: https://en.wikipedia.org/wiki/File:CRISP-DM_Process_Diagram.png.

Leisch, F., 2002. Sweave: Dynamic generation of statistical reports using literate data analysis. In: Härdle, W., Rönz, B. (Eds.). Compstat 2002 - Proceedings in Computational Statistics. pp. 575–580.

Linden, G., Smith, B., York, J., 2003. Amazon.com Recommendations Item-to-Item Collaborative Filtering. IEEE Internet Comput. (3), 76–80.

Loeliger, J., McCullough, M., 2012. Version Control With Git: Powerful Tools and Techniques for Collaborative Software Development. O' Reilly Media.

Lutz, M., 2009. Learning Python. Shroff Publishers & Distributors Pvt Ltd.

McCallum, Q.E., 2012. Bad Data Handbook: Cleaning Up the Data So You Can Get Back to Work. O'Reilly Media.

McKinney, W., 2012. Python for Data Analysis. O' Reilly Media, Available at: http://shop.oreilly.com/product/0636920023784.do.

Montgomery, D.C., 2012. Design and Analysis of Experiments, Eighth ed. Wiley.

Moodie, M., 2012. Pro Apache Ant, First ed. Apress.

PMI, 2013. A Guide to the Project Management Body of Knowledge, Fourth ed. Project Management Institute.

Rasie, E.M., 1999. The McKinsey Way. McGraw Hill.

Redman, T.C., Sweeney, B., 2013. To work with data, you need a lab and a factory. Harv. Bus. Rev. Available at: http://blogs.hbr.org/2013/04/two-departments-for-data-succe/.

Rogers, S., 2012. Facts are Sacred: The Power of Data (Guardian Shorts). Guardian Books.

Sadalage, P.J., Fowler, M., 2012. NoSQL Distilled. Addison Wesley.

Sebastian-Coleman, L., 2013. Measuring Data Quality for Ongoing Improvement: A Data Quality Assessment Framework. Morgan Kaufmann.

Shafranovich, Y., 2005. Common Format and MIE Type for CSV Files. Available at: https://tools.ietf.org/html/rfc4180.

Shearer, C., 2000. The CRISP-DM model: the new blueprint for data mining. J. Data Warehousing 5, 13–22.

Spector, A., Norvig, P., Petrov, S., 2012. Google's hybrid approach to research. Commun. ACM 55 (7), 34.

Tahchiev, P., et al., 2010. JUnit in Action, Second ed. Manning Publications.

Tatroe, K., Lerdorf, R., 2002. Programming PHP, Fourth ed. O' Reilly Media.

Tufte, E.R., 1990. Envisioning Information. Graphics Press.

van Heesch, D., 1997. DOxygen, www.doxygen.org.

Whittaker, J.A., Arbon, J., Carollo, J., 2012. How Google Tests Software. Addison-Wesley Professional.

Witten, I.H., Eibe, F., Hall, M.A., 2011. Data Mining: Practical Machine Learning Tools and Techniques. Morgan Kaufmann.

Yau, N., 2013. Visualize This: The FlowingData Guide to Design, Visualization, and Statistics. Wiley.

Zemeckis, R., 1994. Forest Gump. United States of America.

Index

A

Printed in the United States
By Bookmasters